# BRITAIN'S SECRET TREASURES

## MARY-ANN OCHOTA

headline  The British Museum

First published in 2013
by HEADLINE PUBLISHING GROUP

1

Cataloguing in Publication Data is available from the British Library

ISBN 978 0 7553 6573 9

Editors for ITV: Ed Taylor, Michael Kelpie
Editors for the British Museum: Michael Lewis, Ian Richardson
Researcher: Kate Jarvis
Typeset in Avenir and Legacy by Bobby&Co
Printed and bound in Italy by
Rotolito Lombarda S.p.A

HEADLINE PUBLISHING GROUP
An Hachette UK Company
338 Euston Road
London NW1 3BH

www.headline.co.uk
www.hachette.co.uk

Britain's Secret Treasures first transmitted in the UK in July 2012. The six-part series was devised by Ed
Taylor & Michael Kelpie and commissioned by Katy Thorogood for ITV Network.

The series told the stories of members of the public who had discovered extraordinary artefacts as they
dug in their gardens, walked in fields and strolled along beaches – sometimes literally stumbling on
lost treasures that had lain undetected for many years.

It is testament to the boundless dedication of the British Museum's Portable Antiquities Scheme,
under the leadership of Roger Bland, his team, and their nationwide network of Finds Liaison Officers
that the histories of these amazing artefacts, and the people who found them, have become part of the
ITV series and ultimately now form the heart of this book.

The new series of Britain's Secret Treasures returns to ITV in the Autumn 2013.

An ITV Studios company

# CONTENTS

| DATE | PERIOD | EVENTS | BRITAIN'S SECRET TREASURES |
|---|---|---|---|
| 2.6 Million years ago – 8,300BC | 'Palaeolithic' Early Stone Age | By 800,000 years ago humans control fire<br><br>200,000 years ago *Homo sapiens* evolve in Africa<br><br>100,000 years ago *Homo sapiens* begin to spread across the world<br><br>26,000BC Last Neanderthals die out<br><br>10,000BC First evidence of farming in the world | *Happisburgh Handaxe 500,000BC* |
| 8,300BC – 3,500BC | 'Mesolithic' Middle Stone Age | | |
| 4,000BC – 2,100BC | 'Neolithic' Late Stone Age | 4,000BC First evidence of farming in Britain<br><br>2900BC first phase of building Stonehenge<br><br>2400BC first evidence of copper metalworking in Britain | *Isle of Wight Axehead 3500–2100BC* |
| 2400BC – 800BC | Bronze Age | 2400–2000BC third phase of building Stonehenge, making the monument we see today<br><br>2200BC first evidence of bronze metalworking in Britain | *Tisbury Hoard 2000–700BC, Late Bronze/ Early Iron Age*<br><br>*Ringlemere Cup 1700–1500BC*<br><br>*Near Lewes Hoard 1400–1250BC*<br><br>*Milton Keynes Hoard 1150–750BC*<br><br>*Carpow Bronze Age Logboat 1130–970BC*<br><br>*Tamlaght Hoard around 1050–950BC*<br><br>*Horns and Crotal Musical Instruments around 800BC* |
| 800BC – 100AD | Iron Age | 800BC first evidence of ironworking metallurgy<br><br>450BC–100AD La Tène 'Celtic' art traditions develop across Europe including Britain<br><br>55/54BC attempted invasion of Britain by Julius Caesar | *Blair Drummond Torc Hoard 300–100BC*<br><br>*Nesscliffe Ritual Spoons 300BC–100AD*<br><br>*Sedgeford Hoard 50BC*<br><br>*Helmet Cremation Burial 75–25BC*<br><br>*Pegsdon Mirror 75–25BC*<br><br>*Winchester Gold hoard 75–25BC*<br><br>*Sedgeford Torc around 100BC*<br><br>*Anarevitos Gold Stater 10BC–10AD*<br><br>*Tanworth Comb 25–70AD*<br><br>*Langstone Tankard 1–150AD* |

| DATE | PERIOD | EVENTS | BRITAIN'S SECRET TREASURES |
|---|---|---|---|
| 43AD – 410AD | Roman | 43AD Roman Invasion of Britain<br><br>60/61AD Queen Boudicca's revolt against the Romans<br><br>78AD Romans take control of Anglesey<br><br><br><br><br><br><br><br>122AD Construction begins on Hadrian's Wall<br><br>Around 319AD Emperor Constantine adopts Christianity across Roman Empire<br><br>Late 300s AD First Anglian and Saxon invasions and raids<br><br>410AD End of Roman Rule in Britain | Hallaton Treasure<br>43BC–50AD, Late Iron Age/ Early Roman<br><br>Putney 'Brothel' Token<br>1–50AD<br><br>Leopard Cup<br>1–100AD<br><br>Cautopates Roman Figurine<br>43–307AD<br><br>Syston Knife Handle<br>43–410AD, Roman<br><br>Billingford Amulet<br>60–150AD<br><br>Crosby Garrett Helmet<br>75–250AD, Roman<br><br>County Durham River Assemblage<br>90–400AD<br><br>Staffordshire Moorlands Ilam Pan<br>100–200AD<br><br>Marcus Aurelius Bust<br>160–200AD<br><br>Roman Slave Shackle<br>200–400AD<br><br>Ashwell Hoard and Goddess Senuna<br>200–400AD<br><br>Chalgrove Hoard and Coin of Domitianus<br>251–279AD<br><br>Frome Hoard<br>around 290AD<br><br>Hadrian's Wall Coins<br>406–408AD |
| 400AD – 1100AD | Early Medieval: includes Anglo-Saxon 410–800AD Viking 800–1100AD | 410 Jutes arrive in England<br><br>432 St Patrick arrives in Ireland<br><br>449 Angles and Saxons arrive in England<br><br>793 Vikings attack Lindisfarne Monastery, Northumbria<br><br>878 The Viking King Hálfdan conquers Wessex, forcing King Alfred the Great to hide in a marsh<br><br>886 King Alfred agrees a treaty with Viking leaders to divide England<br><br>927 Athelstan establishes a united English Kingdom for first time in history<br><br>1016 King Cnut of Denmark invades England and re-establishes Viking control<br><br>1066 King of Norway, Harald Hadrada invades England in the North shortly before William the Conqueror attacks England in the south. King Harold II of England is beaten by William and Normans take control | Alnwick Sword<br>around 500–650AD, Early Medieval<br><br>Staffordshire Hoard<br>640–700AD, Anglo-Saxon<br><br>North West Essex Ring<br>580–650AD, Anglo-Saxon<br><br>Clonmore Shrine<br>650–700AD, Irish Christian<br><br>Holderness Cross<br>620–660AD, Anglo-Saxon<br><br>Baldehildis Seal<br>600–700AD, Anglo-Saxon<br><br>Llanbedrgoch Viking Treasure<br>600–1000AD, Viking<br><br>Silverdale Hoard<br>900–910AD, Viking<br><br>West Yorkshire Ring Hoard<br>900–1000AD<br><br>Vale of York Viking Hoard<br>around 928AD, Viking<br><br>Saltfleetby Spindle Whorl<br>1000–1050AD, Viking |

5

| DATE | PERIOD | EVENTS | BRITAIN'S SECRET TREASURES |
|---|---|---|---|
| 1066AD – 1500AD | Medieval | 1086 Domesday Book completed | *Newton Stewart Dog Lead around 1100–1200* |
| | | 1096–99 First Crusade | *Carlton Knight 1150–1250* |
| | | 1170 Thomas Becket murdered at Canterbury Cathedral | *Seal Matrix of Stone Priory 1260–1300* |
| | | 1305 Scottish rebel William Wallace executed by the English | *Canterbury Pilgrim Badges 1300–1500* |
| | | 1315–22 Great Famine sweeps Europe | *Kirkcaldy Heart Brooch around 1350* |
| | | 1348 Black Death in England kills an estimated 1.5 million people out of 4 million total population | *Raglan Ring 1440–1475* |
| | | 1387 Geoffrey Chaucer's *The Canterbury Tales* appears | *Boar Badge of Richard III 1470–1485* |
| | | 1455–85 Wars of the Roses | |
| | | 1476 William Caxton uses first printing press in England | |
| 1500AD – 1800AD | Post Medieval | 1533 Henry VIII marries Anne Boleyn | *Ursula's Virgin Badge around 1500–1530, Medieval/ Post Medieval* |
| | | 1536–40 Henry VIII establishes Church of England, and dissolves the monasteries | *Hockley Pendant 1500–1550, Medieval/Post Medieval* |
| | | 1588 Spanish Armada sails to attack England | *Bentley Miniature Book 1500–1550, Medieval/Post Medieval* |
| | | 1590/1 First Shakespeare play performed | *Daventry Visard Mask 1600–1700* |
| | | | *Beddingham Nose 1500–1700* |
| | | | *Cloth Seals from Durham 1550–1650* |
| | | | *Holy Island Mason Hoard around 1562* |
| | | | *Girona Wreck Cameo 1588* |
| | | | *Epsom Horse Harness Boss 1603–1664* |
| | | | *Hawking Vervel 1610–1612* |
| | | 1620 'Pilgrim Fathers' sail for America | *Nether Stowey Hoard 1642–1651* |
| | | 1642–51 English Civil War | *Dartmoor Sword around 1650* |
| | | 1649 King Charles I executed for Treason | *Chinese Coin Hoard 1659–1850* |
| | | 1660 King Charles II restored to the throne – period known as the 'Restoration' | *Rochester Cufflink 1660–1700* |
| | | 1666 Great Fire of London | *Pitminster Toy Cannon 1700–1750* |
| | | 1688–1746 Series of conflicts and uprisings in Scotland and Ireland | *Rosemarkie Trade Weights 1707–1725* |
| | | 1746 Jacobites defeated at Battle of Culloden, the last battle fought on British soil | *French Forgery Hoard around 1711* |
| | | 1771 First cotton mill factory opens in Britain | *Mourning Ring 1735* |
| | | 1789–1802 Revolutionary Wars between France and Britain | *Fort George Toy Soldiers 1748–1768* |
| | | 1802–1815 Napoleonic Wars between France and Britain | *Spanish-American Doubloons 1790–1801* |

| DATE | PERIOD | EVENTS | BRITAIN'S SECRET TREASURES |
|------|--------|--------|----------------------------|
| | | | *Inverness Shoulder-belt Plate*<br>*1794–1816*<br><br>*HMS Colossus Shipwreck*<br>*1798* |
| 1800 –<br>Present Day | Modern | 1825 First Steam Train passenger service runs between Darlington and Stockton<br>1837 Queen Victoria comes to the throne<br>1843 Slavery abolished in all Britain's colonies<br>1867 Joseph Lister publishes his research about antiseptic surgery<br>1914–18 World War One<br>1918 Women over 30 given the right to vote<br>1926 John Logie Baird publicly demonstrates television<br>1933 Adolf Hitler comes to power in Germany<br>1939–45 World War Two | *Navenby Witch Bottle*<br>*1820–1880*<br><br>*Kellington Dental Block*<br>*1890–1930*<br><br>*Great War Victory Medal*<br>*1919*<br><br>*George Humber's Distinguished Conduct Medal*<br>*1919*<br><br><br><br>*Prisoner of War Farthing Pendant*<br>*1939–1948*<br><br>*Hackney WWII Hoard*<br>*1940* |

# Introduction

The treasures in this book span 500,000 years of life in Britain, and they were all discovered by members of the public. Some treasures were found by chance when people were going about their everyday lives, walking the dog, digging the garden, on a school trip, farming, or doing building work. Other treasures were found by people intentionally searching using metal detectors, hoping there might be something there, waiting to be discovered.

However you make a find, it comes with an electrifying sense of discovery – knowing that the last person to touch this unique object was a stranger from a distant generation. The find might have come from a small, personal moment of fear or triumph, or be part of a grand account of kings and queens. The shiny golden treasure hoards that grab the news and make the finders millionaires are few and far between – most searchers only ever find ordinary things that belonged to ordinary people – but even when an item is financially worthless, it can still have an incredible power to reach through time and connect you to a person from the past. The promise of that magical connection is addictive. It's what gets many metal detectorists and other searchers out in the cold and rain every weekend.

The excitement of making a discovery comes with the responsibility to share that find – to make sure each crucial piece of our past is recorded and preserved for future generations.

In England and Wales all finds should be recorded through the Portable Antiquities Scheme, which is managed (in England) by the British Museum and (in Wales) through the National Museums Wales. Locally based archaeologists, known as Finds Liaison Officers, undertake the work of logging and recording these finds. Scotland and Northern Ireland have their own systems they use for recording archaeological objects (see p296 for more details).

When a Finds Liaison Officer or curator gets a call or email bringing them the first glimpse of an artefact for assessment, they too share the thrill of discovery. It's their job to establish just how important a find is, and what its discovery might mean for our understanding of the past. Working together, amateurs and professionals unearth, record and preserve the finds that tell our history.

We throng to see these objects, to learn about them and the contexts they came from, to discover what that can tell us about our ancestors' lives.

Museum curators understand the power of objects, and many have finds-handling sessions where you can handle precious, ancient and intriguing objects from their collections. The power of touching objects is so potent that researchers are now even bringing heritage artefacts into hospitals and care homes.

Touching and handling can damage artefacts – the oils from our skin, our breath, and exposing the artefact to a non-controlled climate can all take their toll – but although much of our past is fragile, it shouldn't be shut away. Conservators, fundraisers and educators ensure that these treasures are preserved for future research and enjoyment, and that our heritage is protected.

To select just a few dozen artefacts from the 900,000 finds that have been discovered, investigated and logged on the national Portable Antiquities Scheme (PAS) database (see p295), as well as finds of significance from Scotland and Northern Ireland, was an astonishingly difficult job. A team of experts shortlisted finds that were of national importance (like the Vale of York Viking Hoard, p234), had deep cultural significance (like the Roman Slave Shackle, p180), were considered to be exquisitely beautiful (like the Leopard Cup, p104), and some that had a weird or wonderful find story.

These secret treasures invite us to explore the personal worlds of our ancestors: their homes and families, their passions, fears and beliefs. The incredible stories of how these objects were made, handled, cherished and discarded are ours to enjoy. The ITV show *Britain's Secret Treasures* – a collaboration with the British Museum and now into its second series – immediately fired the interest of the wider public, and got them sending in pictures of their own previously unrecorded finds, visiting local museums, and exploring the PAS database online. This book presents the stories behind just eighty of Britain's secret treasures. Each one invites us into an intriguing past and, above all, these treasures demonstrate how important ordinary people are in the quest to secure our national heritage.

1 - SALTFLEETBY SPINDLE WHORL
2 - SPANISH AMERICAN GOLD DOUBLOONS
3 - NAVENBY WITCH BOTTLE
4 - CARLTON KNIGHT
5 - SYSTON KNIFE HANDLE
6 - HAWKING VERVEL
7 - SEDGEFORD COIN HOARD
8 - SEDGEFORD TORC
9 - HAPPISBURGH HANDAXE
10 - BILLINGFORD AMULET
11 - BALDEHILDIS SEAL

**MOSTLY LOW-LYING** and sometimes overlooked, the large, fertile areas of the East Midlands and East Anglia are tucked between damp fenland and rolling hills. Some people who live in the coastal areas of this region are struggling to stop their homes and communities being claimed by the sea. But in the process of erosion, this dynamic coastline is giving up secrets from its extremely ancient past – including the very earliest evidence for human habitation in Britain. The **Happisburgh Handaxe (p45)** is a stone tool more than half a million years old. It comes from a time when mainland Britain was attached to continental Europe and our early ancestors could walk from Amsterdam to Norwich without getting their feet wet.

It's difficult to grasp just how old this tool is, or how important in the great scheme of human achievement. Similar to the moments when we first controlled fire, when we first cooked food, when we first made marks on the rock walls of cave shelters – this flint tool marks a step-change. All the treasures in this book build on that simple flint tool. Putting a man on the moon, modelling quantum physics or finding a cure for cancer are simply further along the ladder of human problem-solving.

In the much more recent past, people continued to be drawn to the sea and the fertile lands of the East. People made, traded and used items like the **Sedgeford Torc (p27)**, the **Syston Knife Handle (p40)**, and the **Billingford Amulet (p43)** in Iron Age and Roman times. When the Romans left, the Angles arrived, from modern-day Denmark and Germany, establishing their eastern Kingdom, East Anglia, which was later divided into the North Folk and the South Folk (Norfolk and Suffolk).

Hundreds of years later the next inevitable wave of foreign invaders and settlers arrived – the Vikings – and they brought with them a rich heritage that still exists in the place names and family names of many people in the East, as well as in everyday treasures like the **Saltfleetby Spindle Whorl (p30)**. Ancient centres of power across the region include Lincoln, Ely and Norwich, and you can experience the wealth and power of this area by exploring the historic houses, castles and monuments that have been preserved. In some parts, a sense of isolation lingers. But elsewhere, new communities of incomers are once again influencing the culture and ethnic make-up of the East. It's not a new trend – it's one with a most ancient pedigree.

# Spanish-American Gold Doubloons

## Treasure Trove in a Lincolnshire hedgerow

Sue Green and her brother Dave Wilkinson often metal detect together. They're both members of the Lincoln Historic Search Society, and have found their share of the usual detecting finds from Lincolnshire – Roman brooches and coins, medieval metal work as well as Victorian and modern items.

Just like many new detectorists, it took Sue a while to get permission to practise her hobby on a promising piece of land. But in 2010, with a year's experience under her belt, she invested in a new machine and got

> **Date:** 1790–1801, Post Medieval
>
> **Where, when and how found:** South East Lincolnshire; 1928, 2010 & 2011; farm work & metal detecting
>
> **Finders:** Father and son, Fredrick and John Kingswood (1928); sister and brother, Sue Green and David Wilkinson (2010 & 2011)
>
> **Official valuation:** £6,650
>
> **Where are they now?** Collection Museum, Lincoln www.thecollectionmuseum.com

permission for a new piece of land. After a couple of hours' searching, she hit a strong signal which looked like it had come from a jam-jar lid in the ground. As she lifted the item she realised it was a big, fat, gold coin. And it wasn't alone – together with her brother, she got the signals for five more big, fat, gold coins. Sue took them home and alerted her local Finds Liaison Officer (FLO), Adam Daubney, who recorded the discovery and reported it to the coroner.

## The coins

The gold pieces Sue found are all 8-escudos coins, minted between 1790 to 1801, from across what was then the Spanish-controlled New World, in Chile, Colombia, Mexico and Bolivia. They're 37mm in diameter, 24.5g each, and made from 88% gold. The name 'Doubloon' was originally only used for 2-escudos coins, but grew to encompass all denominations of escudos – ½, 1, 2, 4 and 8. The term 'Pieces of Eight' was never used for 8-escudos coins, but for silver coins worth 8-reales.

The escudos have a profile of Charles IV of Spain on the front (obverse) and the Spanish royal coat of arms on the reverse, along with the mint mark, assayer's initials, and the inscription, **AUSPICE.DEO IN UTRO Q.FELIX**. which means 'Under God's Will we will prosper'.

The escudos were struck in Spanish-controlled areas and were used for bullion and coinage, circulating around the world. During the decades of European war following the French Revolution in 1789, and throughout the Napoleonic Wars of 1803–1815, gold coinage was hoarded in Britain and across Europe. Coin hoards are rarely found from the period between the end of the English Civil War (which ended in 1651) and the 1790s, but in the years around 1800 coin hoards, particularly of gold, rapidly increase in frequency. It fits with the pattern archaeologists see of hoarding increasing at times of social and military unrest.

## The burial

Sue's pet theory is that a pirate might have dropped his golden loot whilst riding along a nearby bridleway. It's possible that she's right, there's no way to know. Another theory comes from documentary research conducted by the landowner and Adam, the FLO. The landowner has studied the land deeds and indentures of the parish fields around the hoard find site, and identified the likely owner at the time of deposition as Lord Robert Hobart. Lord Robert was 4th Earl of Buckinghamshire and Secretary of State for War and the Colonies between 1801 and 1804 – which makes him very likely to have had significant access to these precious gold coins. Perhaps he gave the doubloons to an employee or relative as a gift or payment. Perhaps they were buried on Lord Robert's behalf, and there's even a slim chance that he buried them himself.

Some people intrigued by this treasure mystery have noted that Lord Robert died falling from his horse in February 1816. It's no more than speculation, but maybe his tragic early death is the reason the hoard was never recovered.

## A village farce

Initially it was thought that Sue's mini hoard of six coins was unique. But research revealed that there had been a previous discovery of 'Spanish gold coins' in the same field in 1928. A father and son labouring team, Fred and John Kingswood, had been digging in the field and found 18 gold coins. They took them to the local pub to show their friends and tried to discover if they were of value. They didn't find out what they were but in the excitement of the following days, the landowner, Mr Frank Waterhouse, heard about the coins and engaged a private detective to get them back. Meanwhile, the village baker took one of the coins to test it with acid, another got 'lost', and a few were taken to a local fair. One of Fred's friends wanted to hang one from his watch chain, but Fred refused to sell.

The landowner, Mr Waterhouse, eventually visited the Kingswoods' house and 'bluffed' John into giving up some of the coins. But the Kingswoods didn't reveal the full number that they'd found, and Fred and John decided to rebury the coins under their own apple tree. They resolved that they'd only give them up to a police officer. But Mr Waterhouse's private detective discovered the plot, confronted the Kingswoods and the coins were eventually recovered. The whole hoard was ultimately claimed by the Crown under the old law of Treasure Trove, and the coins were valued at £3 6s each, a hefty sum in 1928.

More than a year and a half after their 2010 discovery, Sue and David returned to the field and discovered two more coins, which were perhaps dislodged by a new round of deep ploughing. In total, 26 escudos have come out of the field. Thorough subsequent searches have revealed nothing more – the whole hoard has at last been recovered – but the real mystery of the Lincoln doubloons may never be solved.

> "Initially it was thought that Sue's mini hoard of six coins was unique. But research revealed that there had been a previous discovery of 'Spanish gold coins' in the same field in 1928"

**See also:**
Hackney WWII Hoard
Frome Hoard

# Carlton Knight

## *A bronze horseman found in a garden*

This finder had been metal detecting for twenty years when he was asked to look for a lost ring in a back garden. Instead, he found this 5cm-high solid bronze figurine of a knight on horseback so close to the surface that he could see it before he started digging.

The knight has a moustache and conical helmet, and holds a shield in his left hand and the warhorse's reins in his right. The horse wears a saddle cloth and caparison, an ornate cloth covering its back and legs, with its hooves peeping out at the bottom. The knight's kite-shaped shield, conical helmet and armour stylistically dates the object to the second half of the 12th or early 13th century. Traces of silvering have been found on the surface – it's likely that when it was new, the knight would have been a bright shiny, white-silver colour.

Although the little knight is listed in the Portable Antiquities Scheme database as a 'chess piece', there's debate about his identity.

The Carlton Knight looks a lot like the Lewis Chessmen, a group of 93 walrus ivory and whale-teeth chess pieces from the same period, discovered on the Isle of Lewis, in the Outer Hebrides, and dating to about 1150–1200. But the Lewis Chessmen have strong Scandinavian influences, whereas the Carlton Knight doesn't. No other pieces have ever been found that would match the Carlton Knight in a chess set, and the Carlton Knight seems to have evidence of solder underneath it, suggesting that it was perhaps fixed to a larger object as a decoration. What's certain is that the piece is a compelling character portrait of a medieval horseman.

**Date:** 1150–1250, Medieval
**Where, when and how found:** Carlton in Lindrick, Nottinghamshire; 2004; metal detecting in a back garden
**Finder:** Anonymous
**Where is it now?** Bassetlaw Museum, Retford, Nottinghamshire
www.bassetlawmuseum.org.uk

## The medieval knight

The 'High Middle Ages', the period in which the Carlton Knight was made, was a time of prosperity and growth for many in Europe. Some of the finest cathedrals were built, intellectuals were flocking to new universities like Oxford and Cambridge, and trade was booming in newly chartered market towns. Wealthy lords funded expeditions to new lands, including the Crusades, the series of Holy Wars to seize Jerusalem and other lands from Muslim Turks and 'barbarian' tribes. Famous orders of knights were established – not least the Knights Templar – and tales about legendary warriors like the Knights of the Round Table were popular across Europe.

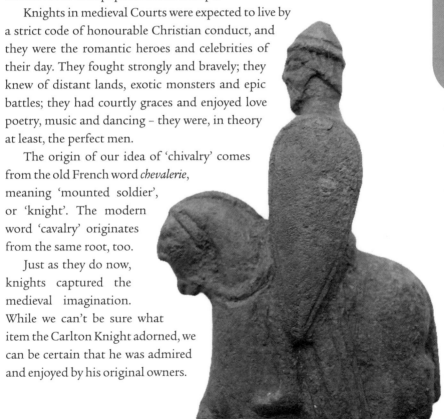

Knights in medieval Courts were expected to live by a strict code of honourable Christian conduct, and they were the romantic heroes and celebrities of their day. They fought strongly and bravely; they knew of distant lands, exotic monsters and epic battles; they had courtly graces and enjoyed love poetry, music and dancing – they were, in theory at least, the perfect men.

The origin of our idea of 'chivalry' comes from the old French word *chevalerie*, meaning 'mounted soldier', or 'knight'. The modern word 'cavalry' originates from the same root, too.

Just as they do now, knights captured the medieval imagination. While we can't be sure what item the Carlton Knight adorned, we can be certain that he was admired and enjoyed by his original owners.

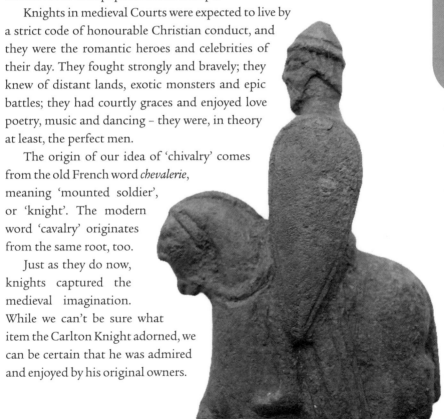

See also:
Clonmore Shrine
Ursula's Virgin Badge
Newton Stewart Dog Lead

# Hawking Vervel

## A royal hawk's foot ring

This tiny silver ring weighs just 1.37g, and is less than 0.5mm thick. When it was discovered, the detectorist recognised it as a hawking ring, or 'vervel', that would have been attached to the jesses (leather straps) on a bird of prey's legs to identify its owner. Hawking is the sport of using a trained bird of prey to hunt and capture small mammals, birds and sometimes fish. Evidence of hawking stretches for thousands of years – both as a functional way of catching food, but also as a prestigious activity – it's known as the 'Sport of Kings'.

**Date:** 1610–1612, Post Medieval

**Where, when and how found:** Cley-next-the-Sea, Norfolk; 2012; metal detecting

**Finder:** Anonymous

**Official valuation:** £6,000

**Where is it now?** Norwich Castle Museum, Norwich www.museums.norfolk.gov.uk

**Also visit:** Birds of prey centres throughout the country; National Portrait Gallery, London www.npg.org.uk

This hawking ring is made from solid silver and it bears an intriguing inscription. On the outer face is the name, '**Henrye Prince \***', and on the flat shield-shaped plate is an engraving of the three feathers badge of the Prince of Wales.

The Royal badge and name on this vervel refer to Henry Frederick Stuart, son of James I and Anne of Denmark. Henry was born in 1594, made Prince of Wales in 1610, and died suddenly in 1612 from typhoid fever. Given that Henry was only Prince of Wales for two years, we can date the vervel closely to around 1610 to 1612.

## The king we never had

Henry was the eldest son of James I, and was in line to become King of England after his father. Henry was intelligent, handsome, popular with the public and at court, and was considered a strong leader who would make an excellent king. He enjoyed the leisure pursuits of the nobility – hawking, hunting, jousting, and was renowned for his athleticism, but he also took

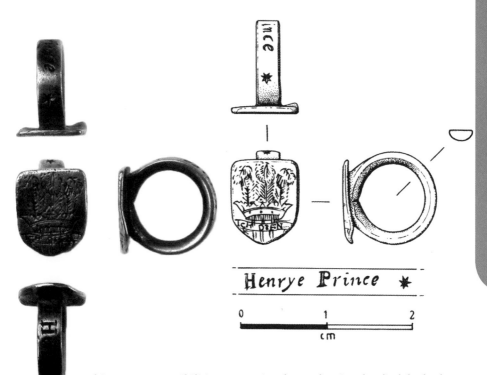

Henrye Prince ✳

0          1          2
cm

his state responsibilities very seriously. At the time he died, he had been planning to build the first bridge across the River Thames at Westminster. The Venetian Ambassador wrote, 'His designs were vast; his temper was grave, severe, reserved, brief in speech. All the hopes of these kingdoms were built on his high qualities.' The whole country went into mourning when their beloved prince died of fever aged just 18. Distraught citizens wept openly in the London streets, and his funeral procession was over a mile long.

Henry's younger brother, Charles, was thrust into the spotlight – just twelve, Charles led the procession at his brother's funeral – his father, King James, was said to be too distraught to appear in public.

Charles ascended the throne in 1625 as King Charles I, and served a tumultuous reign facing challenges to his authority at home and abroad. He refused to accept a constitutional monarchy, set high taxes and caused more upset by marrying Henrietta Maria, a French Catholic. In 1649, after years of Civil War, Charles was captured, charged with treason against his own country and executed. The monarchy was only restored in 1660, with Charles II (Charles I's son) on the throne.

Historians have long wondered whether any of this would have happened, had Henry, a committed Protestant, survived his fever and served as king instead of his little brother.

## Hawking in Norfolk

We don't have any specific evidence Henry ever came to north Norfolk, but his birds could have been brought here for training with a member of his royal entourage, or they could have been with the Prince himself – the fact that we don't have surviving records is not evidence that he *didn't* visit Cley-next-the-Sea. It's a quiet place now and the estuary is silted up, but at the time it was a busy port.

Training hunting birds took time and patience, and noblemen would have had servants specifically employed to keep their hunt animals – hounds, horses and hawks – up to snuff. The key to keeping a hunting hawk keen was to feed it very carefully – too full and it wouldn't bother flying after the prey, too hungry, and it could die. Little chicks and mice would be given, as well as scraps of rabbit meat and fish. Each trainer would have his own special 'recipe' for keeping his birds in tip-top hunting condition.

Our phrase 'fed up', meaning you've had enough, comes from hawking and falconry, as does 'hoodwink', to fool someone – the hoodwink was a small leather cap that fitted over a hawk's eyes so it would stay calm and quiet regardless of what was going on around it.

Falconry and hawking became less popular during the 17th century – under Charles I and then during the brutal years of Civil War and rule under Oliver Cromwell, the British nobility had other things to worry about. Without a king keen on hawking, and then without a king at all, the 'Sport of Kings' lost its figurehead.

See also:
Newton Stewart Dog Lead
Epsom Horse Harness Boss
Dartmoor Sword

# Baldehildis Seal

## *The gold seal of a medieval queen*

In 1998, on farmland near Norwich, a tiny gold disc was unearthed by a metal detectorist. He'd been going to the site for twenty years, and has continued to detect on the land for the fifteen years since, but has never found anything like it from the same period. It's a remarkable find – just 12mm across, made from 98% pure gold, and dated to 600-700AD. It's uniquely rare, very valuable and intriguingly odd.

Date: 600–700AD, Merovingian Early Medieval

Where, when and how found: Postwick, Norfolk; 1998; metal detecting

Finder: Anonymous

Where is it now? Norwich Castle Museum, Norwich
www.museums.norfolk.gov.uk

The disc is a double-sided seal matrix, used to stamp a personal identifying imprint in wax.

It was designed to attach to a finger ring by a pivoting pin that allowed the seal matrix to swivel and both engraved sides to be used. On one side, a cross hangs above two figures – a long-haired woman, and a bearded man with large oval eyes. They're embracing each other, apparently naked, possibly in sexual intercourse.

On the other side is an engraved head-and-shoulders image of a man or woman with long hair with an inscription around the edge spelling out the female name '**BALDEHILDIS**'.

Baldehildis, Baldehilde or Balthild, means 'bold spear', or 'bold sword'. The elements of the name were common in Anglo-Saxon England, as well as France, but the combination to make the name Balthild is only recorded for one person. Inscriptions on seals can't always be linked to specific people – the details of individuals are often lost through the ages. But a solid gold seal with this woman's name narrows down the focus considerably – our best candidate for the original owner of this precious, prestigious ring is a 7th-century queen linked to a fairytale life story.

At this time, England was divided into a number of Anglo-Saxon kingdoms. The elites had strong contacts with their continental counterparts – particularly the Franks, who reigned across what is now France and part of Germany. One of the Franks' greatest queens was Balthild, and she is said to have been Saxon, and come from 'over the sea', normally used by the writers to mean from Anglo-Saxon England.

## The life of Balthild

*The Vita Domnae Balthildis*, 'The Life of Lady Balthild', written not long after her death, was designed to explain why she should be made a saint. It describes how she was sold as a slave at a 'cheap price', and brought to serve in the palace of a Frankish mayor, Erchinoald.

She was 'graceful in form ... a beautiful woman with a smiling face', 'kind-hearted, sober and prudent in all her ways', and well-loved by all in the household. When the mayor's wife died, he wanted to marry Balthild. In principle this was a great honour, but Balthild wasn't keen and fled the palace until Erchinoald gave up and married someone else. When she returned, the Frankish king, Clovis II, saw her, made her a free woman and married her himself, in 648AD.

Balthild had three sons by the King, all of whom lived to serve as kings themselves, but as none were old enough to succeed when Clovis died in 656AD, Balthild ruled as Queen Regent. She founded a number of hospitals, charitable and religious institutions, including the Abbey of Chelles outside Paris, and banned the selling of captive Christians in Frankish territories. The *Life* says that Balthild personally bought many slaves simply so she could free them.

Although this story of slave girl to Queen of the Franks is a charming one, it's probably not quite true. Many biographies of the medieval saints suggest they had very lowly beginnings, or were slaves, to romantically demonstrate their humble and godly ways. It's more likely that Balthild was a member of an East Anglian royal dynasty, a princess, when she married King Clovis.

## The mystery of the ring

There is no tradition of swivel seal rings known from Anglo-Saxon England, and no rings at all with women's names. There are, however, a number of surviving Frankish gold rings of high status and royal women's names on them, and some other rings with male names have engraved busts. One ring in the British Museum collections parallels the image of the two people embracing – it's a betrothal ring, dated to the 600s AD. It's quite possible that the Balthild seal was commissioned as a betrothal ring on the occasion of her and Clovis' marriage.

We have no idea how it ended up in Norfolk. Perhaps it was sent back to Balthild's family some time in the Early medieval period, or it may have been sent as a token during diplomatic business between the kingdoms. It's also possible that it was lost much later, in circumstances we can only guess at.

The beautiful ring has been acquired by the Norwich Castle Museum, and can now be appreciated by us all. Balthild is once again riding high.

See also:
Raglan Ring
Staffordshire Hoard
North West Essex Ring

# Sedgeford Coin Hoard

### Twenty golden coins stuffed inside a cow bone

Established in 1996, the Sedgeford Historical and Archaeological Research Project, or SHARP, is one of the largest independent archaeology projects in the country. Every year they welcome members of the public to dig with them, with the aim of uncovering the rich history of this small village. And it's quite a history – from Late Stone Age and Iron Age burials, to Roman, Anglo-Saxon, medieval and WWI sites, this little corner of Norfolk has seen a lot.

Alongside professional archaeologists, SHARP keeps its members involved in every stage of the archaeological process, from planning to publication. It's been called 'democratic archaeology' – archaeology of the people, for the people and by the people.

In August 2003, during an excavation at one of the local field sites that had already revealed some strange horse burials, a metal detectorist picked up a signal and discovered a cow's pelvis with a separate cow leg bone buried underneath it. The leg bone was unusually heavy, made a jangling noise and something metal was jutting out of the end.

The project co-director, Chris Mackie, took the bone to a local hospital and asked for it to be x-rayed. Chris was still in his muddy wellies and imaging manager Heather Masters thought the whole situation was a bit strange. But once she developed the x-ray film, the results were astonishing and the excitement was immediate – the bone was stuffed with coins.

Further inspection revealed twenty Iron Age gold coins dating to around

> "The leg bone was unusually heavy, made a jangling noise and something metal was jutting out of the end"

| |
|---|
| **Date:** About 50BC, Iron Age |
| **Where, when and how found:** Sedgeford, Norfolk; 2003; metal detecting as part of a community dig |
| **Finders:** Members of the Sedgeford Historical and Archaeological Research Project |
| **Official valuation:** £7,700 |
| **Where is it now?** Lynn Museum, King's Lynn, Norfolk www.museums.norfolk.gov.uk |
| **Get involved:** SHARP welcomes members of the public to join their courses and excavations www.sharp.org.uk |

50BC. They were identical to eight other coins found in previous seasons of the dig, and eleven more that had been scattered around the cow bone. All thirty-nine were a type known as a 'Gallo-Belgic Type E Stater'. Made from a blend of 50% gold, silver and copper, these coins are stamped with a stylised horse on one side and are plain on the other side (known as 'uniface'). Because there were more than two coins which were more than 300 years old, the finders knew that they had officially unearthed Treasure, and immediately reported it.

The Sedgeford coin hoard either represents wealth stashed for security, an act of fear at a time of danger, or more likely an offering to the gods for something as peaceful as a good harvest, a mild winter, or the health of a child.

It's relatively rare to find a coin hoard during an excavation, but finding one inside a bone is so far unique. It's possible that people regularly used hollow bones to store coins in, but it's more realistic to imagine them using leather or fabric purses for everyday storage. Whether the burial was

# "But it's equally likely that these popular coins reached Norfolk through ongoing exchange, and perhaps as diplomatic gifts"

made as an offering during a ritual (known as 'votive deposition'), or for safekeeping, we don't know.

## Gallo-Belgic coins

Around 60 to 50BC, the Roman Army was waging war against the native tribes living in ancient Gaul (modern-day northern France and Belgium) with the aim of taking control of the territory and expanding the frontiers of the Roman World. It's thought that Gallic tribal leaders paid native British warriors to travel across the English Channel and help them fight the Romans.

Experts previously thought that Gallo-Belgic staters were all minted in northern Gaul, and brought to southern England either by hired mercenary fighters returning home with their payments, or by Gallic refugees fleeing across the sea with the valuables and coins they could carry.

But it's equally likely that these popular coins reached Norfolk through ongoing exchange, and perhaps as diplomatic gifts.

This was a time of threat from Rome, with potentially complex and risky politics between different tribal leaders. But it was also a time with rich opportunity for trading and building allegiances.

See also:
Helmet Cremation Burial
Sedgeford Torc

# Sedgeford Torc

## Two pieces of a 2,000-year-old necklace discovered 40 years apart

During the Easter holidays in 2004, the Sedgeford Historical and Archaeological Research Project (SHARP) had organised a group of fieldwalkers and metal detectorists to survey a field together. One of the metal detectorists, Dr Steve Hammond, a retired chemistry lecturer, got a signal. And the piece of gold he unearthed was clearly ancient – the end piece, or terminal, of an Iron Age torc.

## Torcs

A torc is a neck ornament made of metal that would sit at the base of the wearer's neck. They were popular across Europe throughout the Bronze and Iron Ages, from around 2000BC–100AD. The styles of torcs changed, but the principle remained the same. The name 'torc' originates from the Latin word *torquere*, meaning 'to twist'. They were often made by twisting metal, as in this example. Most torcs only have a small gap in the ring, so they would have been difficult to put on and take off. It's been suggested that they were only worn for special occasions, or put on without the intention of taking them off again, like a modern wedding ring.

Peculiarly, the terminal Steve found looked familiar. Very quickly the researchers discovered that it was the missing part of a torc that had been found in 1965 just 400 metres away. The original piece was in the British Museum, claimed by the Crown as Treasure Trove

> "The name 'torc' originates from the Latin word *torquere*, meaning 'to twist'"

**Date:** Around 100BC, Iron Age

**Where, when and how found:** Sedgeford, Norfolk, 1965 & 2004; farm work (1965) & metal detecting as part of a Community Archaeology survey (2004)

**Finders:** A. E. Middleton (1965) & Steve Hammond (2004)

**Official valuation:** £65,000

**Where is it now?** Both pieces of the torc are displayed together at the British Museum, London www.britishmuseum.org

**Also visit:** Norwich Castle Museum, Norfolk www.museums.norfolk.gov.uk

**Get involved:** SHARP (Sedgeford Historical and Archaeological Research Project) welcomes volunteers www.sharp.org.uk

from the farmer who had dug it up when he was harrowing a field. The farmer had been given a reward of £3,300, an enormous sum in a time when fish and chips cost 6p and the average annual wage was £950.

After forty years, the Sedgeford Torc was finally reunited with its terminal, and its beauty was once again revealed. It's made of 25 metres of twisted gold and silver wire. Each wire, just 2mm thick, has been twisted with another, and then the pairs of wires twisted in threes to make eight six-stranded ropes. These ropes have again been twisted on themselves to create the intricate neck section. The hooped terminals have been cast in moulds with a distinctive 'trumpet swirl' pattern and raised beads. This kind of decoration style is known as *La Tène* art.

*La Tène* art is the technical term for what's popularly known as early 'Celtic' art. Plant motifs, animal patterns and swirling geometric designs popular across northern Europe were developed in Britain from around 450BC, and after 300BC British and Irish craftspeople developed their own distinctive styles. They were so accomplished that modern smiths struggle to copy their designs.

" *La Tène* art is the technical term for what's popularly known as early 'Celtic' art. Plant motifs, animal patterns and swirling geometric designs popular across northern Europe were developed in Britain from around 450BC "

See also:
Blair Drummond Hoard
Sedgeford Coin Hoard
Tanworth Comb

# Saltfleetby Spindle Whorl

### *Weaving magic in Viking clothes*

This little spindle whorl from Saltfleetby St Clement, in Lincolnshire, looks at first like a common archaeological find used for what was once an everyday activity – spinning.

The process of hand-spinning a sheep's fleece into yarn involves a few key steps. First, the wool is washed, dried and combed out. The end of the bundle of wool is then teased out into a strand and attached to

**Date:** 1000–1050AD, Viking

**Where, when and how found:** Saltfleetby St Clement, Lincolnshire; 2010; metal detecting

**Finder:** Denise Moncaster

**Where is it now?** Returned to finder

**Visit:** Jorvik Viking Centre, York www.jorvik-viking-centre.co.uk

a spindle, formed of a wooden pen-shaped 'spindle shaft', weighted with a small stone or lead bead with a hole in the middle, known as a 'spindle whorl'. Different sizes of spindle whorl are used to make different weight threads – the smaller the whorl, the finer the thread.

The spinner sets the spindle off in a circling motion, allowing it to sink towards the floor. As the spindle rotates, it pulls out and twists the fibres against each other into a neat, strong and even thread.

The smallest whorls are no bigger than beads, the largest, up to around 100g, would have been used to make thick, coarse yarn for outer garments, or for twisting more than one thread together to make a 'ply' yarn.

Although wooden, spindle shafts and actual fabrics rarely survive in archaeological contexts. The whorls, made of stone, chunky metal or other materials, are relatively common finds.

But this whorl is special. It's uniquely inscribed on the sides and flat face with Norse runes, the writing of the Vikings.

## The Vikings in Lincolnshire

The first definite record of raiding parties from Scandinavia is the attack on the monastery of Lindisfarne in 793AD. The English chroniclers refer to the raiders as Danes, or Northmen, sometimes 'the host', but in fact different groups came from Denmark, Norway and Sweden. The common acceptance of

the term 'Viking' really only began during the 1700s, along with the romantic idea of brave warrior men coming from across the sea to seek treasure and wage brutal but heroic battle.

In the 800s AD, Viking groups began to settle in north and east areas of the British Isles. When they settled Christian lands, Vikings often started to worship the Christian god alongside their traditional Norse gods. As part of the trade and peace treaty that King Alfred the Great brokered in 878AD with the Vikings, Viking leader Guthrum had to agree to convert to Christianity. Alfred acted as his godfather, and in exchange Alfred recognised Guthrum as the Christian ruler of East Anglia.

These evangelical urges were only partly to do with converting pagans to the Christian faith. The other, and perhaps more pressing, need to convert the Vikings was because Church teaching at the time stated that Christians should not trade with non-Christians. In some circumstances, Viking leaders would have the sign of the cross made over them, a practice known as being 'primsigned', which was considered an interim step towards baptism. In other cases Viking leaders and their people willingly and thoroughly adopted Christianity. Archaeologically, conversion to Christianity is most distinctively marked by graves without traditional Viking grave goods.

## Viking fashion

Experts have noted that the shape and style of the Saltfleetby Whorl would be quite unusual if it was found on a Viking site in Norway, which confirms that the Vikings living in Britain had developed their own regional styles, both for their clothes, and also for their tools and trinkets.

Vikings didn't write descriptions of what, to them, were everyday things – what they wore, how cloth was made, and other daily functions were understood by everyone and didn't need to be recorded. Most of our written sources from this period are either Anglo-Saxon records of battles, famines, kings and queens, or the epic story poems of the Icelandic and Orcadian sagas.

But from the archaeological evidence, as well as tiny details in written sources and illustrations, we can build a picture of what people wore, and the importance of clothes and personal adornment in Viking culture.

Fabric for clothes was made from linen or wool woven on an upright loom. It's also possible that exotic fabrics like silk reached Viking communities through trade and war spoils, and the sagas mention wedding gifts of cloth with gold woven into them. Embroidery and braid around cuffs, collars and hems would have been popular, and jewellery including strings of beads, brooches and hair clips were worn just as they are today.

> "Viking clothes were designed and made to last for years, and it's likely their clothes were finished to a higher quality than most of our clothes are today"

Men wore tunics with belts, and trousers that were either loose or tight along the leg. Some wore cloth bandages wrapped around their calves over their trousers, protecting their legs and keeping their trousers clean. Women wore long shift dresses with sleeves, with outer, more elaborate over-dresses. Both men and women wore thick woollen cloaks, wool socks and leather shoes. Vikings didn't know knitting techniques, instead they used *nålbinding*, 'needle-binding', using a single thick needle to create a knotted textile that could be shaped into hats, mittens and socks.

Modern experiments show that to make enough yarn to produce a typical set of clothes for an adult man and woman in the 11th century, you'd need about 6kg of raw wool (one sheep gives 1–2kg), spun into 40,000m of yarn, then woven into cloth and finally sewed into garments. It would require weeks of work, and all clothes would have been carefully cared for and repaired until they wore out. Some undershirts have been discovered made from odd patchworks of cloth, and it's quite likely that people were cutting out the less worn sections of old clothes and patching them together to make a new item, rather than throwing the whole thing away.

The archaeological evidence we do have for Viking textiles reveals fine-quality cloth and intricate and precise sewing – Viking clothes were designed and made to last for years, and it's likely their clothes were finished to a higher quality than most of our clothes are today.

## The inscribed whorl

Runes were the written letters of the Scandinavian cultures. By the 11th century, a new form of their alphabet, known as the *futhork*, or 'Medieval Runes', was evolving with 27 characters and dots between strings of letters.

The inscription on the Saltfleetby Spindle Whorl runs around the vertical wall and the flat face of the whorl. The form of the lettering has been dated to 1000–1100AD, but only half of it is easy to decipher.

Along the wall, it says:

**.oþen.ok.einmtalr.ok.þalfa.þeir.**
which was translated by Professor John Hines at Cardiff University as
**Óðinn and Heimdallr and Thjalfi, they...**

Odin and Heimdallr are important Viking gods that were worshipped before Viking communities converted to Christianity. Thjalfi is a name associated with a servant boy of the god Thor, but in the form on the whorl, this might be a female name, or a poetic word referencing the sea.

Along the face of the whorl, it says:

**ielba.þeruolflt.ok.kiriuesf.**
which is translated as **... help thee, Úlfljótr and** [*xxx*]

Úlfljótr is probably a man's name, but experts are uncertain about the meaning of 'kiriuesf'.

So the summary meaning is 'The gods Odin and Heimdallr and Thjalfi will help you, Úlfljótr and [xxx]'.

By the 11th century Vikings were Christian and had built a number of churches in the region dedicated to St Clement, a patron saint linked to seafaring communities. This spindle whorl proves that the Old Gods were still called upon, and woven into everyday life.

## Weaving magic

We often make the dangerous error of thinking that housework isn't as important as the work that goes on 'out there' in the public domain. In fact our modern term for an unmarried woman is still *spinster*. But the Vikings believed that work that was done in the home, traditionally women's work, wasn't just important practically, it was also important spiritually.

Old Norse literature often connects spinning and weaving with fate and magical activity. There was a folk belief that goddesses would examine women's spindles at Midwinter, the shortest day of the year, and if the women clearly worked hard, the goddesses would bless the household with good fortune and a good harvest; if the women were not industrious, disaster would befall the house in the coming year. The fate of the whole household rested on women's work.

Children's fate and health were also wound up with spinning. A tradition amongst pregnant Swedish Viking women was to spin three linen threads and dye one black, one red and one white. The White would be used to tie off the umbilical cord at the birth, the Red would be tied around the baby's wrist to ward off the evil eye, and the Black, a sign of death and misfortune, would be burned in the fire.

Other spindle whorls, cut from rock crystal, have been discovered in Viking graves, which would flash as they spun, and others from amber or jet, which were considered to be made from the fertility goddess Freyja's tears. Just like the Saltfleetby Spindle Whorl, these were ways to imbue every thread with protective magic. There were also magical incantations that could be used to weave either good or ill into the cloth being made on a loom – mothers and sisters were said to be able to weave protective shirts for their menfolk going into battle, and other stories describe women weaving poisoned shirts to cause misfortune and death to enemies.

Churchmen were so concerned about women practising magic during spinning and weaving that they specifically outlawed it. Around the year 1010, Bishop Burchard of Worms described a common belief in the community that threads become so intertwined during weaving that unless spells are cast at the same time, a loved one's fate might end up entangled and they'd die. The bishop determined that if you consented to this practice, or were present when it happened, you needed to do thirty days' penance on bread and water to atone for the sin.

We still have special and potent textiles now – from religious clothes and woven prayer mats, to wedding veils, military uniforms and the more prosaic 'lucky socks'.

See also:
Vale of York Viking Hoard
Llanbedrgoch Viking Treasure

# Navenby Witch Bottle

## *A magical belief from the 1800s*

Jo and Michael Butler were having some building work done at their home in Navenby, Lincolnshire, when they discovered a small green glass bottle nestled in the foundations. It looked old-fashioned, and had some bits and pieces inside it, but it wasn't obviously anything more than an odd little bottle. Jo put it under the stairs and there it sat.

**Date:** 1820–1880, Post Medieval

**Where, when and how found:** Navenby, Lincolnshire; found 1999, reported 2003; discovered during building work

**Finders:** Jo and Michael Butler

**Where is it now?** Museum of Lincolnshire Life, Lincoln www.lincolnshire.gov.uk/ visiting/museums

Four years later, Lincolnshire County Council held an archaeology evening and the Butlers decided to show their bottle to the local Finds Liaison Officer, Adam Daubney. He immediately knew exactly what it was – a witch bottle.

Made from an old inkwell bottle with a strap of leather, bent pins, iron hooks, human hair and possibly urine inside, the bottle had been sealed into the floor of the building for at least 180 years. Witch bottles like this one were intended to bounce bad spells or evil intentions away from the victim and the home, and back on to the person who was sending them. Even if you didn't know who the spell-caster was, the bottle would protect you. If a person in the village became sick or died shortly after you created your witch bottle, you would know that they were the witch and had been targeted by their own spell.

Belief in witchcraft and magic was particularly common in Britain up until quite modern times. In a time before modern scientific explanations, people thought that illness, disability or accidents could be caused by evil forces – perhaps as a result of a sin they'd committed or because a curse had been set against them. These beliefs were woven into a world view that combined Christian religion, spells, curses and charms, as well as a whole cast of strange and powerful semi-human and spirit creatures. Witches were thought to control these powerful and potentially dangerous forces.

## Who were witches?

Many 'witches' were lone, older women who practised folk healing and midwifery and were relied on by the community to create herbal remedies, love potions and protective charms. It would have seemed like they had power over sickness and health, and even life and death. Until around the late 1500s, this 'white magic' was considered an unproblematic, normal part of life and belief.

But then Christian Church and secular leaders began to demonise these folk magic practitioners as being in league with the devil, and in many places 'witches' were tortured and murdered.

Some people, known as 'cunning-folk', did continue practising white magic without persecution. They were seen to be useful and on the side

"Experts estimate that more than 12,000 people have been executed as witches in Europe since the medieval period" of 'good', and helped to protect people against 'bad' witches. But dabbling in magic was risky, potentially exposing you to accusations of harmful witchcraft.

'Ordeals' to discover whether someone was a witch included dropping them, bound, into water to see if they floated, dunking them in rivers tied to a 'ducking stool' to see if they drowned, or weighing them against the Bible to see which was heavier. This was in addition to the usual practices of torturing someone until they confessed, and encouraging 'witnesses' to testify against suspected witches.

Some of the most famous witchcraft trials in Britain are the North Berwick trials of 1590 and the Pendle witch trials of 1612. Experts estimate that more than 12,000 people have been executed as witches in Europe since the medieval period. People around the world are still executed for crimes of witchcraft today, and others have been murdered or mutilated for body parts to be used in witchcraft rituals.

The tide change in Britain came when the Witchcraft Act of 1735 was passed by British Parliament, making it a crime to *accuse* someone of witchcraft, rather than the previous century's crime of *being* a witch. Embracing the scientific rationalism of the modern age, leaders wanted to eradicate what they saw as the ignorance and superstition of uneducated people.

Clearly, many people held on to beliefs that harm could be caused by magical means, and by magical people, and that's why, in the mid-1800s, someone in Navenby made their witch bottle.

## Counter-magical devices

One theory for the 'recipe' of ingredients in the Navenby bottle is that the urine and bent pins would cause the witch to feel like they were passing pins when they went to the toilet – a heartily unpleasant experience at the best of times, and excruciating in an era before modern painkillers and antibiotics.

The other possible rationale behind the bottle is that evil forces trying to enter the home would be lured by the smell of the hair, snagged on the bent pins, then drowned in the urine.

One of the earliest known accounts of preparing witch bottles is from Joseph Glanvill's 1681 treatise 'Evidence concerning Witches and Apparitions'. Glanvill recounts the case of a man whose wife was ill and plagued by a 'thing in the shape of a bird'. An old travelling man advised that this must be a dead sprite, and to cure her of her bewitchment the husband was instructed to:

> 'Take your Wife's Urine ... Cork it in a Bottle with Nails, Pins and Needles, and bury it in the Earth; and that will do the feat [to cure her].'

Glanvill tells us the dutiful husband did as he was told and his wife began to 'mend sensibly'.

Counter-magical devices seem to have been buried into the foundations and walls of buildings since prehistoric times – Neolithic (late Stone Age, around 3000BC) roundhouses have revealed animal and human bones buried in the floors, Green Men and other folk images were carved into medieval Christian churches, and some of the buried treasures described in this book may well have been deposited to protect the occupants of a home or community from perceived evil.

Witch Bottles weren't the only tool available – old shoes, cats entombed while alive and horses' skulls have all been found built into walls, doorways and chimney breasts to protect occupants and 'catch' evil. Pinning a horseshoe above a door is a continuation of this ancient tradition, and hidden human shoes are regularly found during building work in British homes. Northampton Museum keeps a 'Concealed Shoe Index' and invites people who find shoes hidden in the floors, walls and chimneys of old buildings to report them. Their database already holds details of more than 1,900 concealed shoes.

See also:
Billingford Amulet
Saltfleetby Spindle Whorl

# Syston Knife Handle

### *An erotic depiction of a man, a woman, another man and a severed head*

David Baker was metal detecting on farmland in Syston when he got a signal, dug down and discovered this very unusual copper-alloy Roman knife handle. At 64mm long, it would have been riveted to a short fixed blade, making a functional domestic knife. What's most striking is the three-dimensional design that forms the handle.

**Date:** 43–410AD, Roman

**Where, when and how found:** Syston, Lincolnshire; 2007; metal detecting

**Finder:** David Baker

**Where is it now?** Collection Museum, Lincoln www.thecollectionmuseum.com

The design depicts a rather acrobatic sex scene – an adult male on the right is being straddled by a woman in the middle, who is in turn leaning on the back of a smaller man on the left, who is holding what appears to be a severed human head. The smaller man could perhaps be a juvenile or a dwarf, and all three figures have their heads turned, looking out to right and left. Careful inspection of the Syston handle shows that the tall man on the right isn't actually having sexual intercourse with the lady in the middle, but is directing his attentions towards the smaller chap at the end.

Decorative knife handles are quite common from the Roman period. The most popular design is of a hound chasing a hare, others include figures in wrestling embraces and gladiators. Other erotic knife handles have been found from Roman Britain, including a crouching woman straddling a man lying down, found in North Yorkshire, a nude standing female figure, from Worcestershire, and two knives similar to the Syston knife handle. The other 'threesome' knife handles show the same three figures but minus the severed head. So far this addition is unique.

> "An adult male on the right is being straddled by a woman in the middle, who is in turn leaning on the back of a smaller man on the left, who is holding what appears to be a severed human head"

The design is certainly eye-catching, but what could it mean? The discovery of more than one knife handle showing variants of the same 'threesome' scene suggest that they refer to a well-known story, song or myth. No 'threesome' knife handles have been found outside Britain, so it's likely that this was a story with a British provenance and these knife handles were manufactured here.

## Rude Britannia

We don't have written evidence of the folk traditions of Roman Britain – the native Britons didn't keep written records, and Roman historians and writers tended to restrict their accounts to matters of 'importance' rather than the folk entertainment or rituals of provincial Romano-British society. Romans often incorporated native traditions into their ritual and religious practices and it's more than likely that they also enjoyed songs and stories from the native British repertoire. Perhaps the characters featured in a bawdy tale, poem, or raucous song.

It's easy to interpret the Syston Knife Handle as a bit of Romano-British smut, but some experts have suggested that this interpretation reveals more about our own modern attitudes to sex, rather than those of Roman-Britons. Perhaps this knife handle reflects a fertility or rebirth story, something with ritual importance, rather than a playful and saucy trinket. It's also possible that the knife handle represents Roman attitudes to the 'barbarian' practices of the natives. Head-hunting cults may well have existed in native British cultures, and it's possible that this strange sex scene is mocking, satirical and demeaning.

We can't be sure, and archaeology will struggle to offer us the answers. What remains is our modern response to this strange, charming and intriguing object – and if it entertains us, then perhaps it entertained its Roman owners as well.

See also:
Putney 'Brothel' Token
Roman Slave Shackle

# Billingford Amulet

## A Roman magical charm inscribed with a secret message

This beautiful gold sheet known as a *lamella* (meaning 'small tablet' in Latin) was discovered accidentally in a Norfolk garden. Originally it would have been tightly rolled up and hung in a tubular pendant around the neck as a protective talisman. Its protective power is contained in the inscription scratched on to its surface,

**Date:** 60–150AD, Roman

**Where, when and how found:** Billingford, Norfolk; 2003; chance find in a garden

**Finder:** Anonymous

**Official valuation:** £10,000

**Where is it now?** Norwich Castle Museum, Norfolk
www.museums.norfolk.gov.uk

a mysterious spell offering an intriguing insight into one man's life and belief in Roman Britain almost two thousand years ago.

The gold sheet, 4cm by 3cm, weighing just 1.93g and 91% pure (almost 22 carat), is soft enough to easily inscribe. Using a fine, needle-point stylus, someone has confidently written a series of words and symbols in Greek, Latin and magical characters across nine lines and two side-lines, that give the formula of a protective charm.

The text begins with a series of magical symbols that look a bit like Greek, and then the inscription continues:

> **Iao, Abrasax [ ... ], ablanathanalba,**
> **give health and victory (to)**
> **Tiberius Claudius Similis whom Herennia Marcellina bore**

*Iao* and *Abrasax*, written in Greek, are the names of gods. Incredibly, the word *ablanathanalba* is a well-known magical word, the Roman equivalent of our 'Abracadabra'.

The bottom lines reveal that this treasure was originally owned by Tiberius Claudius Similis. Similis was a common name in Roman Germany, and the owner was probably a citizen from the Lower Rhine area, posted as a soldier

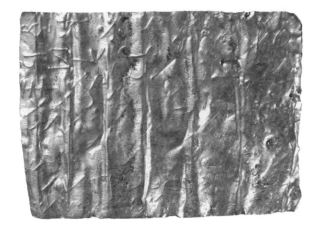

to the new northern Roman province, Britannia, after the initial conquest in 43AD.

Although these magical amulets would have been quite common in the Roman Empire, there are only seventy survivals in the world. Quite how this one ended up sitting in the grass of 21st century Norfolk, we will never know. It's most likely that it was simply dropped or fell off and, incredibly, neither destroyed nor discovered in twenty centuries.

Just like modern-day lucky charms, it's not always easy to work out how much someone believes in magical power, even if they do wear a 'magical' artefact. People across cultures and throughout time have always tried to control and manage 'fate', the unknown, and luck. Often we have conflicting and competing belief systems that we turn to in different circumstances. For example, people who go to church at Christmas may still blow on their dice for luck, wear a grandparent's treasured jewellery for a job interview and not step on the cracks in the pavement on the way out of the house. The social, psychological and spiritual importance of artefacts are always entwined; most of the time, we don't stop to unravel and analyse our beliefs.

The situation was probably the same for Tiberius Claudius. Perhaps a family member commissioned the amulet from a professional magician or priest; perhaps he paid to have it made himself. Certainly, the person who wrote the inscription was well-versed in Greek, Latin and the strange magical symbols. We don't know whether this lamella helped Tiberius Claudius, but it's certainly a triumph that it was discovered, reported and is now displayed for us all to appreciate.

**See also:**
Cautopates Figurine
Ashwell Hoard
Hockley Pendant

# Happisburgh Handaxe

## *Evidence of the earliest Britons*

Mike Chambers was walking his dog in Happisburgh (pronounced 'Haze-bruh'), Norfolk, when a shaped black stone on the beach caught his eye.

As Mike lifted the stone out of the thick clay it was sitting in, he immediately recognised it as an ancient tool known as a 'handaxe' – a tool designed to be held directly in the hand rather than attached to a handle. This was an extraordinary find. It had eroded out of the ancient mud and sand levels that had once been the ground surface 500,000 years ago – meaning it was at least that old.

> **Date:** 500,000BC, Palaeolithic (Early Stone Age)
>
> **Where, when and how found:** Happisburgh beach, Norfolk; 2000; chance find while dog walking
>
> **Finder:** Mike Chambers
>
> **Where is it now?** Norwich Castle Museum, Norwich www.museums.norfolk.gov.uk
>
> **Visit online:** Natural History Museum online resources www.nhm.ac.uk/nature-online/life/human-origins/

Shaped from a natural chunk of flint, this tool has been systematically struck to remove sharp flakes of stone until it's the ideal shape and sharpness. It's been worked on both sides and is designed to fit well into a human hand. Analysis of the patterns of scratches and surface damage, called 'use-wear analysis', reveals that handaxes were multi-functional, used for scraping and cutting hides, bones, wood and meat. They were the Swiss Army knives of their day, and based on the position of Mike's find we know that it's one of the earliest handaxes we have.

Simpler human stone tools have been discovered in sites nearby dating to an incredible 800,000 years ago. It means that early human species reached northern Europe much earlier than we'd previously thought.

> "This tool has been systematically struck to remove sharp flakes of stone until it's the ideal shape and sharpness"

The earliest humans evolved in Africa, and reached southern Europe perhaps around 1.5 million years ago. Experts didn't think they moved

north of the Alps until 500,000 years ago, but evidence from Happisburgh pushes the dates back by another 300,000 years. At that time, the climate was colder than it is now – the habitat was mainly pine forest and the winters were long, similar to modern southern Scandinavia. To have survived these conditions means that these early humans were smarter, better equipped and more mobile than we'd thought.

## Early humans

The people who made the Happisburgh handaxe weren't modern humans – *Homo sapiens* – they belonged to an earlier ancestor species, but until human fossils are discovered in the area, we can't be sure which species we're dealing with. The likely candidate is *Homo heidelbergensis*, who were tall, agile tool-makers with brains almost as big as ours. It's very likely that they wore furs or hides, could control fire, worked together to hunt and forage, and cooked their food. We don't know if they had language, but it's suspected that they could speak simply.

The landscape of Happisburgh would have looked very different at the time these people were living here. Mike's find was in an area that used to be a riverbank in an ancient valley. At this time Britain was connected to continental Europe by a wide land-bridge. Sea levels were probably similar to today, but a chalk ridge between Kent and northern France, and an area known to archaeologists as 'Doggerland', were above sea level. The chalk was breached by the sea about 450,000 years ago, forming the English Channel, and now Doggerland is under the North Sea.

Although the climate was colder, the banks along the river were lush and grazed by lots of animals – fossils of deer, bison, rhino, carnivores and aquatic animals reveal that this was an area where the river was slow-flowing, and food for herbivores and carnivores was plentiful. It would have been a bountiful habitat for these smart ape-men with their stone tools and well-honed survival tactics.

The person who made and used this handaxe understood his or her materials and environment, and wouldn't have thrown this tool away lightly. Their sophisticated tool technology marks this species out as special, and there's some evidence that handaxes became the first 'prestige' items ever – beautifully shaped and worked to a level beyond anything that improved their usefulness. Just like so many other treasures in this book, this handaxe shows that humans have always found unique ways to express themselves.

When Mike discovered and picked up the handaxe, he was the first person to hold it for more than half a million years. Something about that stone meant he saw the human 'signature', and in that instant, he shared an incredible connection to a person half a million years away.

See also:
Isle of Wight Axehead
Syston Knife Handle
Dartmoor Sword

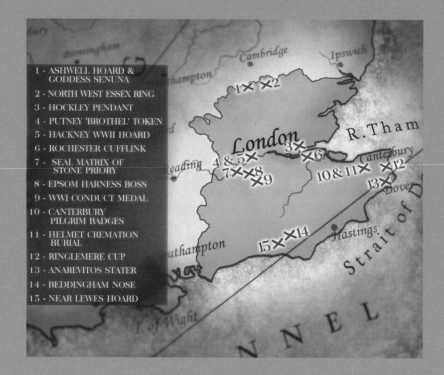

1 - ASHWELL HOARD &
    GODDESS SENUNA

2 - NORTH WEST ESSEX RING

3 - HOCKLEY PENDANT

4 - PUTNEY 'BROTHEL' TOKEN

5 - HACKNEY WWII HOARD

6 - ROCHESTER CUFFLINK

7 - SEAL MATRIX OF
    STONE PRIORY

8 - EPSOM HARNESS BOSS

9 - WWI CONDUCT MEDAL

10 - CANTERBURY
     PILGRIM BADGES

11 - HELMET CREMATION
     BURIAL

12 - RINGLEMERE CUP

13 - ANAREVITOS STATER

14 - BEDDINGHAM NOSE

15 - NEAR LEWES HOARD

THE SOUTH EAST has borne witness to some pivotal moments in Britain's history. Ancient centres of power, like Canterbury, Colchester and Royal Tunbridge Wells have shaped our nation in ways we often underappreciate. And being so close to the continent, the South East has seen more than just the weather come across the Channel.

When the Romans invaded in 43AD, they built Dover Lighthouse, coastal forts like Richborough, and developed thriving civilian centres like Verulamium (St Albans). Saxon shore forts reveal the next wave of neighbours to arrive and radically transform our country. A few hundred years later, William the Conqueror's 1066 victory is memorialised in his castle at Hastings and the abbey at Battle, and defences from almost every generation onwards are apparent in the landscape and in the artefacts we find. The **Hackney WWII Hoard (p68)** captures a moment when a terrified citizen feared the next invaders were on their way.

Ever mindful of that delicate relationship with close neighbours, the people of the South East have played clever political games through the years. A number of the finds from this region hint at political scheming in camps, courts and castles – from the Iron Age **Anarevitos Stater (p80)**, to the Anglo-Saxon ruler who wore the **North West Essex Ring (p58)**, to the 17th-century **Rochester Cufflink (p60)** and the **Epsom Horse Harness Boss (p72)**.

Generations of residents in the South East have felt threats from across the water, but have also experienced times of power. The **Ringlemere Cup (p54)** and **Helmet Cremation Burial (p75)** are incredible finds that reveal the prestigious networks South Eastern people have been involved with. More intimate possessions, like **George Humber's Distinguished Conduct Medal (p90)** and the **Canterbury Pilgrim Badges (p86)** are poignant reminders that extraordinary historical events are always played out in the personal experiences of everyday people.

The South East is the most densely populated region in the British Isles and London dominates, of course, with its 8.5 million residents. The mighty River Thames has been a focus of activity since humans arrived in Britain, and it's been described as the largest archaeological site in Britain. This liquid history begins in Gloucestershire and flows out to the sea in Kent, via royal Windsor and through the heart of London. The **Putney 'Brothel' Token (p95)** is just one tiny, evocative artefact that represents the millions of people who've lived and worked along this ancient riverside.

# Ashwell Hoard and the Goddess Senuna

## A *unique Roman temple treasure that reveals a new British goddess*

Alan Meek was detecting in an ordinary field in Hertfordshire when he thought that he'd picked up a sandwich wrapper. He quickly realised it was actually a very ancient piece of silver, and it wasn't alone.

Alan had pinpointed a rare assemblage of twenty 'votive plaques' – thin sheets of gold and silver with religious words and images inscribed on them, some items of jewellery, two small silver arms and a silver statuette.

Over the next few years, the Ashwell site was excavated by professional archaeologists and the local community archaeological society. It's helped us build a picture of how these precious treasures ended up where they did.

Each of the objects in the Ashwell Hoard was a personal offering made at a Roman temple shrine honouring a goddess. Romans in Britain, as well as Britons who had adopted a Roman way of life ('Romanised' Britons), worshipped many different gods and goddesses and would travel to local shrines to pray for assistance and protection with specific troubles. Many would vow that if they did get help from the god or goddess, they'd return to the shrine to make an offering in thanks.

You could either bring a precious offering of your own, or leave a votive 'plaque', a shaped and decorated metal strip specifically crafted as a temple gift. The pieces of jewellery in the hoard are probably personal items that were offered at the temple by different people. The votive plaques are all similar in style, so it's possible that they were purchased from a stall selling standard plaques that could then be personalised by engraving your own prayer or vow. Silver votive plaques have been found elsewhere, but gold

> **Date:** 200–400AD, Roman
> **Where, when and how found:** Ashwell, Hertfordshire; 2002; metal detecting rally
> **Finder:** Alan Meek
> **Official valuation:** £37,137
> **Where is it now?** British Museum, London
> www.britishmuseum.org

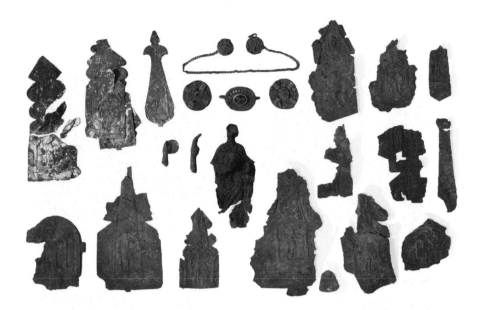

plaques are much rarer, and only two others have been found in Britain – the Ashwell Hoard contains seven.

## Who is Senuna?

Most of the leaf-shaped plaques have been stamped with a standard image of a gabled shrine with Minerva, the well-known Roman Goddess of Wisdom (as well as other things), standing within it in a typical pose. But beneath the image, in the space left for an inscription, the plaques have been dedicated to a different, previously unknown goddess, Senuna.

One plaque is dedicated by a woman called Lucilia, who 'willingly and deservedly fulfilled her vow' to the goddess, another two plaques are inscribed:

**'Servandus Hispani willingly fulfilled his vow to the Goddess Se(nuna)' (DSE SERVANDVS HISPANI V S L)**

It seems clear that Senuna was either a goddess linked to Minerva, or perhaps the local 'version' of the same deity.

It wasn't initially clear to the archaeologists who the statuette represented, as any potentially distinguishing features had broken or corroded away. But incredibly, a year after the original hoard was found, the archaeological

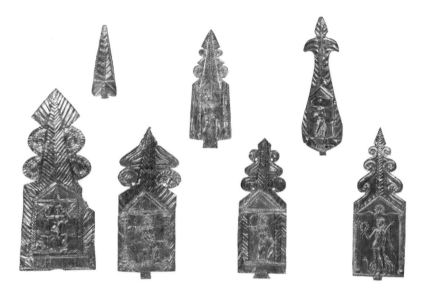

excavation unearthed the base of the same statue, and it had the name 'Senuna' inscribed on it. This mysterious silver figure is the only known representation of Senuna. The statue's face has been lost, but the back of the figure shows a full-length draped garment, probably a dress, and the woman's hair tied neatly in a bun at the nape of her neck.

## Burial

A large number of finds were made during the archaeological excavations that followed Alan's discovery, revealing evidence of centuries of ritual activity in the same area. The hoard itself wasn't inside the shrine building, but buried in a shallow hole on its own. At some point between 200 and 400AD, it seems that a temple official collected up the finest gold and silver gifts from the shrine, carefully packed them in a cloth bag, and buried them a short distance away.

We won't ever know why the valuables were taken out of the shrine, but it may be linked to conflict between newly converted Roman Christians and the people who continued to worship the old gods, including Senuna. For whatever reason, the person who buried the hoard never returned and so the sacred offerings to this British goddess lay undisturbed for more than 1,600 years.

It's a tantalising possibility that there may be many other British gods and goddesses that we don't yet know about.

**See also:**
Cautopates Figurine
County Durham River
    Assemblage

# Ringlemere Cup

## A gold drinking vessel buried in a lost mound

In 2001, the finder was studying archaeology as an adult learner and continuing his hobby of metal detecting – a passion he'd been enjoying for more than eight years. He was searching a recently harvested potato field when he got a strong signal from his machine. He dug down into the soil and saw a shining gold cup. It had been hit by

> **Date:** 1700–1500BC, Bronze Age
>
> **Where, when and how found:** Ringlemere, near Sandwich, Kent; 2001; metal detecting
>
> **Finder:** Anonymous
>
> **Where is it now?** British Museum, London
> www.britishmuseum.org

modern farm machinery so was crushed along its side, but it was immediately clear that this was something very special and probably ancient. If he hadn't found it when he did, it would have almost certainly been utterly destroyed by the next round of ploughing.

The finder took the squashed cup home and did some quick research – he discovered one similar cup had been unearthed in the 1830s in Rillaton, Cornwall, and was now a celebrated item in the British Museum collection dating to the prehistoric Bronze Age. The finder called Michael Lewis, his local Finds Liaison Officer, and the farmers who owned the land, and reported his amazing discovery.

## Ritual cups

Gold is a prized substance across most cultures and throughout history. It's rare, and in its pure state it doesn't tarnish, fade or react to any other substance. It's soft enough to work easily and in the hands of a skilled craftsperson it can be formed into any number of breathtaking pieces. The Ringlemere Cup is one of these pieces – beaten out from a sheet of thick gold, with a wide strip of gold for the handle, it weighs 184g and is about 82% pure gold and 10% silver, which is a common metal mix for naturally-occurring gold found in rivers. It has a simple corrugated design, and tiny diamond-shaped rivets to fix the handle in place. Intriguingly, its base is rounded, meaning that it can't stand up on its own. It would either have had some kind of stand to hold it upright,

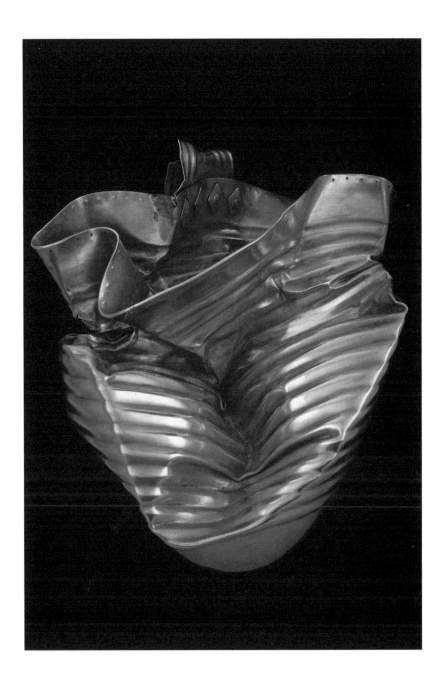

or it was designed to never be put down – perhaps passed from person to person in a ceremony, or held in the hands of one high-status individual.

The Ringlemere Cup dates to the Bronze Age, a period that begins around 2400BC and continues until the Iron Age, which is marked by the introduction of iron-making technology, in around 800BC. The Ringlemere Cup is from the middle of the Bronze Age period, around 1700–1500BC, making it at least 3,500 years old. Prompt reporting to the PAS meant that a thorough excavation of the site could be completed. An initial assessment turned into a five-year project, with geophysics surveys, multiple seasons of excavation, fieldwalking and organised metal-detector surveys. The results have put this incredible cup into an equally remarkable context.

## The ploughed-out mound

A tiny rise in the farmer's field, the area that the finder had been searching, proved to be the remains of a ploughed-out type of monument known as a round barrow, over 50m in diameter. It appears that the first version of the monument was a timber structure, and then a 'henge' was built – a circular ditch and bank with a small entrance passage. This dated from the Neolithic, the late Stone Age, up to 2,000 years before the Ringlemere Cup came into existence. Other smaller monuments and circles were built around the large henge, and later a soil mound, the round barrow, was built right at the heart of the site.

The archaeologists had thought that they would get evidence to show that this was a Bronze Age burial mound which people had sited inside an already-ancient monument, but no evidence of a grave pit, skeleton or cremation has been found. This might be because it simply hasn't survived the passage of time, with generations of farmers ploughing the mound flat, or it might be because there never was any burial, and this mound was for some other purpose.

"The archaeological excavation also showed that Anglo-Saxon people in the 400s and 500s AD had used the field for burials"

The archaeological excavation also showed that Anglo-Saxon people in the 400s and 500s AD had used the field for burials. It looks like an ordinary farmer's field now, but for more than forty generations, this site was very special.

## European union

The extensive investigation of the Ringlemere field revealed large scatters of flints and early pottery, and also, significantly, two amber artefacts near to the site of the cup. Amber was mined from along the Baltic Sea coast – modern-day Poland, Germany and Lithuania – and traded westwards to prehistoric tribes across France, Spain and Britain. The people in Kent at that time appear to have been at the midpoint in a prestigious trade network that stretched from continental Europe into west England and Ireland. Ideas, people and precious goods flowed through their hands from across the sea, and it's likely that they were considered to be important and wealthy people.

We often try to understand prehistoric people and their allegiances with a modern map in our minds, but it doesn't always help: the British Isles weren't a united region, and the sea wasn't considered a barrier – it was an opportunity to travel and trade. People in Kent were much more closely aligned to communities who lived along the coasts of France, Belgium, the Netherlands and north-west Germany, than with people in west and north Britain. Several precious vessels like the Ringlemere Cup have been found across north-west Europe, made from gold, silver, amber and shale. Most of these cups are from sites along the sea coast, which suggests that these cups were an especially important tradition for this network of coastal communities.

Although we don't have standing monuments from this period in Kent (unlike Wiltshire, where we have Stonehenge, Avebury and Silbury Hill, for example), archaeological evidence is pointing to a rich and unique culture that flourished in this area three and a half thousand years ago. The Ringlemere Cup is part of that great society.

The Ringlemere Cup is now displayed next to the only other British example, the majestic Rillaton Cup, in the British Museum, London. It's a treasure of international importance.

See also:
Carpow Logboat
Horns and Crotal Musical
  Instruments
Milton Keynes Hoard

# North West Essex Ring

## *Pagan and Christian belief combined*

This chunky solid gold finger ring, discovered by a metal detectorist in November 2011, tells the enormous story of religious conversion in the British Isles.

A striking image is on the flat top, the bezel, in a frame of engraved dots: A human figure in profile, probably male, and seemingly naked save for a belt, holds a cross in one hand and a bird in the other. A second bird hangs above the figure's head. The whole hoop of the ring is decorated – with birds, a pair of very stylised animal heads and an intricate, abstract interlaced pattern. The size of the ring suggests it was worn by a man.

> **Date:** 580–650AD, Early Medieval
> **Where, when and how found:** North-west Essex; 2011; metal detecting
> **Finder:** Anonymous
> **Where is it now?** Saffron Walden Museum hopes to acquire www.vistsaffronwalden.gov.uk
> **Visit:** Sutton Hoo royal burial site, near Ipswich, Suffolk. www.nationaltrust.org.uk/sutton-hoo/

## Art and belief

Using the form of the ring and the style of the engraving, it has been dated to the late 500s or early 600s AD, a time when the kingdom of Essex was first under the control of the kings of Kent, and then later overlorded by the kingdom of East Anglia.

The *Ecclesiastical History of the English People*, written by the early historian and monk known as the Venerable Bede in 731AD, describes attacks on England by several Germanic tribes from continental Europe in the late 300s and early 400s AD. Initial raiding parties were followed by people wanting to stay, and eventually three tribes – the Angles, Saxons and Jutes – set up small kingdoms in what was to become England. The Anglian kingdoms included East Anglia, and eventually gave the name to the whole of Angle-land – England.

Unlike the Romano-British, who were mostly Christian, the Angles, Saxons and Jutes were pagan, and worshipped a pantheon of gods and goddesses. It's been suggested that the man on the ring is the Anglo-Saxon god Woden (the origin of the day name, 'Wednesday', *Woden's Day*, and aligned with the Norse god 'Odin'). Woden seems to have been the highest of the gods, linked to carrying off the dead and to fury, poetry and inspiration. It's not 100% clear how similar beliefs about Woden and Odin were, but in Viking mythology from a few hundred years later, Odin is said to have had two ravens, Huginn and Muninn, who fly around the world bringing him information. There are also suggestions that Woden himself could transform into a bird, or send his spirit to possess a bird's body. The link between birds, spiritual power and humans is common in many cultural traditions – until more research is done, we can't be sure who the ring represents.

But this intriguing figure is also holding a cross, a distinctly Christian symbol. There isn't evidence for the cross shape being meaningful to any of the European tribes before Christianity was introduced.

Bede describes how, in 597AD, the Pope sent a missionary to England to found a church and convert the people. This missionary was St Augustine, and when he landed in England he first visited the court of Æthelberht, the King of Kent, whose wife was a Christian from the Frankish kingdom (which covered modern-day France and some of Germany). Æthelberht converted to Christianity and gave Augustine land to build a church at Canterbury, which is still the centre of English Christianity. Following Augustine and other missionaries, pagan kings across England converted, although it's not certain that they fully relinquished their attachment to their old gods. According to Bede, some kings worshipped at shrines of the old gods as well as at Christian altars.

But as more Anglo-Saxons converted to Christianity and promised at the baptismal font to forsake their pagan ways, the nature of the old gods began to change. Instead of being forgotten, they began to be incorporated into semi-legendary genealogies of the royal families. By the time Bede wrote his history in the 700s AD, Woden had become the great-great grandfather of the fabled first Anglo-Saxon invaders in England, Hengist and Horsa.

These were extraordinary, dynamic times in English history – brutal, warmongering, but also incredibly religious. The mixed symbolism on this ring is unique, and it reveals the complex integration of belief systems at this time.

See also:
Staffordshire Hoard
Holderness Cross
Baldehildis Seal

# Rochester Cufflink

## A little link to the Merry Monarch

This finder was metal detecting a field in Kent in February 2001, when he got a signal and saw a glint in the soil. He pulled out a small, solid silver button with a stamped decoration on one of the discs. The striking decoration is of two touching hearts under a single crown, and it's probably a cufflink button.

Because it was solid silver and almost certainly more than 300 years old, local Finds Liaison Officer Michael Lewis submitted the little object, weighing just 2g and measuring 15mm across, to the Treasure process. This was the first of its kind ever reported as Treasure – the only similar button had been found in Jamestown, Virginia (USA). But since this find, nearly 200 more buttons have been reported to the PAS, with versions of a crown and heart motif on them. It was an unofficial logo probably first used to celebrate the royal marriage of King Charles II in 1662, and remained popular for decades after.

> **Date:** 1660–1700, Post Medieval
> **Where, when and how found:** Rochester, Kent; 2001; metal detecting
> **Finder:** Anonymous
> **Official valuation:** £150
> **Where is it now?** British Museum, London
> www.britishmuseum.org
> **Visit:** Hampton Court Palace, Surrey, where King Charles II and Catherine of Braganza spent their honeymoon
> www.hrp.org.uk/HamptonCourtPalace/
> Windsor Castle, where the ceilings of the Queen's Presence Chamber in the State Apartments portray Catherine as a goddess

## Charles II, the popular king

Following Charles I's execution in 1649 England became a Republic, known as the Commonwealth. By 1660 the experiment had failed, much blood had been shed and Parliament eventually invited Charles I's son, Charles II, to become king – the monarchy was restored. Charles was known as the 'Merry Monarch' – compared to the puritanical rule of Cromwell during the Commonwealth, life under Charles was one long party (at least for the rich) with a hedonistic court life and flourishing arts, music and bawdy theatre. Charles favoured religious tolerance, but many powerful figures in his parliament were staunchly anti-

Catholic and worked hard to strengthen the power of the Church of England, and penalise Catholics.

It was politically controversial, therefore, when Charles took Catherine of Braganza, a Portuguese noblewoman and a devout Catholic, as his wife. The country nonetheless celebrated the marriage of their beloved king, and Royal memorabilia was manufactured and sold around the country, including silver buttons like the one from Rochester. These decorative buttons could have been used alone, or two could be joined together as cufflinks.

The heart symbol has long had associations with courtly and romantic love, as well as being a symbol of fidelity and faith. It also had Catholic overtones – other buttons have the sacred heart image of Jesus Christ on them. Just like now, people in the 17th century were familiar with heart symbols – on packs of playing cards, on love tokens, in coats of arms and in religious paintings. They would have instantly responded to the royal

"This was the first of its kind ever reported as Treasure – the only similar button had been found in Jamestown, Virginia (USA)"

'branding' of this marriage – Catherine and Charles were united, romantically and politically.

It was certainly a good economic match for both countries, but Catherine didn't speak English and couldn't officially be crowned Queen because she was Catholic. In terms of their personalities, it wasn't an obviously solid union either. Catherine, as Queen Consort, slowly won some favour at court with her polite ways and quiet tolerance of Charles' licentiousness. But Charles continued to unashamedly delight in his mistresses, including Barbara Palmer and Nell Gwynne, and seemed to prioritise horses, hunting and hawking over his pious wife.

The greatest threat to Catherine and Charles' marriage, however, was in their inability to produce an heir to the throne. Catherine suffered at least three miscarriages and a stillbirth, and it became increasingly clear that she might not give birth to any living children. Charles had had at least twelve illegitimate children with his mistresses, and his courtiers encouraged him to divorce Catherine and remarry someone younger, seemingly more fertile and someone who was definitely not Catholic. Charles refused, however, and stuck by his wife until his death, protecting her from demands that she face trial for treason. Charles converted to Catholicism on his deathbed, an act which perhaps reveals his true affection for his wife and her faith.

Because Charles died without any legitimate children, the throne passed to his brother, James II. Remarkably, one of his acknowledged illegitimate children with Louise de Kerouille, Duchess of Portsmouth, is a direct ancestor of Princess Diana and her children, Princes William and Harry. If Prince William is one day crowned king, he will be the first direct descendant of Charles II to sit on the English throne.

See also:
Epsom Horse Harness Boss
Hawking Vervel

# Seal Matrix of Stone Priory

## A stamp of authority from a lost priory

We give our seal of approval, we seal things with a kiss, we seal the deal. And the origin of these phrases is from a very literal act our medieval forebears used to perform. Much like the pin numbers and certified signatures we use now, our ancestors used wax seals to prove their identity and authenticate official documents. Seals are still used

Date: 1260–1300, Medieval
Where, when and how found: Cobham, Surrey; 2011; metal detecting
Finder: Tony Burke
Where is it now? On display at the Church of St Michael & St Wulfad, Stone, Staffordshire
www.stmichaelschurchstone.co.uk

today – the Great Seal of the Realm, Queen Elizabeth II's seal, is put on official documents such as new peerages or Royal proclamations, and is considered to be more official than her personal signature.

Seals came into common use in Britain under the administration-loving Normans in the early 1100s. A blob of beeswax would be melted and a personal identifying imprint would be made into it. The seal would then be fixed to the document to prove it wasn't a forgery.

The item used to make the imprint in the wax is known as a 'seal matrix'. Wealthy families and institutions would commission unique engraved seal matrices which they would protect carefully. Just like now, identity theft was a worry and if you lost your seal, it could be misused by others.

That makes the findspot of this treasure a real mystery.

Tony Burke was metal detecting in a field in Cobham, Surrey, in 2011, when he discovered a large lump of metal, 74mm long, 45mm wide and weighing 84g. Tony immediately recognised the pointed oval as a seal matrix of some kind and reported the artefact to his local Finds Liaison Officer, David Williams.

On one side of the copper alloy matrix is an impressively detailed depiction of the Virgin Mary with the child Jesus on her knee. The child holds a book in his left hand and points upwards with his other hand. Mary is holding a flower in her hand, and around the image is an inscription:

# S'ECCE SCE MARIE ET SCI W(V)LFADI MARTIRIS DE STANIS
*The Seal of the Church of Saint Mary and Saint Wulfad the Martyr of Stone*

At first Tony and local archaeologists thought that the seal might have something to do with Staines, a place name meaning 'stone' that was relatively close to the findspot. But St Wulfad was not a local saint, and an online search immediately revealed his connection to an Augustinian priory in Stone, Staffordshire.

## The destruction of the monasteries

The priory at Stone was founded in the mid-12th century, but in the 1530s it was one of the first victims of Henry VIII's Reformation of the Church and Dissolution of the Monasteries.

Henry aimed to destroy Catholic authority in England and to reclaim the great wealth held within the religious houses. He ordered that monasteries, priories and abbeys be disbanded, their property be reallocated and all the proceeds be paid to the Crown.

The King's agents first targeted small religious houses with an income less than £200 per year, and it's perhaps at this point, in 1536, that the Stone seal matrix was moved. It's possible that a monk from Stone moved to the Newark Augustinian Priory in Surrey (which survived until 1540), taking with him the most portable and important possessions he could. If they were left at Stone Priory they would almost certainly be destroyed or sold. At this point, the seal matrix would already have been more than two hundred years old and as an emblem of the authority of the doomed Priory it would have been one of the most important items to try and save.

The Stone Priory buildings were quickly dismantled and destroyed, but the main church building was saved by local parishioners. They continued to use it as the parish church until 1758 when it was eventually demolished and replaced by the current church of St Michael & St Wulfad.

## Anglo-Saxon saints of Stone

The legend of Stone and St Wulfad tells that when the great Anglo-Saxon King of Mercia, Wulfhere, heard that his sons Wulfad and Rufin had converted to Christianity, he flew into a horrified rage and struck them down where they stood. The boys' mother, distraught with grief, ordered that her murdered sons be buried and the grave marked by a stone cairn. Thus, the town that grew up around the spot took the name Stone. When King Wulfhere also eventually converted to Christianity around 670AD, he had a church built on the site of his martyred sons' graves, in tribute and penitence.

The truth of the matter is a little less clear – certainly there was a pagan King Wulfhere who converted to Christianity and founded a number of religious sites in Mercia. But there isn't any further evidence of his sons Wulfad and Rufin, despite there being local churches dedicated to both names.

Nonetheless the quality and detail of the engraving on the Stone seal matrix makes it very special. It would have been used to authenticate transactions of land and money by the Priory, for levying taxes and accounting for donations.

Incredibly, the Stone seal matrix can still make a very clear impression in wax, over 700 years after it was first used. Tony Burke, the finder, the landowner of the field in Surrey, and the parishioners of Stone were all keen to see the seal matrix return home permanently. The seal matrix is now on display at Stone parish church.

See also:
Baldehildis Seal
Raglan Ring

# Beddingham Nose

## A false copper nose

Ray Wilson was metal detecting on grassland on the South Downs when he discovered a copper alloy nose. Finely moulded with two nostril slits in the base, a flattened rim around the sides and broken attachment holes at the top and on the sides, Ray assumed it must be part of a sculpture or a suit of armour.

But investigations by the Local Finds Liaison officer, Laura Burnett revealed that if the nose had been armour, it would have been cast from iron rather than bronze and if it were sculpture, it probably wouldn't have nostril slits and attachment holes. Experts at the Hunterian Museum and the Science Museum ultimately identified it as a very early prosthetic nose, used in place of one lost through accident or illness. The Danish astronomer Tycho Brahe lost his nose in a sword duel in 1566 and was famously recorded as wearing gold and silver false noses. Copper staining on his skull suggests he may have worn a copper alloy nose as well, and perhaps only worn his precious one on special occasions.

The most common cause of nose loss was disease, particularly syphilis, a bacterial infection that is usually sexually transmitted, but can also be passed from mother to foetus. The final stage of syphilitic disease results in bone destruction, and additional lumpy growths. One of the first areas to show signs of bone loss are the delicate nasal bones and the cartilage of the septum. Many people in the 1500s and 1600s were left severely disfigured, and the social taboo and shame of venereal disease added to the victim's trauma.

Syphilis was very common throughout the post-medieval and modern period across Europe, and it's estimated that more than 12 million people still suffer from the disease around the world today. Syphilis can be treated

---

**Date:** 1500–1700, Post Medieval

**Where, when and how found:** Beddingham, East Sussex; 2009; metal detecting

**Finder:** Ray Wilson

**Where is it now?** Returned to finder

**Visit:** Hunterian Museum, Royal College of Surgeons, London www.rcseng.ac.uk/museums;

Wellcome Collection, London www.wellcomecollection.org;

Science Museum, London www.sciencemuseum.org.uk

with the simple antibiotic penicillin, discovered by Alexander Fleming in 1928, but millions of people still suffer from the disease because of a lack of access to medical care.

Treatment was certainly not available when the Beddingham Nose was commissioned and worn, and a prosthetic would have been the best resolution of the facial disfigurement. It's very possible that if the owner of the Beddingham Nose didn't lose it in an accident or fight, he or she may have lost it to syphilis.

The findspot is near to a historic path, so it's possible that this was an accidental loss. The nose is difficult to date, but similar prosthetic noses made from ivory and silver at the Hunterian Museum and the Science Museum, both in London, suggest a date around the 1500s or 1600s, extraordinarily dynamic times in our nation's history. The Beddingham Nose find overlaps with the Daventry Visard Mask (p173) – it's interesting to imagine two of our ancestors meeting, each wearing their personal face apparatus.

See also:
Daventry Visard Mask

# Hackney WWII Hoard

## *Eighty gold coins lost in the Blitz*

Terry Castle was helping residents dig a frog pond in the garden of a block of flats when one of their spades hit a glass kitchen storage jar in the mud. The heavy contents of the jar were wrapped in greaseproof paper, and as Terry and the others emptied the jar and unwrapped the paper, they were amazed to find they'd struck gold. Inside the jar were eighty large gold coins with an image of Liberty on one side and an American Eagle on the other – 33g each (a modern £1 coin is just 5.5g), and made of 90% gold, these were beautiful, impressive and obviously very valuable.

> **Date:** 1940, Modern
>
> **Where, when and how found:** Hackney, London; 2007; found while digging a garden pond
>
> **Finders:** Two residents with a volunteer and care worker, Terry Castle
>
> **Where is it now?** Privately owned after auction; one coin and the jar are in Hackney Museum www.hackney.gov.uk/cm-museum.htm
>
> **Also visit:** Jewish Museum, Camden, London www.jewishmuseum.org.uk

Terry immediately reported the coins to Kate Sumnall, the Finds Liaison Officer at the Museum of London, who took possession of them for safe keeping.

## The coins

The gold coins were all American $20 coins of a type known as the Double Eagle. 'Double Eagle' isn't a nickname for the coins, but their official title, and they were produced from 1850 until 1933. Most of the Hackney coins had been minted in San Francisco, and dated between 1854 and 1913.

The immediate challenge was to find out how the coins had ended up buried in a Hackney garden. A possibility was that the coins might have been left by an American serviceman posted to the area at some point after 1913, but research on residents during that time drew a blank - no US servicemen had lived there. For three and half years the coins remained at the Museum of London, and in one final attempt to locate the owner, the British Museum put an advert in the *Hackney Gazette* under the headline 'TREASURE MYSTERY'.

Local historian Stephen Selby was intrigued by the headline. In an inspired hunch he searched the national newspaper archives and discovered an article in *The Times* dated 13 March 1952, entitled 'GOLD COINS IN GARDEN': Sixty years ago, a gardener had also found a glass jar in the same garden – it had contained eighty-two $20 gold coins, and the hoard was claimed by a man called Martin Sulzbacher.

An online search revealed that Martin had died, but his son, Max, was still living in Israel. Max was able to fill in the blanks of this treasure mystery story. In 1938, Martin Sulzbacher, a Jewish banker in Oberkassel, Germany, decided that he needed to get his family out of Nazi Germany. He began smuggling money out to his brother Fritz and parents who were living in London, including a large number of $20 gold coins. Quickly following, he moved with his wife and four children (including Max) to the safety of England. Just two months later on 9 November 1938, the night that became known as *Kristallnacht* – the 'Night of Broken Glass' – Nazis across Germany burnt synagogues, destroyed Jewish shops and homes and rounded up Jewish civilians who would later be sent to the death camps.

Martin used some of his smuggled wealth to purchase a house in Hackney, into which he, his family and parents moved. The rest of the coins he stored in a bank safety deposit box.

In May 1940, the Germans invaded France, and the war was suddenly at Britain's door. One immediate response from the British Government was to interview all German and Italian foreign nationals and detain those considered to be a risk to national security. Those who were a 'risk' would be sent to Britain's distant colonies – Canada and Australia. Martin Sulzbacher and his wife were detained and on 30 June 1940, Martin was forced to board a liner, the *Arandora Star*, at Liverpool, bound for Canada. Their children were evacuated to the countryside, but Martin's parents, his brother Fritz, and his sister-in-law remained at the house in Hackney.

Off the coast of Scotland, the *Arandora Star* was torpedoed by a German U-Boat. Incredibly, Martin was rescued from the water and taken to Greenock, Scotland. Shortly afterwards, he was deported again, this time successfully reaching Australia aboard the SS *Dunera*, where he remained until 1941.

In London, Martin's brother Fritz thought his brother's gold in the bank deposit box was at risk, and would be lost if the Germans invaded Britain. Fritz decided to withdraw all the coins bar one from the bank, and hide them elsewhere. He wrapped them up in greaseproof paper, placed them in two glass storage jars, and buried them in the back garden of the house in Hackney. But although the German troops never landed on British soil, the Blitz bombing raids destroyed plenty. The Sulzbacher house in Hackney took a direct hit and Martin's parents, his brother Fritz, and his sister-in-law were all killed, the house and garden were destroyed, and the whereabouts of the gold coins was lost.

Martin returned to Britain in 1942 and was reunited with his wife, his four children, and Fritz's four orphaned children. He discovered just one solitary coin in his safety deposit box, and learned that Fritz had buried the rest, but no one knew where. The family were left with nothing and suffered years of hardship, along with many other distraught, war-torn families. The hoard was lost and the Sulzbachers started from scratch.

The government eventually paid compensation to Martin for his destroyed property. It was a decade before the site was redeveloped and a workman found the first jar and Martin was reunited with eighty-two of his coins. He died in 1981 without ever discovering the fate of the final eighty. It fell to his son Max, at the age of eighty-one, to fly from Israel to London and prove his claim to the coins in 2011. He gave one of the Double Eagles to the finders and one to Hackney Museum, and auctioned the rest at Sotheby's to restore the Sulzbacher family graves, and help his living family.

This moving story reveals the set of complex events that resulted in a hoard being lost. We only know the details because it happened within living memory. No contemporary accounts exist, and no further archaeological evidence is available. The Hackney Hoard indicates just how challenging it can be to piece together the story behind an artefact from deeper in the past.

See also:
Nether Stowey Hoard
Holy Island Mason Hoard
Spanish-American Gold Doubloons

# Epsom Horse Harness Boss

## *The find that points to a night of Royal partying*

Journalist Mark Davison was with members of his local metal detecting group in Epsom, the heart of racehorse country, when he got a strong signal near a gate. He thought he'd found an upturned ashtray, but when he turned the item over, it took his breath away. A bright, shiny, gold-coloured decoration bearing a Royal Coat of Arms.

This large and impressive horse harness decoration is made of a gilded copper alloy and shows the Arms of the Royal House of Stuart, an ancestry which includes the 17th century Kings James I and II, Charles I and his son, Charles II.

The shield in the centre is supported by a lion and a unicorn, a crown sits above the boss, and at the base is a scroll with the motto:

**Date:** 1603–1664, Post Medieval

**Where, when and how found:** Epsom, Surrey; 2009; metal detecting

**Finder:** Mark Davison

**Where is it now?** Finder has given on long-term loan to Bourne Hall Museum, Ewell

**Get involved:** www.epsomandewellhistory explorer.org.uk

### DIEU ET MON DROIT

It's French and literally means, 'God and my Right', referring to the divine right of the monarch to govern. It's sometimes translated as 'My Divine Right', or alternatively 'God and My Right [shall I defend]'. A second inscription, on a belt shaped around the inner circle, is:

### HONI SOIT QUI MAL Y PENSE
which translates as 'Shame upon He who thinks Evil'.

The back of the harness boss is a dished hollow and has incomplete fittings that would have been used to attach it to the horse's harness, either on to the sides of the bridle bit, perhaps on a chest or rump band, or possibly to a carriage. A horse wearing such a high-quality decoration was certainly part of the Royal household.

## Which Royal household?

The 1600s were times of incredible change in Britain, with foreign wars, international trading and philosophical debate challenging ideas that had seemed to be the unquestionable cornerstones of the country. Most fundamentally, thinkers began to challenge the idea that kings and queens had been given the right to rule by God, rather than by Man.

In 1660, with Oliver Cromwell and the ideals of a Republic now dead, Charles II's supporters recalled him from Europe and restored him to the throne. Indebted to the noblemen who supported his claim to the throne, Charles II was keen to bestow land, titles and his Royal favour upon them.

> "The Royal harness boss has remained in such a beautiful state of preservation because it luckily fell on to ground that was never ploughed"

The Earl of Berkeley was a loyal supporter of the King, and owned a grand residence called The Durdans, a house in the Epsom area, very close to the harness boss findspot. Thanks to the famous diary keeping of John Evelyn, we know King Charles II visited The Durdans in 1662 and again in 1664, and we can even pinpoint one particular evening that the friends spent together at the Earl's house.

Under 1 September 1662, Evelyn wrote in his diary: 'Being invited by Lord Berkeley, I went to Durdans, where [I] dined with his Majesty, the Queen, Duke, Duchess, Prince Rupert, Prince Edward and an abundance of noblemen.'

One simple line might reveal the moment the harness boss was lost. Travelling to and from The Durdans with a retinue comprising dozens of horses, it's very likely that the Epsom Harness Boss fell from one of King Charles II's steeds and rolled into a field. Normally archaeology can't pin down artefacts to specific events, but this seems to be a noteworthy exception. The Royal harness boss has remained in such a beautiful state of preservation because it luckily fell on to ground that was never ploughed.

Finder Mark Davison has shared his remarkable discovery with the public by loaning the piece to Bourne Hall Museum in Ewell.

See also:
Inverness Shoulder-belt Plate
Boar Badge of Richard III
Hawking Vervel

# Helmet Cremation Burial

## A rare burial in Iron Age Kent

Trevor Rogers is an experienced metal detectorist, and in late 2012, on farmland outside Canterbury, he made an extraordinary discovery. He carefully lifted his find, buried a bag of lead fishing weights in the hole so he knew where to go back to, and took his Treasure home. When he got home, he called Andrew Richardson, the Finds Manager at the Canterbury Archaeological Trust, and said that he thought he'd found a Celtic bronze helmet. Nothing of the sort had ever been found in Kent, and very few parallels have been found across Britain or even on the continent – if the find really was an early bronze helmet, it would be very rare indeed.

> **Date:** 75–25BC, Iron Age
>
> **Where, when and how found:** near Canterbury, Kent; 2012; metal detecting
>
> **Finder:** Trevor Rogers
>
> **Where is it now?** British Museum, London, undergoing assessment. Canterbury Museum hopes to acquire it through the Treasure process www.canterbury.co.uk/Canterbury-Museums.aspx
>
> **Get involved:** Canterbury Archaeological Trust runs courses and events, and also welcomes volunteers and supporters www.canterburytrust.co.uk Dover Archaeological Group run excavations in the local area

The following morning, at his house, Trevor showed Andrew a Late Iron Age brooch, a fragment of burnt bone and an almost complete Iron Age bronze helmet. The bone had been inside the helmet, and the brooch was from the soil slightly higher up. There was more bone at the findspot, but Trevor hadn't dug more than he had to – once he realised what he'd discovered, he knew that every layer of soil and bone would be incredibly valuable for putting this find in its archaeological context. The find was declared to the Coroner, as the helmet and brooch together constitute Treasure, as a prehistoric base metal assemblage.

A 2m x 2m excavation at the findspot was organised and the full detail of this extraordinary treasure emerged: it was a human cremation burial, where the brooch had probably been used to fasten a textile or leather bag holding the fragments of burned bone. This bag had then been placed

inside the upturned helmet. The helmet had then been buried in a shallow circular hole and covered over. The distinctive style of the brooch dates the cremation to the 1st century BC, placing it firmly in the Late Iron Age.

The actual cremation of the body was completed at a different, unidentified site. The deceased would have been set on a pyre of wood that was allowed to burn down and, once cool, the remaining fragments of burned bone were collected and buried. No other evidence of cremation burials or inhumations (body burials) were found in the area surrounding the helmet findspot – the helmet burial

> "It was sheer luck that the helmet hadn't been struck and destroyed, although a section of damage to the helmet's rim is probably from a glancing blow by a plough blade"

was either isolated, other evidence has been destroyed, or the burials were widely spread out.

Deep, modern plough marks had cut the soil either side of the helmet burial pit – it was sheer luck that the helmet hadn't been struck and destroyed, although a section of damage to the helmet's rim is probably from a glancing blow by a plough blade.

This wasn't a richly furnished chiefly burial, but clearly a person buried with such a beautiful and precious helmet must have been significant.

## Romans in Kent

In 55 and 54BC, Julius Caesar began the first invasion of Britain. He later left to focus on fighting the Gauls on the Continent, but not before Roman troops set foot on British soil. It's possible this helmet was worn by a Roman soldier, and that the grave is Roman. But the tradition of cremating a body and burying the remains in a bag fastened with brooches is a practice linked to native cultures in Late Iron Age Kent, which makes it much more likely that this is the grave of a native man.

He might have acquired the helmet during his lifetime, and as an act of respect his mourners buried him inside his most treasured possession. Perhaps he had fought on the continent during the Gallic Wars of 58–50BC, and brought his exotic helmet home with him. British warriors might have travelled across the English Channel to the areas that are now modern-day France and Belgium to fight with the Gauls against the Romans, and also with the Romans against the Gauls – as mercenaries, they were warriors for hire and would fight for whoever paid them. It's also possible that the helmet was brought over by displaced Gallic refugees making a new home in south-east Britain. One other helmet cremation burial like this has been discovered in Belgium – indicating the extent of the political, military and social links between Iron Age communities even before the Romans arrived to 'civilise' the natives.

Analysis of the finds and of the site is still underway, and much more about this unusual find will be known in the future.

See also:
Anarevitos Stater
Ringlemere Gold Cup

## THE STRANGE AND ANCIENT LAWS THAT GOVERNED 'TREASURE'

Before 1996, the laws concerning Treasure were some of the oldest in the book. 'Treasure Trove' is detailed in a document from 1250, written by a noble called Henry de Bracton. He states that, 'Things such as treasure are said to belong to no one by reason of lapse of time. Also where the owner of the thing does not appear ... by natural law now become the property of the sovereign'.

Anything that couldn't be traced to an original owner, whether it be a stray cow, goods from a shipwreck, or items found in or on the ground, belonged to the King or Queen, not the finder or the landowner. There was initially no suggestion of a reward, or a share in the value – it belonged to the monarch, and that was that. The law was most often used for gold and silver – items made of other materials weren't normally claimed by the Crown. And if you didn't reveal your find, you were no better than a thief and would be treated as such.

Henry de Bracton describes the crime of concealing Treasure Trove as 'a serious act of presumption against the King, his dignity, and Crown'. A Coroner, an official of the Crown also responsible for investigating unexpected deaths, had to go out and investigate suspected cases of people finding Treasure and not declaring it. The tell-tale signs might be that the finder 'carries himself more abundantly in feeding and more richly in dress'. Well-fed, well-dressed peasants were very suspicious. The law was also intended to discourage rich people from hiding their wealth to avoid taxation – if undeclared valuables were found, their owner would either be punished for tax evasion, or the treasure would be claimed by the Crown.

The laws were often unfairly applied – some finders were rewarded for their honesty, others were punished. One case from London in the year 1400 records that a labourer, Peter White from Kensyngton [Kensington], found 35 shillings' worth of silver coins while he was working. When he went to pick them up they were 'mouldy and crumbled like dust'. Peter handed in the surviving coins, 5 shillings' worth, and was promptly arrested. The officers insisted that because he had found 35 shillings, he owed the Crown 35 shillings, and he would have to pay up the extra. Perhaps they suspected he'd stashed a few coins for himself, or perhaps they were simply cruel – either way he was only pardoned when it was clear he was destitute.

Until relatively recently, the historical significance of these Treasure Trove finds was often considered to be less important than the resale value – frequently the weight of actual gold or silver. If you were the finder and you didn't want to risk getting a measly reward, the quickest way to liquidate the value of the treasure, literally, was to melt it down and recast the metal. Sadly this means that many hundreds, if not thousands, of precious artefacts have met their end at the bottom of a jeweller's crucible.

It was only in 1886 that finders became legally entitled to a reward. The change ensured that more finders were willing to come forward, but sometimes even when they did the law didn't protect the finds themselves. For an item to be classed as Treasure Trove in law, it had to be proved that the original owner had intended to return for it. If the items had been buried in a ritual deposit or a grave, with no intention of them ever being recovered, or had been lost accidentally, they weren't Treasure Trove. Discoveries like the Sutton Hoo ship burial, or the **Holderness Cross** in this book (p224) were therefore not Treasure Trove and so the finder and landowner could do what they liked with them. Thankfully, in both these cases, the finders and landowners have ensured that the finds have remained in the public domain.

See the **Get Involved** section (p288) to find out exactly how the current laws work.

# Anarevitos Stater

## A Kentish kings' coalition coin

Amateur archaeologist Danny Baldock was metal detecting in September 2010 when he found a single gold coin of remarkable importance. Dating to the decades just before or after Christ's birth, the coin represents a previously unknown Kentish ruler on one side, with the name of an already-known ruler on the other side.

> **Date/period:** 10BC–10AD, Late Iron Age
> **Where, when and how found:** Near Dover, Kent; 2010; metal detecting
> **Finder:** Danny Baldock
> **Where is it now?** British Museum, London
> www.britishmuseum.org

The type of coin is known as a 'stater', a 5g gold disc that has been stamped on both sides. Most coins have an image of the issuing authority on the front, the obverse, and another, often decorative design on the reverse. On modern British coins the Queen's head is on the obverse. The same pattern often holds true for ancient coins as well, but it isn't always the case for coins in the British Iron Age.

On the obverse of this coin is a back-to-back crescent design with the letters **EPPI** in the segments, standing for Eppillus, a king often associated with the Atrebates and Cantii tribes in southern Britain.

On the reverse is a stylised horseman, and the inscription **ANA** (or **AVA**) above and **REVITO** below, which makes up the native British name, Anarevito, Anarevitos, Avarevito or Avarevitos.

No one knew about this ruler before, and we have no other sources that mention him. Until more evidence is unearthed, we can't be more clear about his true name.

## Two kings

The fact that there are two kings named on the stater Danny found suggests two possible explanations. The first is that the leader Anarevitos was declaring that his authority came directly from the lineage of the well-known and well-regarded Eppillus. Throughout history leaders have claimed authority through their ancestry. By naming Eppillus on one side of his coins, and by issuing coins

at all, Anarevitos was attempting to legitimise his rule. Perhaps the details of him succeeding to power were a little hazy, or he was one of a number of candidates, or he simply wanted to proclaim his greatness – we can't be sure.

The alternative explanation is that Anarevitos ruled at the same time as Eppillus, and this coin represents a leadership coalition. By declaring a power-sharing agreement on coinage, perhaps they were attempting to unite factions in conflict, or bring together a number of local chiefdoms to face an external threat together.

The first attempted invasion of Britain by Rome was in 55–54BC, under Julius Caesar. It was ultimately unsuccessful, and it took almost a hundred years before the Romans tried again (they successfully invaded in 43AD). Julius Caesar wrote an account of his campaign against Britain, and described Kent as being ruled by four kings. This has been interpreted to mean that the region was divided into four smaller independent kingdoms, but perhaps it was a less straightforward arrangement – a shifting network of local leaders all jostling for supremacy over the same lands and people, using a combination of conquest and alliance.

> "The alternative explanation is that Anarevitos ruled at the same time as Eppillus, and this coin represents a leadership coalition"

The later Iron Age population of Kent shared a number of cultural traits with other groups in south-east England and those of northern France, including the tradition of cremation burial and the early adoption of coinage. In the last decades before the Roman invasion of 43AD they also used coins with Roman-influenced designs and Latin inscriptions. By the Roman period the people of the north and east Kent were designated as Cantii or Cantiaci, but it is unclear whether they existed as a unified tribe before the Conquest. It had previously been thought that the kingdoms described by Caesar were unified soon after his invasions, but the discovery of the Anarevitos Stater and other finds over the last fifteen years suggests that rival kings may have continued to wrestle for power for much longer than had been thought.

Early in the 1st century AD, Kent fell under the control of Cunobelinus, whose power was based on territories to the north of the River Thames.

## Cunobelinus

Cunobelinus has secured a place in history as one of the great British kings. He's also known as Cymbeline, in Welsh as Cynfelyn. He's mentioned by the medieval historian Geoffrey of Monmouth, and Shakespeare wrote *Cymbeline* based on his life. Under his rule, the kingdoms of Kent were forced together, and at his peak, Cunobelinus ruled across Essex, Kent, Hertfordshire, Bedfordshire and parts of Buckinghamshire and Cambridgeshire. Cunobelinus died around two years before the Roman invasion, and it's been suggested that power struggles between his sons following his death in fact triggered the Emperor Claudius to invade.

When the Romans invaded in 43AD under Emperor Claudius, they established a number of the south-east tribes as semi-independent entities – each tribal area was made a *civitas*, an administrative county with a capital town. The capital of the Cantii was established at Canterbury.

This precious coin was bought by the British Museum to be displayed and studied. It comes from an incredibly dynamic time in our history, and Danny's find lets us all peek into this two-thousand-year-old power struggle.

See also:
Winchester Gold Hoard
Vale of York Hoard
French Forgery Hoard

# Near Lewes Hoard

## Bronze Age adornments from home and away

David Lange, a veteran detector and archaeology enthusiast, was searching a grass field near Lewes, East Sussex, in March 2011, when he picked up a faint signal. He dug down to reveal a small piece of twisted wire. In the surrounding soil were a couple more pieces of twisted and coiled wire. Then he saw an axe head that he recognised as being Bronze Age – at least 2,800 years old. He then saw the fragmented edge of a large ceramic pot that seemed to be filled with more metal artefacts. To preserve as much evidence as possible, ideally David would have sought archaeological help immediately, but he decided to lift the pot out whole, took it home and carefully began to remove the objects from it. At each stage he took photos, trying to accurately record his find. But the hoard he was trying to record was bigger than he had imagined.

**Date:** 1400–1250BC, Middle Bronze Age

**Where, when and how found:** Near Lewes, East Sussex; 2011; metal detecting

**Finder:** David Lange

**Official valuation:** £15,500

**Where is it now?** Sussex Archaeological Society at Barbican House Museum, Lewes, hopes to acquire www.sussexpast.co.uk

The pot contained parts of approximately seventy-nine objects, including bracelets, necklace fragments, pins, gold discs, torcs, finger rings, clothing ornaments, wires, beads and axe heads. David reported his find to the county Finds Liaison Officer, Stephanie Smith, who arranged for a team of archaeologists to excavate the site and assess the finds.

They all proved to date from the Bronze Age – a prehistoric period running from around 2400BC to around 800BC. It's the time following the Neolithic, or Late Stone Age, where we get the first evidence of metal technology. People first used gold, silver and copper, mostly for prestige ornaments and jewellery. Then, around 2200BC, there was a significant technological leap to making bronze – specifically mixing tin and copper to make a strong and attractive metal.

The crucial thing is that tin ore and copper ore never occur in the same place naturally – so in order to make bronze, not only do you need the

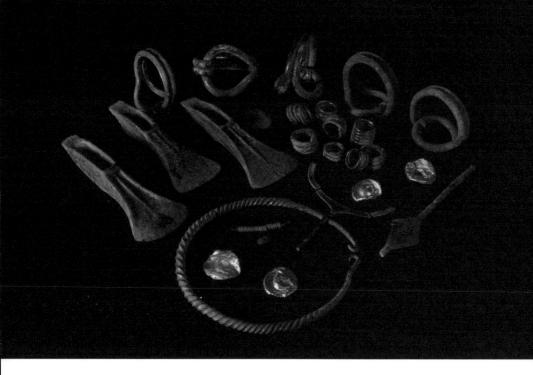

specialist knowledge of how to prepare and mix the metals, you also need a long-distance network of contacts so you can get hold of both the ingredients. This is what makes the Bronze Age such a special period in British prehistory.

The Near Lewes Hoard was deposited some time between 1400 and 1250BC, the Middle Bronze Age, so by this point bronze metallurgy had been practised for almost 1,000 years. Metal working would have been the domain of specialist craftspeople – and it's quite likely that they kept their skills and techniques secret from ordinary farmers and labourers. Part of the appeal of these beautiful, shiny objects was the almost magical way they were made. Heated in a fire hotter than most of us have ever seen, ground-up stone turns into thick, glowing molten liquid which is then poured, spitting and crackling, into a stone mould that transforms it back to a solid – if you had seen a smith at work, he would have looked like an alchemist.

The most distinctive items in the hoard are five bronze 'Sussex-loop' bracelets, a style that has, with one exception, only ever been found close to Brighton, East Sussex. 'Palstave' axe heads are found across Bronze Age Britain – they would have been bound onto a fork-shaped wooden handle with leather or rawhide strips, and used as a functional tool rather than a weapon. The gold appliqué foil discs are a more exotic addition to the hoard – no others have been found anywhere in Britain, and the amber beads are likely to have come from the Baltic Sea coast (modern-day Germany, Poland, Lithuania and Latvia). The period the hoard dates from is called the 'Ornament Horizon', a time when bracelets, necklaces, pins, rings and beads suddenly became incredibly fashionable.

## Why was the pot buried?

At the findspot, the archaeologists found what seems to be a portion of an enclosure or possibly a ditch. The hoard might have been buried inside this special area, but only further excavation will reveal the details. It looks certain that the pot was much more than just a place for the safekeeping of valuables. Both the selection of items for the hoard and the fact that it was buried in a ceramic vessel are unusual features for Middle Bronze Age hoards from southern Britain. We don't know why, but this seems to be a particularly unusual mix of local and continental traditions, probably as a ritual religious offering. It does show how well connected our Bronze Age ancestors were, though, living in a rich and dynamic culture.

We know that Bronze Age people were skilled and confident sailors, travelled to, and traded with, the continent regularly and with the communities along the coastal and river systems, and had sophisticated weapon and craft traditions. They weren't just skilled metal and ceramic workers, but their textile, wood and bone items would have been equally impressive. It's simply that the only materials that normally survive 3,000 years in the ground are pottery and metal – everything else rots away.

The find site isn't an ideal candidate for an extensive dig at this time because it's too exposed – the experts and landowners are worried that the field will become a target for illegal metal detecting. That's why this special hoard will only ever be referred to as 'Near Lewes' – now we've had a glimpse of what this Sussex field has to reveal, it's in everyone's interest to protect its secret treasures.

See also:
Ringlemere Cup
Carpow Logboat
Milton Keynes Hoard

# Canterbury Pilgrim Badges

## *Medieval souvenirs thrown in a Canterbury river*

Ian Smith and Roy Davies spent many days getting wet in the River Stour, the water course that runs through the ancient city of Canterbury. Just as we do now, our ancestors often dropped things into rivers – intentionally and accidentally, and Ian and Roy wanted to recover some of these items. Wading through the thigh-deep water, one shovelled a heap of the gravelly riverbed into a sieve, the other filtered through it to gather any finds.

Amongst other items, over months of searching the pair found dozens of medieval metal badges. Badges have been found at numerous sites across the country, but the sheer number of artefacts retrieved from the river in Canterbury was remarkable. The badges are from a period spanning over two hundred years and most are related to St Thomas Becket, the martyr of Canterbury Cathedral.

> **Date:** 1300–1500, Medieval
>
> **Where, when and how found:** River Stour, Canterbury; 1987; in-water sieving
>
> **Finders:** Ian Smith and Roy Davies
>
> **Where are they now?** Canterbury Museum www.canterbury.co.uk/ Canterbury-Museums.aspx
>
> **Also visit:** Canterbury Cathedral, Canterbury www.canterbury-cathedral.org
>
> Canterbury Tales living history experience, Canterbury www.canterburytales.org.uk
>
> **Read:** Chaucer's *Canterbury Tales*

## The martyrdom of Thomas Becket

In 1161, Thomas Becket was made Archbishop of Canterbury by his friend, King Henry II. It made Thomas the most important person in the English Church, and since he was also Chancellor, the most important person in the country other than the king himself. Henry expected Thomas to govern the Church in a way that would help him rule, supporting him in religious and political matters, both internally and with Rome.

But even though Henry and Thomas had been good friends, once Thomas was made Archbishop, he immediately gave up the Chancellorship and began to challenge the monarch's powers over the Church. He renounced his former lifestyle, which had been a flash affair of feasting, women, hawking and hunting, in favour of an ascetic, monkish existence – a surprise to everyone, not least his friend, the King. Thomas began battling Henry on his political decisions, and stubbornly refused to sign important constitutions, instead supporting Rome and the Church. Thomas seemed to almost delight in antagonising Henry, even going so far as to threaten him with excommunication.

Excommunication was an incredibly serious act in medieval Christianity. People had a strong and very real belief in the eternal torments of Hell, and individuals excommunicated from the Holy Roman Church were condemned to an eternity of torture and suffering. This was a severe and shocking threat.

King and priest argued and undermined one another, and by late 1170, King Henry, in utter frustration, is said to have shouted to his court, 'Who will rid me of this meddlesome priest?' Four of Henry's knights took the king at his word and travelled to Canterbury to silence Becket permanently.

Monks were praying inside the Cathedral at the time the knights arrived, and witnesses saw Becket chased into a corner of the cathedral near the cloisters. The first blow cut Becket down and he dropped to his knees, uttering prayers. Edward Grim, an eyewitness, wrote that:

'the third knight inflicted a terrible wound as [Becket] lay prostrate. By this stroke, the crown of his head was separated from the head in such a way that the blood white with the brain, and the brain no less red from the blood, dyed the floor of the cathedral. The same clerk who had entered with the knights placed his foot on the neck of the holy priest and precious martyr, and, horrible to relate, scattered the brains and blood about the pavements, crying to the others, "Let us away, knights; this fellow will arise no more!"'

Becket's brutal murder on the most hallowed ground in the country shocked the nation, and the scandal was reported across the courts of Europe. Becket's murderers travelled to Rome to seek forgiveness for their crime, and were commanded to each complete fourteen years' penance, by fighting in the Crusades in the Holy Lands. Henry himself, when he heard the news, was racked with grief and guilt – he had killed his friend, and sinned against the Church.

## The rise of a saint

Almost immediately, monks reported that water tinged with Becket's spilled blood had magical healing properties – the very first pilgrims to Becket's murder spot collected this so-called 'Canterbury Water', and there was brisk business making and selling little lead vessels known as 'ampullae', that contained a small amount of the miraculous liquid.

The importance of relics was already firmly established amongst believers, and touching the body or tomb of a saint was thought to give someone a powerful religious experience. Less than three years after his death, the Pope canonised Becket, making him Saint Thomas. Already an important religious site, Canterbury Cathedral became England's most popular pilgrimage destination, and the city grew to accommodate all the new visitors.

Becket's tomb was in the eastern chapel, at the most sacred end of the cathedral and close to the High Altar. Holes were cut into the top of the tomb so pilgrims could stick their hands inside and get close to the martyred Archbishop. They believed that Thomas had the power to improve health, cure sickness and answer prayers, and his spiritual essence

> "The importance of relics was already firmly established, and touching the body or tomb of a saint was thought to give someone a powerful religious experience"

would also be passed on to any item that was placed in contact with him, so visitors also touched religious souvenirs against the saint's tomb.

Just like the stalls and shops around visitor attractions now, stalls opened in Canterbury city to sell souvenirs and religious artefacts to the pilgrims. Along the precinct leading to the cathedral, rows and rows of cheap, mass-produced badges were available to buy, as well as fancier, better-crafted ones if you had more to spend.

Each popular holy shrine across Europe produced a different 'signature' badge shape. Pilgrims could collect the badges on their religious travels, proudly showing off all the shrines they'd been to. For some pilgrims, the journey was difficult and arduous, and that was all part of it – you willingly suffered, knowing that God promised you ultimate redemption. For others, pilgrimage was one of the delights of life – they were both holidays and *holy-days*.

The badges that Roy and Ian found were mostly made from lead cast in the form of Becket's head and shoulders, with him wearing his Bishop's headdress, the mitre. These are actually badges in the shape of the reliquary casket at Canterbury that contained part of Becket's skull, lopped off when he was murdered. The badges have a pin at the back so they could be hooked on to your clothes. Other pilgrim badges were sewn on.

## An offering?

It's not certain why the pilgrim badges were thrown into the River Stour, but they could have been a 'votive offering' – like throwing a penny into a fountain or wishing well, which echoes an ancient tradition of watery offerings that appear in many of the treasure stories in this book.

Perhaps pilgrims bought two badges – one to wear with pride as a souvenir of the trip, imbued with the holy power of Saint Thomas, and one to throw into the river as a gift of thanks for safe arrival and as an offering for a safe journey home.

**See also:**
Ursula's Virgin Badge
Hockley Pendant
County Durham River
   Assemblage

# George Humber's Distinguished Conduct Medal

## The courage of a WWI soldier remembered

Manuel Nicdao was metal detecting near the Surrey-Kent border when he hit a strong signal in a field. He unearthed a cast silver WWI medal with the engraved words, **FOR DISTINGUISHED CONDUCT IN THE FIELD** on one side, and King George V's profile on the other. Around its edge were the details of the person who had won the medal – **35175 Sjt GH Humber RFA** – meaning a Sergeant with the Royal Field Artillery.

Date: 1919, WWI (1914–1918), Modern

Where, when and how found: Limpsfield, Surrey; 2009; metal detecting

Finder: Manuel Nicdao

Where is it now? Returned to George Humber's family

Visit: Firepower! Royal Artillery Museum, Woolwich, London
www.firepower.org.uk

This is a Distinguished Conduct Medal (DCM), awarded for exceptional bravery, and equivalent to the Distinguished Service award given to officers. It is second only to the Victoria Cross.

Manuel reported his discovery to the local Finds Liaison Officers, not because it was a legal requirement, but because he felt such a personal and precious artefact deserved to be recorded and researched and, if possible, returned to the owner or his family. This is the reason many metal detectorists love their hobby – not for the fluke possibility of striking gold or an enormous hoard, but for the small finds that tell a bigger story, for the finds that offer a unique connection to a stranger from the past, someone who has been forgotten by the 'Big History' of kings and queens.

FLOs David Williams and Frank Basford began researching 'GH Humber', in an attempt to trace any living family members. Their hunt led them to a George Humber, who was born in 1889 on the Isle of Wight, and had died there aged 94, in 1985. George had reached the rank of Sergeant, fighting on the Western Front for more than three years with the 38th

Brigade of the Royal Field Artillery during some of the worst battles of WWI. The *London Gazette* reported on the award of the medal in September 1919. It recorded George's wartime exploits, stating that he had 'been through all the heavy fighting ... always commanding his detachment in action with great courage and coolness, often under heavy hostile shell-fire and great difficulties'.

## The Battle of the Lys

By the end of WWI more than 7 million men had served Britain in battle and over 900,000 paid with their lives. The toll on the soldiers who did survive is almost inconceivable, and yet they continued pushing for a victory. Later research revealed that George Humber was awarded his medal for Continuous Gallantry throughout the war, including for his courageous leadership at the Battle of the Lys in Belgium with D Battery of the Royal Field Artillery, in April 1918.

Their objective was to defend the railway line at Hazebrouk, vital for supplying British troops at the Front. The area was attacked by German forces, and the British troops were outnumbered five to one. In George's D Battery, twenty men were wounded and eleven men were killed, including the commanding officer. George took command of the survivors and ordered that they stand their ground. They continued defending their position for days, ultimately preventing a full attack on the railway.

## Finding George's family

Two local papers, one in Surrey, where the medal was found, and one on the Isle of Wight, where George was known to have lived, ran the story of Manuel's medal find. Members of George's family came forward and were able to reveal the likely story behind the location of its loss.

After the war, George took work in the Edenbridge area in Kent, and met Bessie Geal, a farm labourer's daughter. The findspot was just a kilometre away from Bessie's family home, in a secluded field surrounded by woodland. George and Bessie's grandchildren think he must have lost his special medal whilst courting his future wife.

Before he died, George was presented with a duplicate medal at his nursing home. Now, thanks to the efforts of a committed metal detectorist and the Portable Antiquities Scheme working together, George's family has been reunited with the original.

**See also:**
Great War Victory Medal
Boar Badge of Richard III
Prisoner of War Farthing Pendant

# Hockley Pendant

## *The sacred locket in an Essex field*

Five-year-old James Hyatt was playing with his dad's metal detector in a field near Hockley, Essex, when he heard the beep. Dad and son dug the site of the metal detector's response, and they struck gold – a small, beautifully decorated pendant, with a loop at the top so it could be strung on to a chain and worn as a necklace.

Date: 1500–1550, Post Medieval
Where, when and how found: Hockley, Essex; 2009; metal detecting
Finder: James Hyatt
Where is it now? British Museum, London
www.britishmuseum.org

They had discovered a rare treasure dating from the first half of the 16th century, during the reign of the famous Tudor king, Henry VIII. The Hockley Pendant is a personal reliquary – a locket with an inner compartment designed to contain a religious relic, part of the physical remains of a holy person's dead body, or a special item that he or she touched or used.

Relics were incredibly important to Christians throughout and beyond the Medieval period because they were thought to contain the spiritual power and essence of the holy person themselves. It was believed that anyone who came into close personal contact with a relic could be especially protected, healed or helped by the saint and, ultimately, by God – relics were the ultimate lucky charms.

To many modern eyes, the relics that were worshipped are somewhat surreal. Mary Magdalene's shinbone, the fingernails of St Claire, and even the breast milk of the Virgin Mary were venerated and housed in sumptuously decorated cases that celebrated the spiritual treasures inside. They inspired extraordinary devotion from Medieval Christians, and in many places in many faiths, relics continue to be venerated. In fact, the altar in every Catholic church is supposed to have an authentic relic from a saint under or within it, even today.

One of the most powerful and sacred relics in the medieval world was the True Cross – the wooden cross that had been used to crucify Jesus – and the decoration on the Hockley pendant suggests that it was designed to hold a fragment of this powerful object.

On the front of the pendant is a vivid image of a woman supporting a cross splattered in blood, surrounded by plant tendrils. It's most likely Saint Helena, who was said to have discovered the site of the True Cross in Jerusalem around 326AD and brought the remains back to Europe.

St Helena has legendary links with Essex, where the pendant was found, and she's the patron saint of Colchester. The town's coat of arms still represents the True Cross, the red of Jesus' blood and three crowned nails, in Helena's honour.

On the back of the pendant is an engraving of the Five Wounds of Christ – the holes in each of his hands and feet where he was nailed to the cross, and the wound in his side, where a soldier pierced his body with a spear. Coming out of these disembodied wounds are droplets of blood, the gory symbols that helped the pendant's owner focus their prayers and contemplate Jesus' suffering.

Along the sides of the pendant are the names of the Three Kings from the Nativity story – Jasper, Melchior and Balthasar **(IASPAR MELCIOR BALTASAR)**. Along the fourth side is a leaf-shaped decorative pattern. The Three Kings were associated with healing charms, especially to protect from fever and the 'falling-down sickness', which we now know to be epilepsy.

When the pendant was found, the back compartment had been squashed shut. Careful restoration at the British Museum enabled it to be opened again, and the contents of the reliquary were analysed. There were no fragments of wood inside, but instead, matted plant root fibres and unprocessed flax stems. The significance of these fibres remains a mystery, but they might be linked to the plants depicted on the reliquary itself.

A reliquary this small was designed for private prayer and contemplation, as well as to physically declare the owner's religious devotion. It's a very personal treasure, and a remarkable 500-year-old survival.

See also:
Clonmore Shrine
Ursula's Virgin Badge
Canterbury Pilgrim Badges

# Putney 'Brothel' Token

## A saucy token from Roman London

The Thames foreshore is one of the most interesting archaeological sites in Britain. Ninety-five miles long, the 'foreshore' is the area of the riverbank that's covered at high water and exposed at low water.

There are known archaeological sites along the length of the Thames, but twice-daily tides and the thousands of tonnes of water that move across the riverbed every day mean that it's a very dynamic site. Archaeological evidence and artefacts are exposed with every tide, while others are washed away or destroyed.

The earliest evidence we have for human activity along the Thames is early, around 10,000 years old, but it's likely that this great river has been a focus for early humans ever since we first wandered out of Africa and across Europe.

**Date:** Around 1–50AD, Roman

**Where, when and how found:** Thames foreshore, London; 2011; metal detecting/mudlarking

**Finder:** Regis Cursan

**Where is it now?** Donated to the Museum of London www.museumoflondon.org.uk

**Get involved:** Thames Discovery Programme and Foreshore recording group www.thamesdiscovery.org

To get a licence for mudlarking and metal detecting, contact the Port of London Authority www.pla.co.uk

No permit is required for walking on the foreshore and 'eyes only' searching

**NOTE:** River foreshores can be very dangerous – always plan your visit, make sure you can get off the riverside quickly, and beware of environmental hazards – cold water, dangerous and sharp items on the foreshore, wash from vessels and water-borne disease

## Roman London

The Romans arrived in Britain, or Britannia, as they would have called it, in 43AD led by the Emperor Claudius. Their presence here changed British society forever. When the Roman invaders arrived, the native British tribes had two choices – join in, or fight back. Many tribes in the south-east developed diplomatic, military and trade relationships with the Roman newcomers, others were beaten into submission.

London, or Londinium, quickly developed into a bustling, cosmopolitan hub of activity. Citizens and slaves from across the Roman Empire rubbed shoulders with local Britons on the streets of London. Soldiers were sent off to Hadrian's Wall and the Welsh borders to guard the wild frontiers of the Empire, and traders brought in Britain's finest assets to be sold off around the Empire – wool, slaves and agricultural produce.

Alongside the traders, craftsmen, soldiers and politicians of the era were the ladies engaged in the 'oldest profession' – prostitution. Throughout history there have been rules and taboos on who can have sex with whom, and the Romans were no different to us in that matter. Faithful marriage between one man and one woman was considered to be the ideal, but many people, just like now, enjoyed a bit on the side. And from the evidence we have, it seems that Romans liked bawdy humour, dirty jokes and saucy pictures, even though it wasn't considered quite 'appropriate' in polite society. This coin-shaped token, a *spintria*, demonstrates that.

## Mudlarking

In previous centuries, 'Mudlarks' were some of the poorest people in London, earning a meagre living scavenging and reselling trinkets and scrap from the Thames river mud. Nowadays, mudlarks are members of a prestigious society, searching the Thames for archaeological treasures. They need to hold a licence from the Port of London Authority.

Regis Cursan, a licensed mudlark, was metal detecting on the river near Putney when he picked out this copper alloy disc. Just under 2cm across and weighing 4g, it has a design stamped on each side. On one side is a rather unusual version of the number 14 (Roman numerals would normally show XIV, rather than XIIII), and on the other side are a man and a woman in an intimate coupling. Regis had first thought he'd found an odd coin, but when he took it home and searched online, he realised he'd found something very special that day. Only one other spintria has ever been found in the UK, in Skegness. Regis immediately contacted the Finds Liaison Officer at the Museum of London, Kath Creed, and handed the token over to the museum conservators. He's now generously donated the token to the Museum, and it's on public display alongside other artefacts revealing life in Roman London.

## The uses of spintriae

There are two competing theories about Regis' find. The first interpretation is that it is a token that would be used in a brothel. You'd tell the 'receptionist' what you wanted, pay your money, and get a token that showed in pictures what you had paid for. Handing that over to your lady of choice, there'd be no confusion over the services required, even if you didn't speak the same language because you were from two different parts of the cosmopolitan Roman Empire. These tokens have been found throughout the Roman world, and most depict sexual acts, and have a number on the other side. So is the Putney token a novel solution to a time before pocket-size travel dictionaries and smart phone translation apps?

The infinitely more likely explanation is that this 2,000-year-old token is part of a game, and the kinky couple are a bit of saucy decoration. No spintria tokens have been found with a number greater than 16. We don't know what the game was; it's possible that, like a modern pack of playing cards, the tokens could have been used to play all sorts of different games.

The Putney 'brothel' token may have been produced in Britain, but it's more likely that it was imported from elsewhere and could have been made before 43AD. We can't know whether it was lost in or near the Thames in Roman times, or at some point since. What's almost certain is that this little piece of the Roman past would have been lost forever if Regis hadn't been metal detecting that day. That, he says, is why he keeps mudlarking. As you walk along the shoreline of the ancient Thames, you never know what you'll find next.

See also:
Syston Knife Handle
Horns and Crotal Musical
  Instruments
Baldehildis Seal

1 - LLANBEDRGOCH VIKING TREASURE

2 - NESSCLIFFE RITUAL SPOONS

3 - MOURNING RING

4 - POW FARTHING PENDANT

5 - LEOPARD CUP

6 - RAGLAN RING

7 - LANGSTONE TANKARD

8 - GREAT WAR VICTORY MEDAL

9 - FROME HOARD

10 - NETHER STOWEY HOARD

11 - PITMINSTER TOY CANNON

12 - DARTMOOR SWORD

13 - HMS COLOSSUS SHIPWRECK

**THE SOUTH WEST AND THE BORDER COUNTIES** of Shropshire and Herefordshire are lands at the edges of England. Wales is proudly and determinedly beyond England. The shared roots of the Celtic languages reflect the early links between Ireland, Wales, the South West peninsula and France, as well as the sense of cultural and political independence.

In the South West, beyond the marshy levels of Somerset and the temperate farmland of Dorset, are the vast, bleak, high grounds of Exmoor, Dartmoor and Bodmin Moor which block the way to all but determined overland travellers. The granite outcrops of Dartmoor reach a 621m peak at High Willhays, and plunge into dramatic gorges and valleys. Exmoor is gritstone and slate, bracken-covered and unforgiving. The **Dartmoor Sword** (p118) and the **Nether Stowey Hoard (p100)** are discoveries that confirm that even though some of the South West is remote, it has seen its share of the darker moments in our national history.

Wales has its own geographical challenges, including its central spine of high ground running from Snowdon, the highest peak in England and Wales, at 885m, to the Brecon Beacons in South Wales. Culturally and politically, the Wales border has been hugely significant. Yet where there has been conflict, there can also be a strong sense of community. The people who drank together from the **Langstone Tankard (p126)** surely embodied what it means to share a cultural identity. Perhaps the likely owner of **The Raglan Ring (p132)** felt a wrench from the community when he dropped his Welsh name and embraced Englishness to support his king.

The central area of Wales is now thinly populated. The majority of people live along the coast or in the south. As industry and farming have changed, the distribution of people and communities has followed suit.

This is also true in Cornwall, where tin mining began in prehistoric times. It hooked the Cornish natives into a rich and prestigious trade network that stretched across France, Britain and Ireland that's hard to imagine now.

The Roman historian Diodorus the Sicilian wrote in around 60–30BC, that, 'the inhabitants of Britain who dwell about the promontory of Belerion [Cornwall] are especially hospitable to strangers and have adopted a civilised manner of life because of their intercourse with merchants and other peoples'. Although there are barriers to land travel in this region, the sea always offers an alternative route. The **Llanbedrgoch Viking Treasure (p120)** is proof positive.

The coastlines of the region are radically varied. Wild coasts facing the full assaults of the Atlantic, along the Gower in South Wales, and the north coasts of Cornwall and Devon, deliver some of the most terrifying sea states in the British Isles. The Isles of Scilly, 40km west of Cornwall, have been a welcome sight to many seafarers. But **HMS *Colossus* (p140)** didn't find the shelter she needed. Around these coasts, there are many shipwrecks we don't know about, and plenty where no evidence survives. The *Colossus* site is unavoidably deteriorating – we only have it for a short while, and then this secret treasure really will be lost.

Other treasures from this region are small and personal, and it's sheer chance that they were discovered – from the **Mourning Ring (p137)** and **Farthing Pendant (p123)** from Shropshire to the **Toy Cannon (p130)** from Somerset. These are secret and precious treasures we can all admire.

# Nether Stowey Hoard

## Civil War silver hidden for 350 years in a garden

Arthur Haig was metal detecting, helping look for a lost bracelet, when he accidentally located a hoard of silver. Four solid silver spoons, a goblet and a salt pot known as a 'bell salt', all dating to the 1600s, had been concealed in an earthenware vessel and buried in the ground.

All the evidence points to this being a hoard buried for safekeeping, but for some unknown reason, the hoard was never retrieved. The dates make it likely that this hoard was buried because of the English Civil War.

**Date:** Probably buried during the English Civil War, 1642–51, Post Medieval

**Where, when and how found:** Nether Stowey, Somerset; 2008; Chance find when metal detecting for a lost bracelet

**Finder:** Arthur Haig

**Official valuation:** £38,000

**Where is it now?** Museum of Somerset, Taunton

**Get involved:** Two major re-enactment societies bring the Civil War era to life for participants and visitors: English Civil War Society, www.ecws.org.uk; Sealed Knot www.thesealedknot.org.uk

## The items

The spoons all have a crowned leopard's head stamped on to them, the traditional hallmark symbol that indicates they were made in London. Three of them have the same hallmark letter, 'v', for the year 1617, and the fourth has a 'k' within a square shield, representing the year 1587. It's slightly shorter and was made by a different silversmith. All four spoons are marked with the initials of their owner on their backs – a 'G' and an 'A', with a 'C' above, pricked out in tiny dots. This represents the initials of the husband (G) and wife (A) who had a surname beginning with a C who owned the spoons.

English spoons have a distinctive evolution of style, and the four Nether Stowey spoons are known as 'slip top' spoons. The handle, or 'stem', has a hexagonal cross-section, and the end appears to be cut off at an angle, rather than finishing in a knob or other decorative shape. The term 'slip top' comes from the word 'slipped' meaning 'cut', and a slip top spoon looks like it has been cut across the top. Spoons were still prestigious items at this time, but rich families would have easily afforded a matching set of silver spoons like these.

The goblet was found in two pieces – the stem and the beaker, and the beaker section also has the 'G.A.C.' initials on it, suggesting all the objects had one owner. The hallmarks show this piece was made in 1633 in London, and the stem of the goblet was turned on a lathe to make the fine and even shape.

The salt pot has been designed in the shape of a bell, hence it being called a 'bell salt'. It's made from three separate pieces that stack one over another – two lower tiers for holding fine ground salt, and a pepper pot at the top with a screw-on perforated lid so pepper can be shaken out.

The two middle tiers don't have the same date or maker's marks as each other, suggesting that they weren't originally made as a set. They don't fit together perfectly, but that might be due to them spending almost 400 years in the ground, or because they were slightly knocked out of shape during their use.

The ceramic pot that the silverware was packed into came out of the ground in twenty-four sherds, making up about half the original pot. It's a pretty common type of fired and glazed earthenware pot. This itself wasn't a treasured possession, but simply a container to hold the valuables.

A flat silver strip with three little spherical feet was discovered some weeks later by Arthur detecting on the other side of the same garden – it's mangled and broken, but is clearly the base of the bell salt. It does raise a question though – the rest of the silverware was neatly packed into the pottery vessel, and it seems unlikely that the bell salt feet would have been intentionally detached and deposited elsewhere. It leads to the suggestion that the hoard was buried very quickly, and with less care than at first seems evident – was the person in grave and imminent danger, or could the Nether Stowey Hoard actually be the stash of looters, rather than worried owners?

## The owners

In 1642, England was ripped apart by civil war. Resulting from an extraordinary combination of political, social and religious issues, at heart it was a dispute between King Charles I and his Parliament, about how the State should be governed. Oliver Cromwell's Parliamentarian supporters argued that there was no divine right of kings to rule and that the monarchy shouldn't be able to single-handedly control the nation. Depending on your political allegiances, the conflict between Parliament and the king was either a revolution or a rebellion. Bitter and brutal war broke out across the country, sometimes even splitting families.

Across England, Scotland and Ireland, citizens were terrified – their homes and their lives weren't safe, and men and boys were press-ganged into military service for both sides. If you supported the wrong side, you could be branded a traitor, have your lands and assets seized, or even be summarily executed. Fighting continued for nine years, tearing the country apart – historians estimate that 100,000 people died from war-related disease and hunger, and at least 90,000 died in actual battle – from a population of just 5 million.

Stowey Court, a stately home just 800m from the hoard findspot, was used by a garrison of Royalist soldiers supporting the king. A note in the earliest surviving parish register for Nether Stowey states that parishioners removed their 'best goods and things of value' into the great house during the time of the 'Great Rebellion'. It was thought that valuables would perhaps be safer under the care of the Royalist soldiers than they would be in the parishioners' homes. Perhaps they were right, but at some point someone

> "Was the person in grave and imminent danger, or could the Nether Stowey hoard actually be the stash of looters, rather than worried owners?"

clearly decided to bury some valuables in a hole a short distance away from the garrison. Perhaps they were burying their treasures across more than one hiding spot. It's also possible that a soldier with sticky fingers took some of the civilians' valuables and stashed them elsewhere, or that this hoard is the result of looting elsewhere in the country, and was buried by soldiers once they'd settled at Stowey Court in a respite from the campaign.

The initials on the silverware, G.A.C., suggest that these pieces could be associated with the owners of Stowey Court themselves. During the Civil War the house was owned by Mr Angel Grey and his wife, Catherine. The initials A, C, and G don't fall in the expected order to represent their names, though, so this is probably an odd coincidence. The mystery of where the silver came from remains unsolved.

What's certain is that the fear and unrest continued. King Charles I was executed by Parliament on 30 January 1649, but the war continued for another two years and violent recriminations for decades after that. Whoever buried the Nether Stowey silverware wasn't able to successfully retrieve it – perhaps they died, fled the area, or were simply unable to relocate their hiding spot. Their story is lost to us.

See also:
Hackney WWII Hoard
Silverdale Hoard
Hawking Vervel
Rochester Cufflink

# Leopard Cup

## An exotic drinking vessel from an early Roman grave

On a November day in 2002, Gary Mapps was metal detecting in a field outside Abergavenny. He got a signal, and made the find of a lifetime. This copper-alloy drinking vessel, with an evocative leopard-shaped handle, is one of the finest Roman artefacts ever to be found in Wales.

> **Date:** 43–100AD, Roman
> **Where, when and how found:** Llantilio Pertholey, Monmouthshire, Wales; 2002; metal detecting
> **Finder:** Gary Mapps
> **Where is it now?** Amgueddfa Cymru – National Museum Wales, Cardiff
> www.museumwales.ac.uk

## Context is everything

Gary immediately informed the PAS at the National Museum Wales about his star find, and they were able to thoroughly excavate the site, gathering crucial evidence about how and why the cup was deposited. Because it isn't gold or silver, Gary had no legal obligation to inform the archaeologists or museum service about his discovery, but because he did, our understanding is so much richer.

The excavation revealed that the cup had been placed upside down in a small pit containing a human cremation burial with pottery and burnt bone, within a bigger Roman cemetery, beside a major road. It's close to the mid 1st- to early 2nd-century (50–130AD) fort at Abergavenny (Roman *Gobannium*), and would have been a prized possession of a Roman soldier or early visitor to the newly conquered province of Britannia, or perhaps a native Briton who was given the cup as a gift.

This area of Wales had a significant Roman presence, despite the fact that further west the native tribespeople put up a fierce and successful resistance to these new invaders. Many local people collaborated with the Romans, combining elements of Roman lifestyle and art with their own traditional beliefs and practices.

One of the new, popular introductions was wine, giving the natives a new alcoholic option in addition to the mead, beer and grain and fruit spirits they were familiar with. The Romans associated leopards with the

God of Wine, Bacchus, so the beautiful handle is a fitting decoration on a drinking cup.

Leopards were also captured and traded out of Africa and Asia, prized as fighting beasts for shows in arenas and amphitheatres across the Roman Empire, although it's quite possible that the owner of the cup had never seen a real leopard. The cup was almost certainly made in Italy in the 1st century AD, and brought to Britain after the conquest in 43AD. Very similar cups have been found in Pompeii, the Roman city that was destroyed and preserved by a volcanic eruption in 79AD.

The craftsmanship of the cup is exquisite – leaded bronze (copper, tin and lead) was cast in a mould, and then turned on a lathe to achieve the smooth, even, finished look. The leopard handle was cast separately and then finely finished with silver inlay for its spots and probably amber inlay for its eyes.

## Roman burial practices

It's been suggested by some scholars that death for Romans in the 1st century AD was considered to be a definitive end to existence, where the deceased person's spirit would travel to the underworld and that would be it. Following the correct burial rituals would ensure that the person's spirit would successfully depart and not linger on Earth, becoming a danger to the living. The details of these beliefs are hard to pin down in the records. The idea of an eternal, potentially positive, afterlife was slowly introduced from eastern cults, including Christianity, but only became mainstream in the early 300s AD.

Cremations like the one associated with the Leopard Cup would have been performed away from the cemetery, and then the ashes were scooped into a container of some kind and buried or placed in a tomb or cist (pronounced 'kist' like 'crisp', a stone-lined pit) in a marked cemetery. Some inhumations (burial of the body) were also performed – there appears to be regional variation in the common practices. In both cremations and burials, however, archaeologists often find items related to drinking – flagons, flasks, cups and bottles. And just like the Leopard Cup, many are upside down in the grave. Some very bizarre burials also have narrow pipes inserted into

> "Cremations like the one associated with the Leopard Cup would have been performed away from the cemetery"

them from the surface, potentially so that living relatives could continue to provide drinks, libations, to the deceased.

We can't be sure whether people thought that the dead person needed cups and bottles of drink to help them on their journey to the underworld or afterlife, or whether the drinks were intended to pacify malign spirits and keep them away from the living. The alternative is that personal items might have been considered unlucky once their original owners died, so burying them was a way of safely disposing of them. The last option is that it simply became custom to bury something precious with the dead, more as a tribute and memorial, than as a necessity for the afterlife.

The Leopard Cup is now proudly displayed at Amgueddfa Cymru, the Welsh National Museum in Cardif for the admiration and debate to continue.

See also:
Staffordshire Moorlands
   Ilam Pan
Ringlemere Cup

# Frome Hoard

### An enormous Roman pot holding a record-breaking 52,503 coins

Dave Crisp has been metal detecting since the 1980s, and has reported more than 300 finds to his local Finds Liaison Officer. In 2009, he discovered a rare hoard of Roman silver *siliqua* coins buried in a farmer's field – for many detectorists, this would be a find of a lifetime. But the following year, in April 2010, Dave returned to the area to search the field again. He got a signal from his metal detector, and tentatively dug into the earth. Below the surface, he hit some small pottery sherds and a few bronze Roman coins. Dave realised he might have found a hoard – another find of a lifetime! With utter self-control, he stopped digging, marked the position, refilled the hole and called in the archaeologists – he didn't want any information about the context of the hoard to be lost by disturbing more than he had to.

| |
|---|
| **Date:** Around 290AD, Roman |
| **Where, when and how found:** Frome, Somerset; 2010; metal detecting |
| **Finder:** Dave Crisp |
| **Official valuation:** £320,250 |
| **Where is it now?** Museum of Somerset, Taunton www.somerset.gov.uk/museums |

## Three-day excavation

A local archaeologist, Alan Graham, was quickly brought in to excavate the find site. Together with the Finds Liaison Officers, the landowner's family, friends and Dave himself, he began to carefully dig and record the data he collected. The small sherds that Dave had initially discovered turned out not to be the actual container, but a small upturned dish that had been used as a makeshift lid for a much, much bigger vessel beneath. As Alan and his team of excited helpers began to dig out the thick clay around the pot's sides, they realised just how huge it was: 60cm tall and 45cm wide, the grey-ware Roman storage jar was stuffed full of bronze coins. It was a monster, weighing more than 160kg.

> "The grey-ware Roman storage jar was stuffed full of bronze coins. It was a monster, weighing more than 160kg"

There was no way the pot would come out of the ground whole, with the coins in situ. It seemed clear that the pot couldn't have originally been put into the hole full either, but carefully positioned and then filled. Otherwise the sheer weight of the coinage inside would have cracked it instantly.

When people discover hoards and dig them out themselves, information about the way the coins were deposited inside the vessel, and in what order, is invariably lost. Because Dave had stopped digging when he did, the coins were in situ and could be precisely recorded. In order to gather as much data as possible, the team decided to systematically dismantle the pot from the top down following the existing cracks in the pottery, and record the coins in ten layers, immediately bagging and labelling them.

## Conservation of the monster hoard

Before they could be analysed, the coins needed to be cleaned by specialists. Finds are often left to dry naturally, but because the Frome Hoard had been waterlogged in the ground, the coins were carefully washed first, to prevent corrosion from solidifying on their surfaces. It took eight weeks for the staff at the British Museum to wash, dry and count the coins. In total, there were an astonishing, and record-breaking, 52,498 bronze radiate coins and five silver denarius coins – 52,503 in total. This is the biggest hoard ever found in one container.

Thirty-thousand of the coins needed further painstaking conservation, and about 15% of the hoard were so corroded that they were initially entirely illegible. Conservators had to prioritise cleaning just the identifying features on each coin, so that they could be catalogued. On the diagram, see p113, the corrosion over the nose and eyes hasn't been removed, as enough information has already been revealed to identify the coin.

It took ten further weeks for the team to sort the coins by emperor and date. Now they knew where each dated coin came from inside the pot, and patterns started to emerge.

## Patterns in the pot

The earliest coins were from around 253AD, the latest were from around 290AD. All of the latest coins were deposited in the middle of the pot. So the pot wasn't filled slowly over forty years with a series of coin deposits that went from oldest at the bottom to newest at the top. Rather, it seems to have been filled all at once. But not from one source – one group of early coins from Emperor Carausius' reign (286–293AD) are at the top of the pot, while later Carausian coins are in the middle. In normal circulation, all your coins would get mixed together. For groups of coins from different dates to stay distinct, it suggests they were kept in smaller pots and bags, or brought in by different people, and only tipped into the giant pot at the last minute.

## The forgotten British Emperor – Carausius and his coins

Throughout the later 200s, there were a number of breakaway emperors ruling dominions at the edges of Rome's control. Britain and Gaul were at one of these frontiers, and a succession of different rulers took power and then fell – a potentially dangerous time for the military and citizens alike.

One of the men battling for control was Marcus Aurelius Mausaeus Carausius, commonly known as Carausius. Despite his allegedly low birth, by 286AD Carausius had risen to the rank of general and was commander of the Roman naval fleet in the North Sea and English Channel, protecting Roman Britain and Roman Gaul from 'barbarian' raiders.

Roman writers from the time claim that in an 'outrageous act of brigandage', Carausius intercepted a fleet of barbarians with ships full of stolen loot, but instead of returning the valuables to their owners, he kept the treasures for himself and his troops.

For this act of treachery, Emperor Maximian in Rome sentenced Carausius to death. Carausius responded by declaring himself Emperor of Britain and northern Gaul.

Carausius was very keen to prove that he was a legitimate ruler, and the designs on his coins emphasise that – one coin shows the figure of Britannia shaking Carausius by the hand, with a quotation from Virgil, 'Come, long-awaited one' (*Expectate Veni*). Other coins have initials which are likely to stand for another quotation, 'The Golden Age returns, now a new generation comes down from Heaven above'. Like many leaders throughout history, Carausius knew the propaganda power of coins.

Carausius' reign came to an end when he was assassinated by his finance minister, Allectus, in 293AD. We don't know the details, but Allectus managed to rule for around three years before the whole of Britain was reconquered by Rome.

In the Frome Hoard there are around 840 Carausian coins, the largest group ever found in Britain, including five incredibly rare silver *denarii* (singular: *denarius*). There are no coins from Allectus' reign. The latest coins come from the middle of Carausius' reign so it's likely that the hoard was buried a couple of years before, or around the time of Carausius' murder.

# HOW TO READ A ROMAN COIN

by Natalie Mitchell and Ana Tam.
See more of Natalie and Ana's work at www.finds.org.uk/blogs/fromehoard/

The **LEGEND** is the text on a coin which names the emperor (Augustus and Caesar in Latin) ruling at the time. Other titles include commander (*imperator*), pious (*pius*) and blessed (*felix*).

The mintmarks give information about where and when a coin was struck and are often recorded in the format shown at the bottom right of the image. They are found on the reverse of the coin in the areas known as the **FIELDS** and the **EXERGUE**.

On this Carausian coin, the letters 'B' and 'E' are mint control letters in the field of the coin – we don't know what they stand for, but there was a large issue of coins bearing 'B E'.

The '**MLXXI**' in the exergue stands for:

'**Moneta Londiniensis**' (the mint of London) – 1 part silver to 20 parts copper (i.e. 5% silver).

Pax (the personification of peace, as seen on this coin) was the most common image Carausius used on the reverse of his coins.

The coin pictured has been conserved to a point where the text has been revealed enough so it can be identified. The portrait of Carausius on the obverse still has his eyes and nose covered by corrosion because these areas are not a research priority.

The 'IMP' that precedes 'CARAVSIVS' remains hidden by the crystals of corrosion products, as it's common to find IMP before the name of the emperor and there isn't space for much else to fit there.

However, there are instances where a string of extra letters have been included on coins: '**IMP C CARAVSIVS**' means Imperial Caesar Carausius, and '**IMP C M CARAVSIVS**' means Imperial Caesar Mausaeus Carausius. From an inscription on a milestone found near Carlisle, we know that his full name was probably Marcus Aurelius Mausaeus Carausius.

[C]ARAUSIUS

Pius
Felix

[IMP]erator

AVGvstvs

**OBVERSE**

AVGvsti

PAX

B | E
MLXXI

**REVERSE**

## Why did the hoard get deposited?

Although the Frome Hoard is the largest ever found in a single container, hoards of bronze radiate coins that date from 253–296AD are strangely common in Britain. Over 600 have been discovered, including the Cunetio Hoard, Wiltshire (54,951 coins in two containers), the Normanby Hoard in Lincolnshire (47,912 coins), the Blackmoor Hoard in Hampshire (29,802 coins) and the Chalgrove Hoard in Oxfordshire (4,957 coins) (see p155 for the Chalgrove Hoard).

Archaeologists have thought that hoards were deposited at this time because of the military and political instability: in a time before banking or police, the safest place for your valuables may well have been hidden in a hole in a field. But despite the changing emperors, Britain at this time seems to have been relatively peaceful and prosperous. And the Frome Hoard is too big to be easily buried and collected in a hurry.

Dave Crisp's find is forcing us to reconsider the very purpose of Roman hoards. Instead of an act of fear, coin hoarding might have been a celebrated ritual. Throughout the Bronze Age and Iron Age, people deposited metal and precious objects in the ground or in water as offerings to gods. Perhaps burying coins was a similar ritual act for people during the Roman occupation.

The Frome Hoard should be celebrated as a Treasure champion – the story of its discovery, excavation, conservation and display is a shining example of the best ways metal detectorists, land owners and archaeologists can work together to tell the story of our island's incredible past.

See also:
Chalgrove Hoard and
Coin of Domitianus
Hallaton Treasure

# Nesscliffe Ritual Spoons

## *Mysterious, hand-sized 2,000-year-old spoons*

Trevor Brown is a keen and experienced metal detectorist, and in 2005 he made a discovery of international importance. Searching farmland in mid-Shropshire, he got a signal, dug down and discovered these two hand-sized copper alloy spoon-like objects sat one inside another. He took the

Date: 300BC–100AD, Iron Age

Where, when and how found: Nesscliffe, Shropshire; 2005; metal detecting

Finder: Trevor Brown

Where are they now? Shrewsbury Museum & Art Gallery www.shrewsburymuseum.org.uk

artefacts to his local Finds Liaison Officer, Peter Reavill who immediately recognised them as a pair of incredibly rare Iron Age spoons. These aren't ordinary eating or serving spoons, but are likely to have been used for a ritualistic purpose that we can't yet fully comprehend.

Although the spoons are made from copper alloy, because they're prehistoric in date and were found together, they qualify as a 'base metal prehistoric assemblage' and were officially declared Treasure. Shropshire Museums were delighted to be able to acquire them; Trevor and the landowner received the full reward, and the spoons are now on permanent display in Shrewsbury Museum.

## Mystery spoons

Only twenty-three other Iron Age spoons like this have ever been discovered, and Trevor's finds were the first for eighty years. Twenty of these spoons have been found in pairs, and it's thought that the single spoons that have been discovered originally all had a mate that has since been lost. Apart from one pair of spoons discovered in a burial in France, these spoons have only ever been found in Britain and Ireland.

Both the Nesscliffe spoons are made from a single sheet of copper alloy, hammered into shape over a mould, and they're similar enough in shape to be able to sit inside one another. Each spoon has a shallow bowl, pointed at one end, and rounder towards the stub handle end. Both handles are plain,

although other Iron Age spoons are decorated with different designs on each of the handles. On other paired spoons there's clear evidence of wear on the stub handles, showing that the spoons have been held between the forefinger and thumb.

Just like all the other pairs of mysterious spoons, the Nesscliffe pair aren't identical: one is marked with two engraved lines forming a cross through the centre of the bowl, with a small circle highlighting where the two lines intersect.

The other spoon is plain, but usually the plain spoon has a perforated hole on one side, towards the rim. In the Nesscliffe spoon, the bowl is torn at the point where we'd expect to see the perforated hole. Most spoon holes are on the left-hand side; the Nesscliffe spoon appears to have had its hole on the right-hand side. When Trevor discovered the spoons, the 'hole' spoon was sitting inside the 'cross' spoon.

We simply don't know what these spoons were used for, but the current theory is that they were some kind of ritual divination device. Perhaps a spoon was held in each hand, and a thick liquid like blood, oil, honey, or a fine powder, was allowed to flow through the hole in the 'hole' spoon, into the marked quarters of the 'cross' spoon. Depending on where the mixture dropped, the diviner would be able to predict the future or counsel on the best course of action.

An alternative is that the spoons were put together with the bowls facing each other, and a substance was blown in through the hole and allowed to make a pattern inside the bowls, or the substance inside was blown around through the hole.

Like tarot cards, reading tea leaves, or the Roman practice of reading the entrails of a sacrificed animal, the 'truth' is laid out in the otherwise random alignment or pattern, and it requires someone with the appropriate insight to 'translate' what the pattern means.

Many seasonal cycles break into quarters – the annual seasons with their equinox days, or the moon's phases, for example, could perhaps be represented in the spoon quadrants. Maybe people in the British and Irish Iron Age sought advice on when to plant crops, when to marry, begin journeys or commence raiding or warfare. It's possible that ritual specialists (priests, priestesses or 'druids') were resident in every community, or they might have travelled between communities in an area, like holy men and shamans do in many tribal societies nowadays.

The spoons Trevor found were on a slight ridge surrounded by what was once a boggy area, which fits with the nationwide pattern of important artefacts being deposited in or near watery places. Aerial photography has shown that the spoons were placed in a pit or at the end of a ditch within some kind of ritual enclosure with a double ring of earthworks.

Perhaps when a diviner died, their spoons were sacrificed, or if the spoons had been read wrongly or given bad advice, they were given back to the gods. Three pairs of spoons have been found with burials – one pair in Deal, Kent, were placed on either side of the dead person's head; a pair in Burnmouth, Berwick, were placed next to each other on top of the person's face; the third burial pair from Pogny, France, were one inside the other in an organic bag, inside a bronze bowl, next to the body.

Very few Iron Age artefacts have been found in Shropshire, so these add significantly to our knowledge of the regional spread of artefacts. It highlights why it is so important that people record their finds with the Portable Antiquities Scheme. To further our understanding of these enigmatic treasures, archaeological context is everything – and that's why Trevor's careful treatment of his findspot, and his prompt reporting of the find, have proved so significant. The Nesscliffe spoons raise so many questions – the answers have yet to be divined.

See also:
Pegsdon Mirror
Ringlemere Cup
Horns and Crotal Musical Instruments

# Dartmoor Sword

## *A famous sword brand from the Civil War*

This steel sword was found in a village on the outskirts of Dartmoor during building work. The finders took it to a Finds Day at Exeter, and it was recorded with the PAS.

Made from iron forged with carbon and silica to make steel, hammered into shape and then sharpened on both sides, it dates to around 1650, and is a style known as a 'basket-hilted' sword. The 'hilt' is the handle section of a sword, comprising the *grip*, the *guard* to protect the hand, and the *pommel*, the enlarged fitting at the end of the handle to stop the sword slipping and to counterbalance the blade. The basket hilt developed to protect the hand from all angles, and designs became increasingly ornate through the 16th to 18th centuries.

Basket-hilted swords like this were relatively heavy swords, double-edged and up to 1m long. In contrast to the rapier, which was light, thin and flexible, the Dartmoor Sword used the weight of the blade to strike heavy and deadly cuts as well as quicker, thrusting jabs. The skill was to combine the 'cut and thrust' – the origin of the phrase we still use today.

This type of sword is also referred to as a 'mortuary sword' because many of those made after 1649 had an image of the executed king, Charles I, engraved onto the hilt, especially swords being used by Royalist supporters. The men who owned these engraved swords had fought for King Charles, and were now fighting to put his exiled son, Charles II, back on the throne. Oliver Cromwell also owned and used a mortuary sword, although his didn't have a picture of the King on it – you can see Cromwell's sword at the Tower of London. By the 1670s, sword fashions had moved on, and more people chose to use the 'small sword' rather than the longer, heavier mortuary swords.

| |
|---|
| **Date:** Around 1650 |
| **Where, when and how found:** Dartmoor, Devon; 2008; discovered during building work |
| **Finder:** Anonymous |
| **Where is it now?** Returned to finder |
| **Visit:** Royal Armouries Museums at Leeds, the Tower of London and Fort Nelson, Fareham www.armouries.org.uk |

## Ferara swords

The Dartmoor Sword blade doesn't have an image of the King, but is engraved with an intriguing name – 'Andrea' on one side, 'Ferrara' on the other – perhaps the man who made the sword.

An agreement from 1578 details a contract between brothers 'Zanandrea' and 'Zandona' of Ferara, swordsmiths at Belluno, northern Italy, and two London merchants. In the contract, the Ferara brothers agree to supply the merchants with 600 swords 'of the kind used in England', every month for ten years. They agree not to make any swords intended for England for anyone else – an exclusive import deal of 72,000 swords over a decade. It's an incredible number, given that each of these was hand-produced.

In a 1585 treatise on military pursuits, the writer recommends the 'most excellent' sword makers in Italy, picking out Giovan Donato and Andrea, 'ingenious' brothers from the Ferara family of Belluno. Earlier swords have also been discovered with the names Cosmo Ferara and Piero Ferara.

Based on the style of the basket hilt, the Dartmoor Sword has been dated to the mid-1600s, which would mean that a later Ferara, also named Andrea, must have made it. But the spelling of the maker's name differs between the documents and the Dartmoor Sword – Ferara and Ferrara. It's been suggested that this mean it's a fake, engraved by an illiterate person making knock-off swords. It would be like buying a fake Chanel or Gucci handbag that's accidentally spelled 'Channel' or 'Guchi'. But there is another explanation.

It's more likely that the name 'Andrea Ferrara' was engraved to indicate that it was a quality blade, even if it hadn't actually been made by a Ferara swordsmith (like calling a vacuum cleaner a 'Hoover' even though it's a different brand). The final theory is that spelling didn't matter so much in the 16th and 17th centuries, hadn't been formalised yet, and any approximation of the name was as good as any other. That might mean it is a genuine Ferara/Ferrara sword, made by one of the greatest sword-making dynasties in Europe.

See also:
Nether Stowey Hoard
Alnwick Sword

# Llanbedrgoch Viking Treasure

## Life and death in medieval Anglesey

The pattern of Viking raiding and settlement from the 790s AD through to the 1000s has been pieced together with evidence from documentary sources, place name evidence, genetic population study and, of course, archaeology.

Most of the early Viking raids in the British Isles targeted the undefended monasteries that were full of precious Church treasures, like gold crosses and cups and jewelled reliquaries. All along the east coast of England, up and over the northern coast and down along the west coast of the British mainland, *víkingr* parties took what they could during surprise attacks, and carried the spoils, and sometimes people for slavery, back across the sea. Only a small proportion of the Scandinavian population took part in these raiding trips, and it was considered that raiding was a young man's game, and older men should be more focused on family and farming back home.

In the Anglo-Saxon chronicles that record these raids, the attackers are called *Norsemen*, or *Northmen*. The *Northmen* who settled in France ultimately became the 'Normans'. In records written in Iceland, the newcomers are called 'Ostmen' or 'Austmann', meaning 'Men from the East'.

For skilled and efficient Viking sailors, with manoeuvrable and very seaworthy longboats, the sea wasn't a barrier or a defence, it was a highway. It enabled quick and easy access to lucrative targets, and the victims of their raids understood this well. The monastery at Iona, an island off the west coast of Scotland, was ransacked in 795, 802 and 806AD, and eventually the surviving monks decided to abandon their holy island and relocate inland. The risk of smash-and-grab attack if they remained on the coast was too great.

> **Date:** 600–1000, Viking
>
> **Where, when and how found:** Llanbedrgoch, Anglesey, Wales; 2007; metal detecting
>
> **Finders:** Archie Gillespie and Peter Corbett
>
> **Where is it now?** Finds from the site are displayed at Amgueddfa Cymru, the National Museum of Wales, Cardiff www.museumwales.ac.uk

Increasingly, raiders also looked for land that they could settle. Fishing and farming were the main activities for most men back in their Scandinavian homelands – in these new territories, some men took local wives, others took partners in addition to their families back home. Some brought their families over from Scandinavia to settle in the new lands.

The general pattern of settlement is that Danish peoples settled on the eastern side of England, and Norwegian people travelled north and west, settling Orkney, Shetland, the Western Isles and down into the Irish Sea, founding Dublin and other Irish towns, as well as settling and trading with native communities in coastal Wales, the Wirral and Merseyside.

## Anglesey Vikings

The isle of Anglesey was always considered to be an important staging post on these journeys west, but thanks to the work of two metal detectorists, we now know just how important Anglesey really was.

121

In 1992, Archie Gillespie and Peter Corbett reported some Viking weights and coins to the Portable Antiquities Scheme Wales, based at the National Museum and Galleries of Wales. No one knew about any site or settlement there, so it was decided to investigate further. The geophysical survey revealed more than anyone was expecting – a fortified enclosure with large stone walls over an area of 10,000 square metres. Clear evidence of specialist activities in different areas, including metalworking in bronze, tin, silver and iron, farming and food processing was discovered.

Coins, hacksilver (silver jewellery and bullion chopped into chunks to use as currency for trading), whetstones for sharpening knives and ornaments for people and horse harnesses, show that this was a busy and prosperous settlement, occupied for centuries. It's likely that native Welsh people were living on the island before the Vikings arrived, and either tolerated the incomers, or perhaps more likely fled from, or were killed by the new residents.

Just outside the enclosure archaeologists discovered evidence of troubled episodes in the site's history. Five human bodies, dated to the 900s AD, had been unceremoniously dumped into a ditch, and it appears that the adult male in the group had his hands tied behind his back when he was killed. At the time when these people died, Viking communities buried their dead according to traditional Christian principles – laying the body with reverence on the back, aligned East-West. The five in the ditch were dropped in North-South, possibly as an additional insult to their bodies, or their bodies were simply dropped in at random. An alternative explanation is that these were Viking victims of the native Welsh, who considered the Viking incomers to be pagans and not deserving of any Christian respect after death.

The Viking legacy in this area along the west coast of England and Wales is evident in place names and family surnames, and also in our DNA. Thanks to Archie and Peter's discovery, we can add a hugely significant site to our understanding of Anglesey life more than 1,000 years ago.

See also:
West Yorkshire Ring Hoard
Vale of York Hoard
Saltfleetby Spindle Whorl

# Prisoner of War Farthing Pendant

## The craftwork of a German soldier-prisoner

The person who made this pendant took an old bronze farthing of King George V, a coin which was issued throughout his reign, from 1911 to 1936, and carefully drilled, cut out and filed the 'insides' of the coin by hand, to make the King's head stand alone in profile within the frame. They then drilled a hole at the top, so the coin could be hung as a pendant – probably either as a necklace or on a fob watch chain. The work is very precise and neat – someone took a lot of care over making this little piece.

It's interesting in its own right, but what makes this find a real secret treasure is that it was discovered near the site of what used to be a WWII Prisoner of War camp, and is thought to have been made by one of the soldiers interned there.

**Date:** Around 1939–1948, Modern

**Where, when and how found:** Near Ludlow, Shropshire; 2012; metal detecting

**Finder:** Chris Webb

**Where is it now?** Returned to finder

**Get involved:** Many archive documents about POW camps are held at the National Archives, Kew www.nationalarchives.gov.uk

Council for British Archaeology 'Defence of Britain project', where volunteers recorded 20,000 20th century military sites across the UK. Project archive online at www.archaeologyuk.org/cba/projects/dob/

Arborglyph tree graffiti recording information and links at www.wiltshirearborglyphs.weebly.com

## Camp 84

More than 400,000 people, mostly men, were brought to England to be held as Prisoners of War (POWs) until the end of hostilities – fifteen camps of different sizes are known from Shropshire alone. Shropshire was thought to be a good county for keeping prisoners because it's landlocked and rural – if they escaped, they would be easy to spot, and they wouldn't get far. Camp 84, near Ludlow, was classed as a 'German Working Camp' – the most common

designation in the country. Some sites held ordinary citizens from Germany and Italy who'd been living in Britain before the war, and had been interned when war was declared. Other camps had military prisoners from Italy, Ukraine and other non-allied countries. The site of Camp 84 has been demolished and the area redeveloped – the last surviving feature was a derelict water-tower, the only permanent brick feature on site. However, other small pieces of evidence remain in the ground, as well as a rich paper trail in the archives.

A typical POW camp, like Camp 84, had a prisoners' compound area for around 750 men, a guards' compound, recreation area, dining huts, garden plots for growing fruit and veg, a cookhouse, detention block, a sick bay known as a 'camp reception station', toilet blocks, sewage and water works. Many camps didn't have guard towers, but were ringed with barbed-wire entanglements and high rows of fences. Prisoners lived in prefabricated, specially-designed huts made from concrete and steel. Each hut housed twenty men in ten two-man bays.

Prisoners weren't generally considered to be high risk, and it was expected that they'd work to earn their keep. The men were set to agricultural, labouring and construction jobs, picking up the work that British men who were away fighting would have been doing. Compared with the treatment of prisoners of war elsewhere during WWII, conditions in the British camps weren't bad.

Metal detectorist Chris Webb has found a few items that probably once belonged to German POWs from Camp 84, including a silver finger ring fragment with an enamelled Iron Cross motif on it, a symbol linked to the German Army. The prisoners found creative ways to keep themselves occupied, and often made things that might have trading value – a pretty trinket could get you some more cigarettes, food, or other luxury. This farthing pendant is part of this tradition of trench or prisoner art, where soldiers and captives make art out of what is to hand.

One of the most famous pieces of 'prisoner art' is the Italian Chapel on Lamb Holm in the Orkney Islands. Italian POWs, posted to Orkney to help construct sea barrier defences, transformed two temporary Nissen huts into an elaborately decorated place of worship that still stands today. Research groups have also begun to record other categories of military and prisoner activity: trees on Salisbury Plain, Wiltshire, have lots of graffiti carved by American GIs who were waiting to be posted to France. Some of these 'arborglyphs' – tree graffiti – have been traced to specific soldiers – some inevitably leading to war graves, and others to living family members.

## After the war

POWs remained in Britain until as late as 1948 – once hostilities ceased, returning the men to their home territories wasn't a priority for the British government. Many men decided to stay rather than be repatriated – they had made friends, had girlfriends, and many local people didn't consider the POWs the 'enemy' but as unfortunate victims of the same conflict that had taken their own sons and brothers away. After the war ended, some sites were transformed into hostels for agricultural workers, and the very same men who had been POWs moved back in as paid farm labourers. One camp in Cambridgeshire, Friday Bridge Camp, still serves as a hostel for farm workers. Most camps, however, were quickly demolished because they didn't have much reuse potential, and no one considered them to be historically valuable.

We don't actually know exactly how many POW camps there were in Britain. Some camps are only now being identified archaeologically and through archival research, and others have been lost from memory, never existed officially. Records are patchy, and prisoners often weren't told exactly where they were, or allowed to write any identifying address on their correspondence.

Finds of possible trench and prisoner art by members of the public aren't always reported, as they're relatively modern objects. But they are an excellent way to help build our knowledge of these intriguing military sites. Anyone who has any finds like this is encouraged to register them with their local Finds Liaison Officer – together they tell the compelling story of our wartime 'guests'.

**See also:**
Fort George Toy Soldiers
Hackney WWII Hoard

# Langstone Tankard

## *A four-pint tankard dropped in a bog*

This complete wooden tankard was discovered in a peaty layer of a low-lying, waterlogged field on the outskirts of Newport. It holds almost four pints of liquid and was used by our ancestors almost 2,000 years ago, for communal drinking ceremonies using beer and cider. It was deposited at the edge of a bog between 1 and 150AD, possibly around the time of the Roman invasion of South Wales in 47AD. It appears to be a ritual offering.

Made from six strips (or 'staves') of yew wood fitted into a circular base, with undecorated copper alloy bands and a simple handle, it's a large but relatively simple object. What makes it an extraordinary treasure is that the organic component, the wood, has survived for twenty centuries.

> **Date:** 1–150AD Late Iron Age or Early Roman
>
> **Where, when and how found:** Langstone, Newport, Wales; 2007; metal detecting
>
> **Finder:** Craig Mills
>
> **Where is it now?** Amgueddfa Cymru, National Museum Wales, Cardiff (not currently on display) www.museumwales.ac.uk
>
> **Also visit:** National Roman Legion Museum, Caerleon www.museumwales.ac.uk

## Conservation

Normally the only surviving parts of early tankards are the handles, as they're made of solid, chunky metal, but the Langstone tankard is complete. The wood survived this long because the bog it was deposited in kept it waterlogged and without oxygen. If it had been exposed to the air, it would have rotted away a long time ago. Only six complete tankards have ever been found in Britain and Ireland.

The Langstone Tankard was discovered by metal detectorist Craig Mills a few days before Christmas in 2007. When Mark Lewis, the curator at the National Roman Legion Museum at Caerleon saw it, he immediately realised how old and how rare it was. He knew that they would need to act quickly in order to prevent the fragile ancient wood from drying out and disintegrating.

The tankard was taken to the National Museum Wales, Cardiff, where specialist conservators got to work. They soaked the vessel in alcohol to remove

and replace the water in the wood cells, then replaced the alcohol with a volatile compound which evaporated and allowed the organic material to dry without it cracking further or buckling away from the metal fittings. The painstaking work paid off – the Langstone Tankard is now stable and preserved for research and display.

And it's given us some fascinating insights into life in south Wales in the 1st century AD.

## Drinking in Iron Age Britain

To drink from such a big tankard when it was full, you'd have to hold it with two hands rather than by the handle. It's probable that it would have been passed round a group during feasts or ritual events. Each person could take a swig, then pass it on.

Other complete tankards have been found in the south and west of England and Wales and handles and metal bands have been found across Britain, from Orkney to Dorset. The culture for 'competitive feasting' existed across Europe too, where chiefs and nobles would demonstrate their wealth and power by hosting over-the-top feasting and drinking events. Drinking wasn't just for fun, it was an important political and social tool – in many ways that still resonate today. Alcohol could show friendship, demonstrate generosity and mark important occasions.

## Offerings and rituals

A few metres from where the tankard was found, Craig Mills picked up another metal detector signal that identified two decorated bronze bowls and a strainer with traditional 'Celtic' art patterns. They also appear to be linked to ceremonial drinking and drink preparation, and it's possible the strainer was

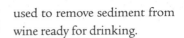

used to remove sediment from wine ready for drinking.

Archaeologists excavated two 'test pits', small trenches at the find site, to find out about the nature of the soil and landscape, and they discovered that both the hoard of bowls and the tankard had been carefully placed (rather than thrown) at the edge of a shallow lake, or a bog with standing water.

There is a vast body of evidence that shows that Iron Age people across north Europe made offerings to their gods in watery places like lakes, rivers and bogs. The favourite sites for these ritual activities are 'liminal' areas – places which are on the boundaries of wet and dry, between cultivated and wild land – and it's thought that these 'edgy' areas might have been where the spirits, ancestors or gods were closest to the living world.

It's not certain, but shellfish and fish don't seem to have been caught or eaten in this period, even amongst coastal communities. This behaviour could also be linked to the idea that water was the domain of the dead, the spirits or the ancestors. Trade networks reveal that people were clearly comfortable using boats along the coast and for deep sea voyages, but there's very little evidence of them eating marine resources.

The bowl hoard wasn't deposited at precisely the same time as the tankard. The bowls were probably made between 25 and 60AD and buried between 50 and 75AD. Both the bowls and the tankard fit the pattern of 'sacrificing' drinking tools at this particular watery place. The big question is 'why?'

## A community in crisis?

We don't know exactly whether the tankard is a Late Iron Age or very Early Roman artefact. There's evidence from the site for both earlier Iron Age activity as well as later Roman activity. The two normal ways of dating an object like this don't help either – the first is based on the style of the tankard, but close analysis shows that the handle might be a later replacement to an earlier vessel, and the bands and woodwork aren't of any particular dateable type. The other way would be to radiocarbon date the wood. Yew wood grows so slowly, though, that yew trees felled for their timber can be hundreds of years old. Radiocarbon dating could give a misleadingly early date – pinning down the date the tree was growing, but not when the tankard was made and used.

The Roman Emperor Claudius successfully invaded Britain in 43AD, and his troops reached Wales by 47AD. They were quickly met with fierce and prolonged opposition from the *Silures* tribe who lived across what is now south Wales. The Roman Army waged war against the Welsh native guerrilla forces for more than thirty years, finally gaining a stronghold across the region.

The Langstone find site is less than 5km from Isca. It's possible that the tankard and the bowls were both offerings to the gods at a particularly crucial time in the battle against Rome.

## TO MAKE IRON AGE BEER
(based loosely on excavation results from the Hochdorf Iron Age site, Germany)
- Soak your barley in a ditch or pit until it sprouts.
- Light a fire at the edge of the ditch, allowing the heat and smoke to add flavour and colour to the grain.
- Bacteria will begin to grow, like in a sourdough bread, to give a tangy note.
- Drop heated stones into your grain mix until it boils, then strain and flavour the liquid with mugwort. Add henbane to make the drink more intoxicating.
- Fermentation can be started with honey or fruit, or the naturally-occuring bacteria in the air.
- Once fermentation is complete, allow the thick sediments to settle, pour into giant tankards, and share with your friends.
- You might like to try your Iron Age beer with a suitable feast, including smoked, salted, roasted or boiled meats (favourites are beef, pork or mutton, house specials include goose and dog), barley and wheat bread, cabbage, parsnips, and a selection of bean stews and porridge. Locally sourced honey and seasonal fruits are available – including apples, pears, cherries and berries. If a cow has just had a calf, you might like a little cheese to finish off.

See also:
Blair Drummond Torc Hoard
Ringlemere Cup
Hallaton Treasure

# Pitminster Toy Cannon

## *A tiny toy war machine*

Despite all our cutting-edge technology, many of us still really love old-fashioned miniature toys – and three hundred years ago there was the same appetite for tiny novelties, particularly toy weapons and artillery miniatures. This toy cannon and wheeled gun carriage were discovered by Kevin Neal while he was metal detecting near Pitminster, Somerset. It dates to the early 1700s, and the level of preservation is exceptional. The cannon is cast copper alloy and the gun carriage is made from copper-alloy sheet and iron, with pins for the cannon to pivot on.

**Date:** 1700–1750, Post Medieval

**Where, when and how found:** Pitminster, Somerset; recorded with PAS in 2010; metal detecting

**Finder:** Kevin Neal

**Where is it now?** Returned to finder

**Visit:** Toy museums around the country

It's not clear whether these miniature cannon were normally played with and used by children, or whether they were more often purchased as entertaining trinkets for adults. It's likely that different-quality miniature cannon were produced at this time – cheaper toys for imaginative play only, and high-quality miniatures that could actually have been fired using gunpowder and mini cannonballs.

"If anyone had ever tried to fire it, this miniature treasure could have exploded in their face"

Many households would have had musket powder that could be used to fire a toy cannon – modern analysis suggests that a miniature would require somewhere between 0.3g and 2.8g of powder. Pistol shot or buckshot could have been used for 'cannonballs', or any household item that could be fashioned into a hard, round projectile. The powder and mini cannonball would be loaded through the muzzle, just like a real cannon. Finally, a fuse, most likely a strand of hemp fibre impregnated with flammable saltpetre solution, known as a 'slow match', would be lit and applied.

It is doubtful that these little cannon were sold with instructions, so a trial and error approach was required. It would have been a very hazardous business – too much powder and the cannon could explode, too little powder and it could misfire or block.

Additionally, it wouldn't always be obvious whether a cannon was a cheap toy with flaws in the metal, or a safe, well-cast working miniature. Attempting to fire a substandard toy cannon could have tragic consequences. Some cannon have been discovered ripped open, the barrels fractured and torn – clear evidence that they've exploded under the firing pressures.

Analysis of the Pitminster Cannon reveals that the muzzle casting was off-centre. One wall of the cannon is 2.7mm thick, the other just 1.7mm. Such an irregular shape means that if anyone had ever tried to fire it, this miniature treasure could have exploded in their face.

Miniature cannon are the most common toys to survive in British archaeological contexts as they're made of thick copper alloy, which survives well in the ground. But the gun carriages that they sat in are incredibly rare survivals. Some must have been made from wood which has since rotted away; experts believe that when fragments of copper-alloy gun carriages *have* been found, they might not have been recognised as such.

The Pitminster Cannon, because of its extraordinary preservation, is a truly exceptional British treasure.

See also:
Fort George Toy Soldiers
Dartmoor Sword

# Raglan Ring

## *The finest gold ring in Wales*

This finder was metal detecting in a field near Raglan Castle in Monmouthshire when he hit the signal for this enormous gold signet ring. The origin of the term 'signet' is from the old French meaning 'small seal'. The flat top, the bezel, is the part used to make an imprint in wax to identify documents as authentic and official, but rings like this were also worn as personal jewellery.

**Date:** 1440–1475, Late Medieval

**Where, when and how found:** Raglan, Monmouthshire, Wales; 1998; metal detecting

**Finder:** Anonymous

**Where is it now?** National Museum Wales, Cardiff www.museumwales.ac.uk

**Also visit:** Raglan Castle, managed by Cadw www.cadw.wales.gov.uk

The bezel of the Raglan Ring is circular and engraved with a prancing lion, known as a 'lion passant' (a heraldic term meaning 'walking to the left'), on a background of flowers and bordered with a phrase written in 'Blackletter', a gothic script. It reads, '*to yow feythfoull*' or '*feythfoull to yow*' (faithful to you), depending on where you start reading the phrase. On either side of the lion are the initials W and A, probably the initials of the owner of the ring. The shoulders of the ring are finely engraved with stylised flowers, stems and leaves. A couple of other gold rings have very similar engraved patterns, for example the Episcopal ring of the Bishop of Hereford, John Stanbury, who served from 1452 to 1474. Along with the lettering, this has helped date the Raglan ring to the middle or third quarter of the 15th century.

The ring is massive – 47.97g of gold, with an internal diameter of 25mm. Most male signet rings are around 20mm in diameter, so this was clearly made for a man with very big fingers, or was perhaps designed to be worn over a glove. We don't know who owned it, but putting together circumstantial evidence with the findspot, the best candidate is William Herbert, first Earl of Pembroke.

## The first Earl

Born around 1423, William decided to take an English form of his name, rather than follow his father, who was known as William ap Thomas. William

married Anne Deveraux in 1449, and they had at least ten children together. It's been tentatively suggested that the W and A initials on the ring refer to 'William and Anne', and that the declaration of faithfulness on the ring ('to you faithful') could be to both his wife *and* his king. William did father at least three illegitimate children, though – sleeping with women who weren't your wife didn't automatically count as being unfaithful in the 15th century.

William Herbert's father began building the grand and fashionable Raglan Castle in the late 1420s, and his son remodelled in grand style. It's unusually late for castle-building, but William's plans put Raglan at the cutting edge of 15th century interior design and architecture. Enormous mullioned windows (mullions are the vertical bars that divide adjacent windows), a polygonal keep and a double drawbridge as well as acres of well-tended estate land with orchards, fishponds and deer parks declared the Earl's wealth and taste.

> "The ring is massive – 47.97g of gold, with an internal diameter of 25mm"

This was a precarious time, however, and the civil wars known as the 'Wars of the Roses' or the 'Cousins' War' raged across the country from 1455 to 1487. It pitted the houses of York and Lancaster against one another for possession of the English throne. William supported the Yorkist claim to the throne, and was ennobled by the Yorkist king, Edward IV, in 1461 as Lord Herbert of Raglan. He was made Earl of Pembroke in 1468 in recognition of his ongoing service and loyalty. King Edward described him as the 'chosen and faithful' – and William ultimately gave his life in support of his king, when he was captured and executed after the Battle of Edgecote Moor in 1469. Before he was killed, William was said to have been allowed to write one last letter to his wife, Anne.

"We don't know whether this ring was lost during William's lifetime, or at some point afterwards. It was an isolated find – a secret treasure that was lucky to be rediscovered"

King Edward IV died in 1483, possibly of typhoid, and his young son Edward V succeeded to the throne. But being only twelve years old, the real power went to Richard, Edward IV's brother, young Edward's uncle. The young Prince disappeared mysteriously in the Tower of London, and Richard declared himself King Richard III (now more famously known as the 'King in the Car Park'). Richard was the last Yorkist king, and the side that William Herbert and thousands of men died for was eventually beaten and Henry Tudor, of the House of Lancaster, claimed the English throne as King Henry VII.

We don't know whether this ring was lost during William's lifetime, or at some point afterwards. It was an isolated find – a secret treasure that was lucky to be rediscovered.

**See also:**
Boar Badge of Richard III
Seal Matrix of Stone Priory

# Great War Victory Medal

## *The universal medal marking the sacrifice of a generation*

Leighton Jones was working for Abertridwr council when his team got a call to unblock a drainage stream. He's a keen metal detectorist, and reckons that it was years of spotting objects while detecting that meant he noticed a muddy, disc-shaped object sitting in the debris of the stream, which turned out to be a WWI Inter-Allied Victory Medal.

> **Date:** 1919, Modern
>
> **Where, when and how found:** Abertridwr, near Cardiff, Wales; 2007; chance find while clearing a stream
>
> **Finder:** Leighton Jones
>
> **Where is it now?** Returned to finder, but he's looking for family of medal owner
>
> **Visit:** Firing Line, Cardiff Castle Museum of the Welsh Soldier www.cardiffcastlemuseum.org.uk

The Victory Medal was created jointly by fourteen allied nations in March 1919 so a single, universal medal could be issued to all allied soldiers across the globe. Different nations did issue slight variations, but the general design is the same: 36mm in diameter, made from bronze, attached to a rainbow-striped ribbon. On the front is the winged figure of Victory holding a palm branch in her right hand, on the reverse, surrounded by a laurel wreath, is the legend:

### The Great / War For / Civilization / 1914–1919

In Britain, the medal was awarded to every person who had served in the armed forces during the war, as well as civilians who worked in the military hospitals, those who served in the Russian operations after 1918, and in mine clearance in the North Sea. In Britain, the Victory Medal was awarded alongside a specifically British war medal – the 1914 Star or the 1914–15 Star, or the British War Medal, depending on when you had entered the 'theatre of war'. More than six and a half million British Victory Medals were awarded.

The medal Leighton found is inscribed around the edge with:

**8-3295 PTE A P BROWN DURH L I**

which means it was awarded to a soldier with the rank of Private, named A P Brown, army number 8-3295, who served with the Durham Light Infantry.

The most likely candidate for the recipient of this medal is Alexander Polson Brown, who served as a Private, acting Lance Corporal, with the Durham Light Infantry. Private Brown was from Boyne, County Durham, and part of the 8th Battalion, drawn from the City of Durham itself. He'd been working as a pony driver in the Langley Moor coal mine in Durham, but when war broke out he joined the effort and arrived in France in July 1915, aged just 19.

In the records, Alexander has two army numbers attached to his name, 8-3295, and 300696. This happened frequently in WWI when soldiers were wounded and returned to another battalion, transferred between battalions, or when a whole battalion was decimated and the survivors were redeployed.

Two million British men voluntarily enlisted for service early in the war – spirits were high and everyone wanted to do their duty. But the death tolls were on an unimaginable scale and battalions that had been formed from a local area, known as 'Pals Battalions', were sometimes worst hit. It meant that whole communities could lose almost all their young men in one or two days.

Alexander did survive the war, and was awarded his Victory Medal, along with the 1914–15 Star and the British War Medal. He married Jane Walker in 1921, had a family and continued to work in mining, moving to the Hatfield mine in Doncaster. He died aged 82, in Stainforth, Doncaster. A long life, through an extraordinary time in history.

It's not clear how Alexander's medal ended up in Abertvidwr, but the finder, Leighton Jones, is keen to reunite such a personal item with the family of the man who earned it.

See also:
George Humber's
Distinguished Conduct Medal
Inverness Shoulder-belt Plate

# Mourning Ring

## *A mother and her baby remembered*

Tony Baker was metal detecting when he got the signal for this pretty, delicate, gold finger ring. He reported it to the Portable Antiquities Scheme, but as it isn't more than 300 years old it wasn't legally Treasure and so the ring was returned to him once recorded. What's remarkable, and moving, is the story the inscription tells – not a story of kings and conquests, but a small story of a tragic event in the life of an ordinary Shropshire family.

The ring is made of gold, with five inlaid and inscribed panels around the hoop, set at the centre with a hexagonal glass or rock-crystal stone. The black inlay is probably enamel. It marks out the lettering very clearly, which reads:

**Date:** 1735, Post Medieval

**Where, when and how found:** Bridgnorth, Shropshire; 2005; metal detecting

**Finder:** Tony Baker

**Where is it now?** Permanently loaned to North Gate Museum, Bridgnorth
www.bridgnorthmuseum.org.uk

**Also visit:** Foundling Museum, London
www.foundlingmuseum.org.uk

Museum of Childhood, London
www.museumofchildhood.org.uk

**MARY / &: SARAH / LITTLETON / OB 7:JUNE / :1735:**

This is a mourning ring, popular from the mid-1600s, which people would commission as a memorial to a loved one who had died.

Tony was intrigued by the people this ring memorialised. He searched for the Littleton family in the parish records in Bridgnorth, and discovered that Thomas Littleton was in fact the parish priest of the local church, St Leonard's. The ring commemorates the death of his wife, Mary, and their baby daughter Sarah.

Mary Littleton most likely died while giving birth to Sarah, or shortly after. Baby Sarah was christened on 7 June 1735 but died the following day. It's quite possible that Sarah was very sick from the beginning – christening a baby quickly was thought to be incredibly important, especially if they were ill or weak. Then, if the baby died, he or she would be assured a place in heaven.

Until recent medical advances in Britain, childbirth was a dangerous event and the most common cause of death in young women. In a time before painkillers, antibiotics and blood transfusions, or modern surgical techniques like caesarean sections, if the labour went on too long or if complications arose, both mother and baby could die. In the 1700s, the average mother had seven or eight live births over 15 years, and in England records suggest that one in six babies died in their first year. Of the children that survived birth, 30% were dead before they reached the age of 15.

## Doctors' hands

Many women died shortly after labour or miscarriage from Childbed Fever. The bacterial infection was often introduced to women by the doctors or midwives who were attending to them. For a long time, it was thought that handwashing wasn't necessary, especially for doctors. One obstetrician practising in America famously declared, 'Doctors are gentlemen, and gentlemen's hands are clean'.

A doctor in Vienna, Ignaz Semmelweis, attempted to encourage the members of his profession to take up handwashing. In his own hospital maternity ward, he insisted that hands be disinfected in antiseptic solution before moving to the next patient, and he saw a drop in deaths from fever from more than 20% to just 1% within the year. He didn't know exactly how, but he knew that handwashing saved lives.

"Until recent medical advances, childbirth was a dangerous event and the most common cause of death in young women"

Dr Semmelweis published his findings, but doctors ridiculed his 'obsession' with handwashing and condemned his work. None of his recommendations were taken up. He eventually fled Vienna and was committed to a mental asylum in 1865, aged 47. He was beaten to death by the guards there, just fourteen days after he arrived.

It would be more than one hundred years after Sarah and Mary Littleton died before the French scientist Louis Pasteur developed the germ theory of infection, and was able to explain what Semmelweis had suspected. Joseph Lister put the theory into practice in surgery and treatment, and published his findings, to great acclaim, in 1867.

## Mourning children

Previously, scholars had thought that people tried to invest less emotion in their children until it became clear that they'd survived the most dangerous childhood fevers and sicknesses. Death was much more a part of 'everyday' life than it is today, and most children would have witnessed the death of a parent or brother or sister, often within the family house. But evidence from letters, diaries and items like this mourning ring suggest that people 300 years ago felt the pain of losing a child as keenly as we do.

Mary's grieving husband Thomas, or perhaps another family member or close friend, commissioned this beautiful piece. The wear pattern on the ring shows that it was well used by the time it was lost. We don't know how the ring ended up in the field where Tony found it. He's permanently loaned the ring to Bridgnorth Museum, as a powerful and moving piece of local history.

See also:
Billingford Amulet
Rochester Cufflink

# HMS *Colossus* Shipwreck

## The rediscovered 1798 wreck of a 74-gun ship-of-the-line

In the 1970s and early '80s, local Scilly man Roland Morris, in conjunction with interested sports divers and the British Museum, thoroughly excavated the known wreck of the warship *Colossus*. By 1984, it was thought that everything of archaeological importance had been recovered, and the site's designation under the Protection of Wrecks Act was revoked.

It was sixteen years later that another group of archaeologically minded divers discovered an extraordinary collection of timbers on the seabed and five enormous iron cannon sticking up out of the seabed, surrounded by a section of the timber hull.

They were 350m away from Roland's site, and it turns out that the site Roland excavated was just the wreckage of the bow (front) section of the ship, and the 2000 discovery was the wreckage of the stern (back) section. The mighty warship had broken up as it sank, and the two major parts of the wreck had settled separately. In between the bow and stern sites is an archaeologically rich debris trail.

**Date:** Built 1787, wrecked 1798, Post Medieval

**Where, when and how found:** St Mary's Roads, Isles of Scilly; 1975 & 2000; designated salvage (1975); accidental discovery by sports divers (2000)

**Finder:** Roland Morris (1975), Todd Stevens, Mac Mace and others (2000–1)

**Where is it now?** Some artefacts at the British Museum, London www.britishmuseum.org

Wreck in situ, south of Samson, depth 15m. This is a designated Protected Wreck and must be dived with a visitor's licence, or through one of the local dive charter boats who will organise a visitor's licence for you. More information at the Cornwall and Isles of Scilly Maritime Archaeology Society www.cismas.org.uk/colossus-dive-trail.php

**Also visit:** Isles of Scilly Museum, St Mary's www.iosmuseum.org

## The *Colossus*

HMS *Colossus* was built in 1787 at Gravesend, around 51m (170 feet) in length, 1,703 imperial tons and designed to carry at least 600 men. She had 74 guns of 32lb, 18lb and 9lb calibre, and was a ship-of-the-line, the finest naval military kit the British Empire had to deploy. Bitter decades of war with France and her allies pushed the British Navy to develop new technologies and new naval battle tactics, and in her eleven-year career, *Colossus* saw action during the Revolutionary Wars at Toulon, off the French coast in the Mediterranean, Groix, in the Bay of Biscay, Cadiz in Spain, and Cape St Vincent, off the southern coast of Portugal.

In December 1798 she was on her way back to England with wounded men from Admiral Nelson's victorious Battle of the Nile, and a cargo including an aristocrat's collection of Greek pottery, spices from Lisbon and the body of Admiral Lord Viscount Shuldham.

On her last leg homeward, *Colossus* sought shelter in the channel known as St Mary's Roads in the Isles of Scilly, awaiting favourable winds. This was before engines or tug boats, so if the wind wasn't coming from the right direction, the ship would simply wait to complete her journey. While *Colossus* was waiting, a winter gale whipped up and, disastrously, her anchor cable snapped. The crew deployed secondary anchors and tried to use the sails to prevent her from drifting on to the rocks, but the force of the storm was too great and she was driven into shallow water. Aground and pounded by the storm, she threatened to break up – all the men on board bar one survived in a hurried evacuation, and by the following day, the mighty ship had rolled on to her beam (side) and began to break up.

Some items, stores and parts were salvaged from the wreck immediately, including the embalmed body of the Lord Admiral. Many other items found a resting place in the sandy seabed, and were discovered by Ronald Morris' team in the 1970s. Morris recovered over 30,000 sherds of the Greek pottery cargo, which were taken back to the British Museum where they remain part of the museum's collection to this day. Some of the pieces were reconstructed and put on display.

So everyone thought they knew where *Colossus* was, which meant that the divers who found the stern site in 2000 couldn't believe what they were seeing – 18-pound guns, with five cannon still in position in their gun ports, muzzles buried in the sand and breech ends sticking up; spreads of glass, piping, pottery and cannonballs; a large flat area of related timbers which appeared to be a significant part of *Colossus*' hull. Most incredible of all was

> **"Aground and pounded by the storm, she threatened to break up – all the men on board bar one survived in a hurried evacuation"**

the vast stern decoration of this formidable ship, including a twice-life-sized wooden carving of a Roman warrior.

The wreck had lain undisturbed for 200 years, but for some reason (still not understood), the seabed was eroding away in this area, exposing the wreck. If it wasn't protected, the timbers would quickly begin to deteriorate and be broken up by storm and wave action. Now that the site had been rediscovered, the race was on to protect it. In 2001 *Colossus* was redesignated a Protected Wreck, and in 2002 part of the carved section of the stern was raised and sent for conservation at the Mary Rose Trust in Portsmouth.

The challenge now is to preserve the wreck for as long as possible. Committed volunteers from the Cornwall and Isles of Scilly Maritime Archaeology Society (CISMAS), in conjunction with professionals from the archaeology and maritime communities and the Receiver of Wreck, are working together to determine the best way to protect the wreck in situ. Some sections may be lifted from the water, but conserving timbers out of the water is incredibly expensive and resource-heavy, and simply isn't possible for a whole warship. Trials of reburying sections of the wreck are ongoing, along with experimental methods to halt or slow the erosion of the seabed around the timbers.

English Heritage have established an underwater heritage trail with key features of the wreck marked by permanent buoys. Armed with a waterproof guide booklet, qualified divers can explore the incredible wreck of *Colossus* while she still exists – one of the most unusual heritage sites open to the public.

**See also:**
Fort George Toy Soldiers
Inverness Shoulder-belt Plate
*Girona* Wreck Cameo

*A digital reconstruction of the majestic warship* Colossus *at anchor.*

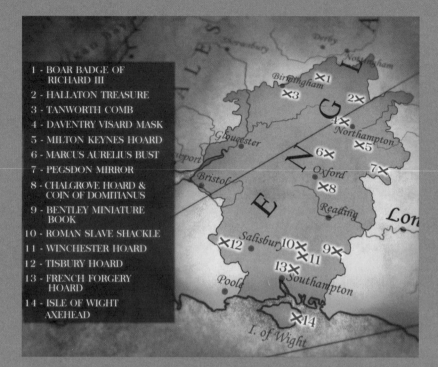

1 - BOAR BADGE OF
    RICHARD III
2 - HALLATON TREASURE
3 - TANWORTH COMB
4 - DAVENTRY VISARD MASK
5 - MILTON KEYNES HOARD
6 - MARCUS AURELIUS BUST
7 - PEGSDON MIRROR
8 - CHALGROVE HOARD &
    COIN OF DOMITIANUS
9 - BENTLEY MINIATURE
    BOOK
10 - ROMAN SLAVE SHACKLE
11 - WINCHESTER HOARD
12 - TISBURY HOARD
13 - FRENCH FORGERY
     HOARD
14 - ISLE OF WIGHT
     AXEHEAD

MELLOW STONE COTTAGES, village greens and ancient churches, winding lanes and gentle hills. It's a quintessential beauty that makes the picture-perfect backdrop for period dramas and tourist photos. This region is still romantically referred to as England's heartland.

This is England as a 'green and pleasant land'. It's the England of ancient hunting counties and forests, market towns and prosperous residents. The **Daventry Visard Mask (p173)** lets us peep into the rituals of a 17th century lady, and also points to the intriguing and strange ways we try to protect ourselves and our homes from the unknown. Just like the people who made deposits in the hoards at **Tisbury (p184)** and **Hallaton (p159)**, making sense of the complexities of life has always been a human pursuit.

This region is where the idea of 'England' was first formed. King Alfred the Great, his son Edward the Elder and his grandson Athelstan were the warrior kings who wrested control of northern and western kingdoms from the Vikings, and united a nation, in name at least. It has witnessed brutal conflict across many centuries – **Richard III's Boar Badge (p164)** allowed us to finally identify the real site of the Battle of Bosworth, the moment when the last English king died on the battlefield.

The deep history of this heartland gives us many secret treasures. On the Isle of Wight, a piece of Neolithic **Axehead (p168)** was discovered on a school trip to a garlic farm. On the mainland, intriguing treasures from Iron Age craftspeople include the **Tanworth Comb (p188)** and the **Pegsdon Mirror (p149)**.

The large river valleys of the Avon and Severn dominate the history and geography of the west of the region. The navigable rivers were key to the blossoming of the prehistoric Wessex culture that gave us monuments like Avebury stone circle and Stonehenge. More than four and a half thousand years later, the rivers brought extraordinary wealth from the British Empire into thriving port cities like Bristol. Artefacts like the **Roman Slave Shackle (p180)** remind us how many 'great' empires have been founded on the sufferings of unfree people.

The Romans successfully invaded in 43AD, but for a significant time before that the local people were in contact with them. The **Winchester Gold Hoard (p176)** is an utterly astonishing find of international importance, and it reveals that the Romans took leaders in their new province of Britannia seriously. The **Coin of Domitianus in the Chalgrove Hoard (p155)** shows that once the Romans arrived, it wasn't all plain sailing.

# Milton Keynes Gold Jewellery Hoard

## *3,000-year-old solid gold jewellery*

In 2000, friends Michael Rutland and Gordon Heritage were metal detecting in a field near Milton Keynes when they made an extraordinary find. They found two solid gold neckrings, three gold bracelets and a tiny scrap of copper-alloy wire in a pottery vessel that dates back more than three thousand years, into the British Bronze Age. Between them, the five gold pieces make up one of the biggest collections

> **Date:** 1150–750BC, Late Bronze Age
>
> **Where, when and how found:** Milton Keynes; 2000; metal detecting
>
> **Finders:** Michael Rutland and Gordon Heritage
>
> **Official valuation:** £290,000
>
> **Where is it now?** British Museum, London
> www.britishmuseum.org

of gold ever found from Bronze Age Britain, and the only one ever to have been found with pottery that can date it.

Because of the style of the pot, a brown fineware bowl, we can pinpoint the gold jewellery to the late Bronze Age, around 1150–750BC. One neckring is 76% pure gold (18 Carat), the others are around 85% – about 20 Carat gold, and together they weigh more than 2kg.

The neckrings, or 'torcs', are 'pennanular', meaning an incomplete circle, and are decorated with incised lines and grooves. Neckrings like this have been found along the whole of the east Atlantic seaboard – from Spain and Portugal, through France, Britain and Ireland. What would have made them so impressive is not only their decoration, but their sheer size – the largest one weighs 627g - a chunky and likely uncomfortable ornament to wear, but one that unequivocally declares status and wealth.

These neckrings would have been difficult to put on and take off, as they're entirely rigid and 1cm in diameter thickness. Neckrings from other sites have evidence of breaks at the back, where the pressure of squeezing them off and on has eventually snapped the metal. That isn't the case with the Milton Keynes neckrings – these items were either worn rarely, for very special occasions, or were worn continually like a modern-day wedding ring.

Two of the bracelets are a massive, matching pair of C-shaped bracelets with their ends ground flat; the other bracelet has an octagonal cross-section and curves round into a D-shape. The bracelets are also a relatively common type, but again, the size is what makes them stand out. The C-shaped pieces are 383g and 408g – which perhaps suggests that these were special occasion ornaments, rather than everyday wear.

## Life circa 1000BC

We don't know whether the Milton Keynes Hoard was buried for safekeeping or as a votive offering to the gods. People probably worshipped a number of gods, possibly related to nature and seasonal processes, and some of the monuments that we know about are aligned to Sun and Moon cycles. The majority of people lived a relatively simple agricultural existence in settled villages, surrounded by their crops and animals, but clearly they devoted quite a lot of time and resources to their religious practices.

Before the Bronze Age people were buried in communal tombs, and it's thought that the emphasis was on the 'Ancestors' rather than individuals.

The Milton Keynes gold was deposited at the end of the Bronze Age, and life was very different. People were either cremated or buried in individual graves in cemeteries, often with grave goods. Children have also been found with richly furnished graves, suggesting that power and status was passed down through family lineages, as well as being 'earned' by efforts in battle or other adult activities.

Valuables as precious as the Milton Keynes Hoard may well have been passed between generations of a family or community. We do know that towards the end of the Bronze Age, there was a downturn in the climate, leading to wetter and colder growing seasons. People may well have been suffering if harvests failed, if there were fewer sources of wild game and if animals weren't thriving. Bone evidence shows an increase in people with diet deficiencies causing conditions like rickets, and smaller children's bones with evidence of malnutrition.

As the environment got harsher, territorial tensions increased – around 1000BC there's the first evidence of large fortifications being constructed, that would eventually evolve into Iron Age hillforts. Perhaps it was a community crisis that meant the gold ornaments were buried – and they were either intentionally or accidentally never retrieved.

## Written proof

After the find was made and reported, the landowners disputed that Michael and Gordon had been given permission to search on the land. The Treasure Valuation Committee determined that the detectorists had been searching legally and with permission. Because of the nature of the dispute, the Committee reduced the reward the landowners received. The case highlights why getting agreement in writing before you begin metal detecting is of the utmost importance, for all parties involved.

There are search agreement templates online, and they're also available from landowners' organisations like the National Farmers' Union (NFU) and the Country Land and Business Association (CLA). Responsible metal detectors and landowners are always recognised for their input in understanding our past.

See also:
Blair Drummond Hoard
Winchester Hoard

# Pegsdon Mirror

### *An exquisite find from an intriguing burial*

This treasure, a copper-alloy mirror, looks immediately familiar even though it's more than 2,000 years old. Mirrors from the Iron Age period (dating from around 800BC to the Roman invasion in 43AD) are a peculiarly British phenomenon – more than fifty-five have been found in Britain and Ireland from the Scilly Isles to east Yorkshire, but fewer than ten anywhere else in pre-Roman Europe.

> **Date:** 80–20BC, Iron Age
>
> **Where, when and how found:** Pegsdon, Bedfordshire; 2000; metal detecting
>
> **Finders:** Anonymous
>
> **Official valuation:** £35,000
>
> **Where is it now?** Luton Museum and Art Gallery, Stockwood Discovery Centre, Luton www.stockwooddiscoverycentre.com

## The find

The Pegsdon Mirror was discovered by two metal detectorists in 2000, in an area that had already given up other Iron Age objects. When they got the signal, the detectorists dug down through the plough soil and discovered the mirror lying at the bottom of a shallow pit. Its polished metal face was uppermost, and thirty sherds of pottery and a silver brooch were all in the soil together.

The mirror is made from three parts – the plate, decorated on one side and plain, flat and highly polished on the other; a Y-shaped handle that was riveted to the plate; and two small rings that sit against the plate between the arms of the handle. In total, it weighs 370.7g.

It would have taken many hours to polish the mirror side to a point where it gave an accurate and clear reflection. Nowadays we have machines to aid polishing; back then, it required long, patient hours with increasingly fine natural abrasives.

A compass was probably used to draw out the complicated asymmetrical pattern on the mirror back, and a basketry design has been used to fill in the pattern. It's from an Iron Age art tradition known as La Tène, often described as 'Celtic' art. Iron Age mirror designs use 'positive' patterned sections and

'negative' empty sections equally. The Pegsdon Mirror decoration is very fine, and the accuracy points to it being the work of a master craftsman.

There's one point, on the left-hand side, where the engraver hasn't filled in a triangle with the basket weave design. There's a small chance that it's a deliberate 'signature', but it's more likely to have been a mistake.

## Treasure

The Pegsdon find was made before the nationwide system of Finds Liaison Officers was set up, so instead the finders contacted Gil Burleigh, the Keeper of Field Archaeology in the County museum service. Immediately, Gil thought the finders must have stumbled across an Iron Age burial.

Even though the mirror was not made of silver or gold, because it was associated with the silver brooch, the whole assemblage fell under the rules of the Treasure Act. The Coroner was informed, and news of the incredible find on the hill was announced.

Gil, helped by the finders, returned to the findspot the following year and fully excavated the site. This was indeed a cremation burial, typical for the region.

The original grave pit had been seriously damaged by decades of deep ploughing, and most of the remaining soil had been dislodged when the detectorists made their first discovery. A small patch of soil hadn't been disturbed, however, and from it the excavators discovered four more sherds of pottery and a piece of burned human bone. The burned bone had become 'calcined' – reduced to its mineral constituents. Calcined bone can still sometimes be dated, but a profile of the person – age, sex and health – can't be established.

Based on the pottery fragments, there were at least two pots in the grave, and the mirror. The brooch seems to have been one of a pair, linked together with a connecting chain, now lost. Despite an intensive search, the second brooch has never been found.

The burial is within a complex, multi-period site combining enclosures, possible houses, trackways and other graves. We don't know what the features and structures around the burial were – a lot of the archaeology has been destroyed by ploughing over the years.

It was previously assumed that all Iron Age mirrors were linked to female burials, but we can't be sure of this. There are no definite cases of mirrors being buried with men, but there are a number of burials that we can't tell the sex from the remains – including the Pegsdon grave. Assuming that mirrors must be women's objects says more about our own cultural assumptions than it does about Iron Age culture.

## The importance of reflections

We take glass and polished surfaces for granted now, but besides still water, the only clear reflections available to Iron Age people would have been in polished metalwork. Polished items like the Pegsdon Mirror would have been very expensive, highly prized, and it's quite possible that access to them, using them, touching them and looking in them, would have been restricted.

We live in a society saturated with realistic images of ourselves – we can always see what we look like from the 'outside', and we're encouraged to care about that image. It's extraordinary to think that most people in Britain, through history, have lived their lives not really knowing what they looked like. The modern writer Margaret Atwood has said that 'to live without mirrors is to live without the self'.

The Iron Age is often thought to be a time when people truly embraced being 'individuals'. Being part of a tribe and focusing on the collective good became less important than personal success and status.

But this mirror may have been much more than a functional looking glass for vanity purposes. Mirrored surfaces allow you to control light, reflect and signal; you can see two ways at once, and perhaps look 'in' to somewhere totally different. Fairytales often feature enchanted or magical mirrors that have some kind of spirit within them, have the power to 'trap' people or souls, or mirrors that can act as a portal to a different world or dimension.

Perhaps these Iron Age mirrors were primarily for 'ritual' purposes – fortune telling or accessing the spirits maybe, rather than doing your hair and make-up. Some mirror burials have evidence that the polished and decorated plate was carefully wrapped in a cloth covering. This is either to simply protect it from scratches, or perhaps to 'contain' its power when it wasn't in use. It's possible that the brooch found at Pegsdon had been used to cover the mirror in this way.

The Iron Age Britons didn't write, so we have no first-hand accounts of their practices. These 2,000-year-old mirrors will always retain some of their secrets.

See also:
Ashwell Hoard and the
Goddess Senuna
Tanworth Comb
Nesscliffe Ritual Spoons

# French Forgery Hoard

## *7,083 imitation coins under a Hampshire shop floor*

This hoard of coins is a mystery in many ways. They were discovered in 2010 under the floorboards of a shop when the plumbing was being repaired.

The copper-alloy coins are very corroded, with many stuck together, and the painstaking work of cataloguing enough coins to properly identify them fell to Paul Wragg, a student at the University of Winchester, supported by Rob Webley, the local FLO, and others. Paul carefully examined the areas showing the date and mintmarks of 700 coins, a 10% sample. Every single one of the sample coins appeared to be a French 30-denier piece, dated 1711, with a mintmark 'D', which represents the city of Lyon, France.

> **Date:** 1711, Post Medieval
>
> **Where, when and how found:** Bishop's Waltham, Hampshire; 2010; discovered under the floorboards of a shop
>
> **Finder:** Anonymous
>
> **Where are they now?** Returned to finder
>
> **Explore:** The history and science of coins www.royalmint.com/discover

Thirty-denier pieces were only ever minted between 1709 and 1713 under the rule of King Louis XIV, for use in the French colonies of Canada and Louisiana (named after Louis). They were made of 80% copper, with a thin coating of silver. On the front side are back-to-back letter Ls, with a crown above and a ring of fleurs-de-lis. On the reverse is a cross with decorative dots and more fleurs-de-lis. The cross resembles the emblem of the royal guard, and for this reason the coin was known as a *mousquetaire* – a musketeer.

No other 30-denier pieces have ever been found in Britain, which makes the existence of more than 7,000 in one corroded pile, a bit of mystery.

Expert analysis of the coins suggests that they were all made with the same die (the 'die' is the stamp used to press the pattern of a coin into the 'flan', the blank disc of metal), but there is unusual variation in the size and weight of the flans used. There is always a bit of variation in stamped coins like this, but there appear to be too many very large and very small coins. The average weight was 3.61g, but two coins in the sample weighed less than

2g. The average diameter of the coins was 25.1mm, but some of the smallest coins were 19mm across.

In the hoard there were also blank flans, cut flans and coins that had been struck off-centre. Most do not have the expected silver coating. The experts have concluded that this is a hoard of forged coins, albeit ones from sophisticated forgers who probably used an official, stolen, die.

We simply don't know why they were deposited under the floor of a building in Hampshire. Perhaps they were stolen and then the thieves realised that they weren't of any value; perhaps they're evidence of a failed English attempt to flood French colonies with fake coins. Forged coins are still a problem – the Royal Mint estimates that three in every hundred £1 coins are fakes, meaning that 44 million forgeries are in circulation at this moment in the UK.

Because the French coins were just under 300 years old when they were discovered and made largely of copper, they weren't defined as Treasure. Once the PAS recorded the find, the coins were returned to the finders to sell or keep as they pleased. What's certain is that the coins are worth more now than they were in 1711.

**See also:**
Chinese Coin Hoard
Rosemarkie Trade Weights
Spanish-American Gold
Doubloons

# Chalgrove Hoard and Coin of Domitianus

## *The coin hoard that revealed a lost Roman emperor*

In 1901 a small, rough coin was discovered and shown to the Bibliothèque Nationale in Paris. It appeared to be Roman, from the 3rd century AD, but it had the face and name of a unknown ruler on it – Domitianus. The curators took a cautious approach and decided that 'unknown' meant 'unlikely'. An influential scholar in Italy didn't see the coin himself, but nonetheless dismissed it as a fake. The small, rough coin was recorded with the condemning verdict: 'of doubtful authenticity'.

**Date:** 251–279AD, Roman

**Where, when and how found:** Chalgrove, Oxfordshire; 2003; metal detecting

**Finder:** Brian Malin

**Official valuation:** £40,000

**Where is it now?** Ashmolean Museum, Oxford
www.ashmolean.org

It was ignored for close to 100 years, until the discoveries of a metal detectorist in a field in Chalgrove, Oxfordshire, gave Domitianus and his coin an extraordinary reprieve.

Brian Malin, a keen detector, unearthed a coarse greyware pot with a hoard of almost 5,000 bronze coins in it, dating from 251–279AD.

Between 260 and 274, Britain was part of a breakaway 'Gallic Empire', but was eventually retaken by the 'official' Roman leaders based in Italy. More than 200 Romano-British coin hoards have been found from this breakaway era. The war was expensive, lots of soldiers needed paying and more coins were being struck. Ordinary people feared for their safety and valuables, and the economy was suffering. Each coin could buy you less, so people were having to store more – often in the ground. So although the Chalgrove Hoard was special, it wasn't thought to be extraordinary. Hoards like this might make the local papers, but they don't normally re-write the history books.

The Chalgrove Hoard reached the British Museum for assessment under the Treasure process. One coin out of the 4,957 coins stood out. The name was unfamiliar for a Gallic Emperor – Domitianus – but a directory of Roman names identified the 1901 'doubtful authenticity' piece. Could this one coin in the new hoard add evidence for the existence of a lost emperor?

Digital images of the French and British Domitianus coins were compared side by side. French and British colleagues agreed – both coins had been stamped from the same die, and they were both genuine.

We don't know anything else about Domitianus – perhaps his reign was so short that he was never documented by the official Roman historians, and only just long enough to start stamping his own coins. He's now referred to as Domitian II or Domitian of Gaul, so he's not confused with the better-known earlier Roman ruler Domitian, from the 1st century AD.

The Ashmolean Museum in Oxford acquired the Chalgrove Hoard for £40,000. But the real reward is that Domitian of Gaul has won his place in history – and that's thanks to an amateur metal detector and professional specialists working together.

See also:
Anarevitos Stater
Ashwell Hoard and the
Goddess Senuna

# Marcus Aurelius Bust

## *The Roman sculpture sat in a fireplace for thirty years*

John Lewis was ploughing a field in April 1976 when he felt something 'clunk' beneath his tractor. The something was a 16cm-high head and shoulders bust of a man with curly hair and blue glass eyes. It looked unusual, but when John showed it to the landowner, he was told he could keep it. John took the bust

Date: 160–200AD, Roman
Where, when and how found: Brackley, Northamptonshire; 1976; found during farmwork
Finder: John Lewis
Where is it now? Ashmolean Museum, Oxford
www.ashmolean.org

to the local museum, who thought that it might be a Victorian imitation of a Roman portrait bust, didn't want to buy it and told him he could keep it.

'Ol' Blue Eyes' lived in the Lewises' fireplace for thirty years, a quirky ornament and nothing more.

But in 2009, John and his wife Joan decided to take their quirky bust to a Finds Day at Banbury Museum organised by the local Finds Liaison Officer, Anni Byard. When Anni saw their object, she 'almost fell off her chair'. The half-life-size bust was so perfectly preserved it was hard to believe it wasn't a fake. But X-Ray Fluorescence testing, which analyses the chemical composition of glass, ceramic and metal, proved its authenticity – it was Roman, made from two kilos of heavily leaded bronze, with deep blue almond-shaped eyes made from glass discs. The glass had been decoloured with manganese and antimony, typical for Roman glass, then coloured deep blue by adding cobalt.

This unique treasure was never part of a bigger sculpture. Instead, it was crafted to be freestanding: A haughty man with head tipped back and mouth turned down, neat curly hair, a stylised moustache and a fancy beard twisted into two pointed prongs of hair.

The bust was made by the lost wax process, a casting technique where a mould is made from a wax model, which is then melted and poured away, to be replaced by molten metal that forms the sculpture.

Although very rare, other portrait busts have been found in Britain. Bronze busts from Cambridge-shire, Norfolk, Suffolk and Northamptonshire share stylistic elements with the Brackley bust, including the slanting eyes and textured hair. This has led experts to conclude that the Brackley bust was manufactured around 160–200AD in a Romano-British workshop that was creating heads and busts of emperors and deities in a unique provincial style.

The man represented in the bust is most likely the Emperor Marcus Aurelius, who ruled from 161–180AD. He was famous as a philosopher too, and his book *Meditations*, about how to fulfil your duty and manage conflict, has been cited as a favourite of philosopher John Stuart Mill, the writer and poet Goethe and politician Bill Clinton.

By comparing the bust profile with other known depictions of Marcus Aurelius, it appears that the bust was designed using a profile image from a coin. The twisted tufts of beard, however, are a distinctly British way of dressing facial hair, and don't appear on any authorised Roman coins. It's quite possible that the British craftspeople started with the 'authorised' image of the emperor, and then added a certain local flair to his beard.

The field where John Lewis found the bust is close to a number of known Roman villas. It's possible that the bust was purchased by a villa owner, as a show of loyalty to Rome or in admiration of the emperor himself; alternatively the bust may have been commissioned for a temple.

The Marcus Aurelius bust has finally been restored to its rightful status as a find of national significance. Ol' Blue Eyes was purchased by the Ashmolean Museum, Oxford, in 2011 and is on permanent display in the Rome gallery.

See also:
Leopard Cup
Syston Knife Handle
Cautopates Figurine

# Hallaton Treasure

## *A helmet, a hoard and hundreds of pigs*

Ken Wallace was metal detecting with his amateur archaeology group, the Hallaton Field Work Group, when he picked up signals for a scatter of Iron Age and Roman coins on a hilltop. The group reported his discoveries, and the site was earmarked for further archaeological investigation. Over the course of the following weeks, and then in successive seasons of excavation and survey, the Hallaton Field Work Group and the University of Leicester Archaeological Services, professionals and skilled amateurs working together, have pieced together the intriguing evidence: this was an open-air 2,000-year old pagan shrine.

The Hallaton site dates to the late Iron Age and early Roman period. The Iron Age is the period considered to be the end of British Prehistory – it begins with the introduction of iron-working technology after the Bronze Age, in around 800BC, and continues until the time of the Roman invasion of Britain in 43AD. The labels are useful to get a sense of the broad changes that happened, but it's a relatively arbitrary system that favours technology and non-perishable material because they are clearer in the archaeological record than the 'Wood Age' or the 'Rise of Worshipping Nature Gods Age'. For some people living through these times there was no overnight switch, no revolution, and no big ideological change. In fact, for a few people in the more secluded corners of Britain, the Roman invasion may not have made any difference to their lives at all.

**Date:** Mostly around 50BC–50AD, but activity continuing through the Roman period to 4th century AD; Late Iron Age/Roman

**Where, when and how found:** Hallaton, Leicestershire; 2000–2005; metal detecting with a local archaeology group

**Finder:** Ken Wallace

**Where is it now?** Harborough Museum, Leicestershire; also at Hallaton Village Museum, and some artefacts in a travelling exhibition. An online gallery is at www.leics.gov.uk/index/leisure_tourism/museums/harboroughmuseum/treasure.htm

**Get involved:** Hallaton Field Work Group www.leicestershirevillages.com/hallaton/fieldworking-group.html; other local groups include: Hinckley Archaeological Society www.fieldwalking.org.uk

The Iron Age is a period where lifestyles, quality of life and social organisation were probably very different in different regions of the country. The traditional image, however, has been of a chiefly ruling class, with warriors, artists and priests below them, and agricultural and domestic peasants and slaves living under their regional commander's protection, but also in his control.

## The finds

Ken discovered 146 British Iron Age coins and 59 Roman coins from the site. During the excavation that followed, large soil blocks were dug out and taken to the British Museum to be excavated by conservators in the laboratory. In total, the Hallaton Treasure comprises 334 Roman coins, 4,952 Iron Age coins, 6,901 pieces of bone, some glass and pottery and 88 metal artefacts including fragments of silver and copper-alloy brooches, silver and copper ingots, folded silver sheet metal, scrap metal, a silver bowl and the extraordinary fragments of at least one silver-gilt iron cavalry helmet, a very prestigious Roman artefact.

The excavators first thought the corroded remains of the helmet were a modern bucket, but it soon became clear that this was no ordinary heap of rust. The helmet has been painstakingly conserved and pieced together over ten years and is now on display, revealing how stunning it would have been when it was first placed in the ground. It dates to the first half of the 1st century AD.

The majority of the Iron Age coins are associated with the *Corieltavi* group, a federation of smaller tribes who lived across the east Midlands. This was a rich and well-populated area, where people seem to have lived peacefully in large villages. There is evidence that suggests that some communities in the region were building defences at this time, so perhaps not all leaders were pro-Roman, and strategies differed.

The find also included a number of coins from other tribes across Iron Age Britain, including some issued by the ruler Cunobelin in south-east England. The majority of the coins date from about 20–50AD. The Roman coins include a number dating to before the Conquest, and other silver and bronze coins from throughout the Roman period.

> ## "On the Hallaton site, the right legs were either buried elsewhere or destroyed in some way"

It isn't just the amazing metal finds from Hallaton that have got the experts and amateurs excited. On the site were the bones of 82 slaughtered, quartered and buried pigs, but the experts estimate that up to 300 pigs may be represented across the whole site. Butchered remains suggest that the meat was probably cooked and may have been eaten, but some legs were 'articulated', which could mean that they were buried whole with the flesh and sinews still attached and that the meat was not eaten. Taken as a whole assemblage, there's a shortage of right pig legs – they appear to be missing from the site altogether.

The fact that the carcasses were missing their right legs is intriguing. Throughout the archaeological record, right-hand and left-hand sides of bodies have different importance – from late Stone Age feasting around Stonehenge to the medieval hunting ritual of 'unmaking' a deer, the different sides of carcasses are treated in different ways. On the Hallaton site, the right legs were either buried elsewhere or destroyed in some way.

The pigs were less than a year old when they were slaughtered, and it's likely that they were killed and eaten in the winter months.

The bodies of three dogs were also discovered, sacrificed and buried – perhaps as spiritual guardians of the site. The most complete skeleton shows the dog was placed in a hole with its head drawn back and its feet gathered under it – its feet were possibly bound when it was put in the ground. All three dogs were big – about the size of German Shepherds – and old when they were killed.

Only one human bone was found – a broken upper arm bone. Many Iron Age domestic and ritual sites have a smattering of human bones, so their absence from Hallaton is unusual.

A pair of glass eyes were discovered, perhaps the only surviving remnants of a wooden statue that has long since rotted away, and an elaborate tankard handle.

From 50BC to the 300s AD, this hill clearly held special importance for the people of Leicestershire. The crucial question is 'why?'

## Sign of the shrine

There's no evidence of a building or structure on the top of the hill, although there may have been a ditch and a wooden palisade fence along the east side.

The coins and other artefacts were buried in discrete pits across the site at different times, although most of them were near the entranceway and buried during the 30s, 40s and 50s AD. We don't know whether these were offerings collected from the whole community, or the wealth of one or two high-status individuals.

What's certain is that this was a place where ritual deposits of precious artefacts were intentionally buried with no plan to retrieve them. It may have been an open site with no central focus, or perhaps there was a natural feature, a grove of trees, or stones, that was considered sacred – we can't be sure for certain.

Access to an internal enclosure may have been limited to special groups of people – priests or chiefs – but the quantity of pigs slaughtered suggests that at least some of the ritual practices involved large groups of the community enjoying a ritual barbeque. Given the age of the pigs at slaughter, perhaps this was a seasonal shrine, celebrating the dark days and the coming of the spring.

One of the last big deposits was the beautiful Roman helmet, probably placed in the ground around the 40s AD. This was clearly a British shrine, rather than one taken over by Roman worshippers, so the deposit was probably made by a native person. Whether the helmet was a diplomatic gift from the Romans, a stolen trophy, or payment for some kind of mercenary service, we won't ever know.

As the Romans extended their control over the east Midlands, activity at the shrine declined but didn't stop. Hallaton remained a special place for generations of people. Its importance has now been restored.

See also:
Crosby Garrett Helmet
Anarevitos Stater
Langstone Tankard

# Boar Badge of Richard III

### The find that reveals more about the 'King in the Car Park'

Carl Dawson was in a field two miles from the Bosworth Battlefield Heritage Centre, when he got the signal. The 3cm-long find he unearthed was immediately, obviously important. It was a little badge in the shape of a boar, made of silver, which was once delicately gilded with a thin coating of gold.

Carl was part of the metal detecting team in the Battle of Bosworth Survey project. The project had received five years' of Heritage Lottery Funding to bring together surveyors, landscape archaeologists, documentary and medieval warfare experts, as well as a team of metal detectorists to help finally pin down the location of the Battle of Bosworth – the 1485 battle that saw King Richard III killed, more than a thousand men slain, and the English crown claimed by Henry Tudor (King Henry VII).

> **Date:** 1470–1485, Medieval
>
> **Where, when and how found:** Bosworth, Leicestershire; 2009; metal detecting as part of an archaeological investigation
>
> **Finder:** Carl Dawson
>
> **Official valuation:** £2,250
>
> **Where is it now?** Bosworth Battlefield Centre, Leicestershire www.bosworthbattlefield.com
>
> **Also visit:** A Richard III Museum is planned for Leicester in 2014; Richard III Museum, York www.richardiiimuseum.co.uk

Richard III was the last English king to die on the battlefield, and his grave was recently, and famously, found in a car park in Leicester, a spot which had originally been the monastic Church of the Greyfriars. The discovery of his remains captured people's imaginations; this boar badge is one of the finds that has revealed more about the last, tragic movements of the fallen king.

## Wars of the Roses

Between 1454 and 1485, a vicious civil war raged between two branches of the same royal family – the House of York and the House of Lancaster – who both claimed the English throne. At the time, it was known as the Cousins' War. We know it as the War of the Roses; the white rose of York versus the red rose of Lancaster.

Between 1454 and 1471, thirteen battles were fought, costing the lives and livelihoods of thousands of people who were forced to fight for their noblemen. Edward IV, from the House of York, came out as the initial winner, and England enjoyed relative peace until his death in 1483. When Edward died, his brother Richard was made Lord Protector, tasked with ensuring that his brother's young son was safely crowned king.

Prince Edward was just twelve years old when he was recognised as king. But powerful nobles saw an opportunity. Young Edward was publicly declared illegitimate, his uncle Richard claimed the crown and took the title King Richard III. Edward and his nine-year-old brother, Prince Richard, were taken to the Tower of London, allegedly for their own protection, and were never seen again.

Richard was accused of ordering the murder of his nephews, the Princes in the Tower, a charge that was never resolved. His reputation is often debated – Shakespeare portrayed him as a deformed and vicious man, hungry for power and willing to do anything to secure it. Others represent an excellent and experienced fighter and leader with loyal followers, who had a legitimate claim to the throne.

Between 1470 and 1485, the white boar was used by the court and followers of Richard III as a symbol to show their allegiance. It's thought that the reason Richard used a boar was because of a play on words: Richard's family was the Royal House of York, and the Roman Latin name for York city was *Eboracum*, which sounds a bit like 'boar' in English. Hence, supporters of Richard would wear a boar badge to show who they were loyal to, normally on their tunic or cap.

Royal accounts show that the King paid for thousands of boar badges to be made for his coronation in July 1483. Most badges would have been made from pewter or copper alloy – but the badge Carl discovered in Bosworth

is gilded silver – clearly owned by a high-ranking nobleman, perhaps even someone in Richard's inner retinue of knights.

By 1485, the forces of the House of Lancaster were gathering again, and Richard's exiled cousin, 28-year-old Henry Tudor, Earl of Richmond, returned from France to lay claim to the English throne. It resulted in a pivotal battle in the War of the Roses, fourteen years after the last one.

## The Battle of Bosworth

Henry Tudor had gathered a small rebel army – French mercenaries who would fight for whoever paid them, some English exiles, and Welsh supporters. In all, his army numbered about 5,000 men. King Richard commanded 12,000 men, and marched out of Leicester to intercept Henry on his way towards London.

On the 22 August 1485, the two armies engaged one another near Ambion Hill, Bosworth. After ferocious fighting, Richard saw an opportunity to personally attack Henry. If he killed Henry outright, the battle would be won. Richard galloped towards Henry's retinue, but his lance broke on impact with a standard bearer. At that point, a group of soldiers who had been waiting to see which side to support, decided to join Henry's forces against the King, and moved towards Richard and his retinue. Richard was instantly and overwhelmingly outnumbered, his horse became mired in a marshy area, and he was unseated. Shakespeare immortalises Richard's final moments in his play *Richard III*: anguished and betrayed, Richard cries out 'A horse, a horse, my Kingdom for a horse!'

Richard was quickly killed, his crown removed and his body stripped and brutalised. Contemporary records state that the dead king was tied across the back of a horse and ridden into Leicester. His body was laid out for people to see that he was really dead, and then he was finally, quietly, laid to rest in Greyfriars church in Leicester. The famous, recent excavation has finally and definitively identified this site, and recovered King Richard's remains from underneath a council car park. Once the scientific analyses are complete, he'll be reburied in consecrated ground.

Richard's skeletal remains show he had a severe scoliosis (curvature) of his spine. It would probably have meant that one shoulder was always higher than the other, and it ties in with contemporary descriptions of him being a 'hunchback'. The fatal injury he sustained is a massive trauma to the back of the head, probably caused by blows from a sword and a halberd (a two-handed pole with a blade on one side and a spike on the other). Further non-fatal injuries may be 'humiliation injuries' inflicted on the King's dead body as he was carried off the battlefield and into Leicester.

After the battle, Henry Tudor was crowned king, and quickly married Richard's niece, Elizabeth, in order to join the two warring houses of York and Lancaster. Yorkist revolts continued for another fifteen years, but failed to damage the King – the Tudor family were on the throne, and they would continue to hold power for 122 more years.

## The lost battlefield

Despite the Battle of Bosworth being so famous and so important, experts weren't certain of the exact location of the battlefield. Contemporary accounts conflicted, and historical maps weren't detailed enough to pinpoint the site. It's been suggested that for the first couple of hundred years, the site was so well known that no one thought it necessary to document it. As time passed, the detail was lost from memory.

It's only following the work of the Battlefield Survey that we can be truly sure of the battlefield and death site of Richard. The discovery of crucial evidence came from the dozens of hours of systematic metal detecting completed by Carl and his group, including a silver livery badge close to the death site of the Duke of Norfolk, one of Richard's supporters, and the largest assemblage of artillery roundshot ever found on a European medieval battlefield.

Carl's silver-gilt boar, however, was the clincher. It was discovered at the edge of an area that was marshy in medieval times, fitting perfectly with the accounts that the King was killed when his horse was mired. The boar could have dropped or ripped from a knight's clothes or armour as he rode next to his king in a final charge. Its loss wouldn't even have been noticed – instantly, the battle was over and the King was dead.

This little boar badge would wait more than 500 years, but thanks to the efforts of a committed metal detecting team, it's treasured once again.

**See also:**
Great War Victory Medal
Kirkcaldy Heart Brooch
Raglan Ring

# Isle of Wight Axehead

## Stone Age axe on a garlic farm

Nine-year-old Imogen Rickman was at a garlic farm on the Isle of Wight on a school trip, when she spotted a rough stone in the soil – she picked it up, and knew it was something special right away. Imogen had discovered an incomplete Stone Age flint axehead.

> **Date:** 3500–2100BC, Neolithic
> **Where, when and how found:** Newchurch, Isle of Wight; 2012; chance find on farmland during a school trip
> **Finder:** Imogen Rickman
> **Where is it now?** On display at The Garlic Farm, Isle of Wight www.thegarlicfarm.co.uk

The find dates to the Neolithic, or Late Stone Age, around 3500–2100BC. For comparison, the most significant phase of building at Stonehenge in Wiltshire took place from 2620–2480BC, towards the end of the Neolithic. Made from one of the natural flint pebbles that occur in the chalk cliffs about 5km from the findspot, the axehead has been shaped by striking the pebble with another flint to break off flakes from the edges, a process known as 'knapping'.

The axehead would have been a slender, tapering triangle shape, with a sharp cutting edge on both sides and was used for chopping down trees and carpentry. Imogen only found the butt-end – the striking end is missing. From the discoloration, it appears that the end broke off a long time ago – perhaps in the Neolithic itself, and that's why the axe was discarded. This was a functional tool, rather than an item of prestige, so it would have been chucked away if it wasn't useful.

Originally the axehead would have been attached to a wood or bone handle, secured with leather binding and possibly an organic glue to hold it firmly in place.

We know from other excavations that Neolithic people were very good at woodworking – some people have even suggested that we shouldn't call it the 'Stone Age', as they probably had more tools made from bone, wood, antler, leather and textile than they ever had in stone.

## Life in the Neolithic

Neolithic Britain had a similar climate to modern Britain, and people lived in small-scale tribes, farming and herding animals, and probably using wild resources too. They ate cattle, sheep and goats, and particularly enjoyed pork for feasting. It's likely that they used early types of wheat and barley to make bread and beer, and traces of mead (honey wine) have been found on fragments of pottery. Cloth-weaving techniques were known elsewhere in the world at this time, but we don't have any surviving evidence from Britain. Most clothing was probably made from leather and animal hides, sewn into well-fitting, warm clothes. The hides would have been preserved by tanning; they probably used a process called 'brain-tanning', where the animal skin is scraped and cleaned, then the brains are rubbed into the skin to help preserve it, before it's rinsed and smoked over a cool fire to make it supple, strong and not smelly.

People probably lived within extended family groups – parents, children, grandparents and aunts and uncles all living and working together, and

> "The people who used this axehead hadn't developed metal working technology yet"

getting together with other people from the wider region for important ritual and religious occasions.

We aren't certain about what kind of houses Neolithic people lived in – in some places, archaeologists have discovered marks in the earth from large timber longhouses, but many other buildings are smaller and not quite so regular and there are also some areas with roundhouses built in small villages.

In other areas we don't seem to have any evidence for dwellings at all – which either means the evidence has simply been lost over time, we haven't found it yet, or the people could have been living in homes that didn't make a significant mark on the ground, such as yurt-style homes with animal hides covering the roof and walls, that are erected temporarily and sit on the ground without foundations.

The people who used this axehead hadn't developed metal-working technology yet. In Britain the first simple items of copper and gold were made from around 2400BC, with bronze working beginning at about 2200BC. They were well-connected and sophisticated though, and trade networks stretched to the continent and all along the British coast as far north as Orkney and Shetland.

The axehead fragment was a remarkable discovery by Imogen – many other people wouldn't have recognised its importance. Every time a find like this is reported, it helps us understand the 'big picture' of where people lived, how they used their land and what technology and tools they had – the everyday lives of ancient people.

See also:
Happisburgh Handaxe
Tisbury Hoard

# Bentley Miniature Book

## *A tiny trinket dedicated to a saint*

Barry Wood discovered this treasure while metal detecting in a field in Hampshire in 1997. This was before the Portable Antiquities Scheme was set up and before there were local Finds Liaison Officers across the country recording objects found by the public.

Barry watched the first series of *Britain's Secret Treasures* in 2012, and like many other people, submitted his find to be assessed by the expert panel. The experts agreed that this tiny bronze book, dating from the early 1500s, is unique.

**Date:** 1500–1550, Late Medieval

**Where, when and how found:** Bentley, Hampshire; 1997; metal detecting

**Finder:** Barry Wood

**Where is it now?** Donated to the British Museum

**Also visit:** Winchester Cathedral, Winchester
www.winchester-cathedral.org.uk

British Library, London
www.bl.uk

**Explore:** Pilgrim routes along the North Downs Way
www.nationaltrail.co.uk/northdowns/

Made from 18g of cast copper alloy, this book-shaped trinket is 31mm by 22.5mm. The spine and covers have been stamped to make it look like the book has leather covers, with parallel lines imitating the spine.

Late medieval books were rare and valuable artefacts. As the printing press had only just been introduced to England, and most books were still hand-stamped, creating them was a very time-consuming and expensive process.

The miniature has an engraved Latin inscription on the open 'pages'.

On the first page across four lines, **PAX / TIBI / MAR / CE**, and on the second page, **EVAN / GELI / STA / MEUS**.

This translates as **'Peace (*Pax*) to you (*tibi*), Mark (*Marce*) my Evangelist (*Evangelista meus*)'**, and is an inscription linked to St Mark's Cathedral Basilica in Venice. Mark is traditionally said to be the author of one of the four Gospels in the Bible, and to have founded the Church of Alexandria in Egypt, one of the four main early churches.

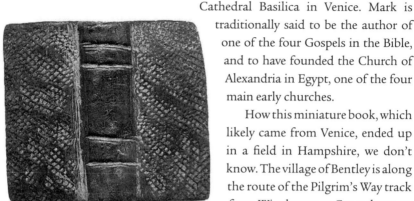

How this miniature book, which likely came from Venice, ended up in a field in Hampshire, we don't know. The village of Bentley is along the route of the Pilgrim's Way track from Winchester to Canterbury, so it may have been dropped by a pilgrim in the early 1500s. There's no evidence of any pin fastening that would have allowed the metal book to attach to your clothes, so it may have been kept in a bag, pouch or pocket instead.

Perhaps the person who lost this was an international pilgrim who had acquired the token on a trip to Venice. Perhaps they had bought it from or been given it by someone local, or perhaps the original owner lived near Bentley but had made the exotic journey to Venice and back themselves. There are many sites associated with St Mark in Europe, including dozens of English parish churches dedicated to this saint, but this kind of item isn't common. Shrines such as St Thomas Becket's at Canterbury were destroyed on the orders of King Henry VIII in the mid-16th century, and pilgrimage was discouraged under his new Church of England. So if the miniature book was dropped by a pilgrim, it would probably have been before this time.

The alternative explanation is that the book was a devotional object associated with a large church or a library. Churches and monasteries were centres of learning and held most of the books in circulation in the 16th century, as not many other people could read. It's possible this intriguing token was lost when someone was moving valuables from one location to another, and it then lay undisturbed for 500 years.

**See also:**
Canterbury Pilgrim Badges
Seal Matrix of Stone Priory
Clonmore Shrine

# Daventry Visard Mask

## *A lady's face protector hidden in a wall*

In 2010, a builder was doing some work on an old internal wall when he discovered something unusual. The wall, probably dating to the 16th century, was four feet thick, and constructed with an inner core of soil, straw and horsehair. In a small niche amongst the straw and hair was a carefully folded velvet mask, with holes for eyes and mouth, and a black glass bead. The finders took the mask to the Northamptonshire Finds Liaison Officer, Julie Cassidy, who identified it as a rare survival of a 1600s visard mask.

Date: 1600–1700, Post Medieval

Where, when and how found: Daventry, Northamptonshire; 2010; found hidden in a wall during building work

Finder: Anonymous

Where is it now? Returned to landowner

Visit: Victoria and Albert Museum, London
www.vam.ac.uk

University of Southampton concealed garments project
www.concealedgarments.org

'Visard' or 'vizard' masks were worn by upper-class women from the 1500s up to the early 1700s. One reason for the wearing of these masks was so women could protect their faces from the sun when they were out of the house. Unlike today, where for most people a tan represents health, wealth and fashion, in the 16th century a tan suggested that you were poor and had to work outside – only gentlewomen were able to keep plump and pale skinned. Women would use white lead powder, lemon juice and sulphur to whiten their faces, but the best way to protect your reputation as a lady of distinction was to cover your face in the first place.

The Daventry Mask appears to be a unique survival – it was identified because of the existence of the complete wardrobe of the 'Lady Clapham' 17th century doll on display at the Victoria and Albert Museum in London. The doll has a small version of a mask almost identical to the Daventry Mask.

The outer layer of the mask is black velvet, the lining is silk, and the inner layers are pressed paper, shaped so that there's space for the nose and with almond eye holes and a lip-shaped mouth hole. There are no attachments or holes for a ribbon or string to be used to tie the mask to the face. Instead, a

small black glass bead has been secured to the inner lining near the mouth using a white thread – the wearer would have gritted the bead between her teeth to secure the mask in place.

A contemporary description confirms the extraordinary way the mask would have been secured:

'A mask ... Gentlewomen used to put over their Faces when they travel to keep them from sun burning ... [It] covers the whole face ... holes for the eyes, a case for the nose and a slit for the mouth ... this kind of Mask is taken off and put[on] in a moment of time, being only held in the Teeth by means of a round bead fastened on the inside ... against the mouth.'

(Randle Holme, *The Academie of Armorie*, 1688)

It's not clear why this unusual, and probably uncomfortable, system of wearing the mask came about. It's possible that women could move their masks around in the way that fans or masquerade masks were used, to 'choreograph' social interactions, exposing the face then concealing it in a flirtatious peekaboo. Or perhaps they just didn't want to muss their fancy hair/hat/wig arrangements with a string tied round their heads.

These masks were not just peculiar to our eyes. Phillip Stubbes, a puritan who detested the fashions of the day, wrote in his 1583 book *Anatomie of Abuses*, about these 'visors made of velvet':

'...if a man, who knew not their guise before, should chance to meet one of them, he would think he met a monster or a devil; for face he can see none, but two broad holes against her eyes.'

It's not clear why the Visard Mask was carefully placed inside the wall of a house, but a team at the University of Southampton are currently researching the history of concealing used garments and items in walls and floors of homes. It seems that people thought they were powerful tools to give protection from witchcraft or evil spirits. They're often hidden near openings and thresholds, like fireplaces, chimneys and doorways, and it's thought that used clothes and shoes, or bottles containing urine, hair or fingernails were considered more powerful because they were personal.

The Daventry Visard Mask was definitely a very personal item, so perhaps that's why it was put inside the wall. Or maybe it was a family heirloom, incorporated into the house as good luck, or a way of keeping your ancestors with you. What's certain is that its strange resting place is the reason this rare and bizarre treasure survived for more than 400 years.

"A mask ... Gentlewomen used to put over their Faces when they travel to keep them from sun burning ..."

See also:
Navenby Witch Bottle
Beddingham Nose

# Winchester Gold Hoard

## *A unique collection of prehistoric gold jewellery*

In 2000, just outside Winchester, retired florist and amateur metal detectorist Kevan Halls was carefully searching a ploughed field with a slight natural hill. He got a signal, dug down a few centimetres, and found the source: a gold Iron Age brooch. He reported his find and his stunned local Finds Liaison Officer, Sally Worrell, took the brooch for assessment to the British Museum. They immediately knew this was very important, as fewer than a dozen gold Iron Age brooches have ever been found in the whole of northern Europe.

> **Date:** Around 75–25BC, Iron Age
> **Where, when and how found:** Winchester, Hampshire; 2000; metal detecting
> **Finder:** Kevan Halls
> **Where is it now?** British Museum, London
> www.britishmuseum.org
> **Also visit:** Butser Ancient Farm, Waterlooville, Hampshire
> www.butserancientfarm.co.uk

Kevan was asked to mark the locations of any other finds he made. He returned to the field over the following months and discovered an extraordinary series of artefacts – a gold rope necklace of a type that had never been seen before, three more gold brooches, a chain for linking two of the brooches together, two solid gold bracelets and another, smaller gold rope necklace. In total, Kevan found more than 1kg of jewellery, made with 22 and 24 Carat (91–99% pure) gold.

The nine items were declared Treasure by the Coroner, an excavation was conducted at the find site, and the jewellery was acquired by the British Museum as an utterly unique assemblage of 2,000-year-old jewellery.

## The jewellery styles

It's been suggested that the Winchester Hoard is a 'his and hers' set of personal adornments: he would wear the 516g necklace and a pair of brooches with a chain between them attached to the front of his woollen cloak; she would wear the smaller necklace (332g) with paired brooches on her cloak or dress, and a pair of bracelets at her wrists.

The brooches are bow-shaped 'fibula', the Iron Age ancestor of the modern safety pin, and would have been both functional and decorative.

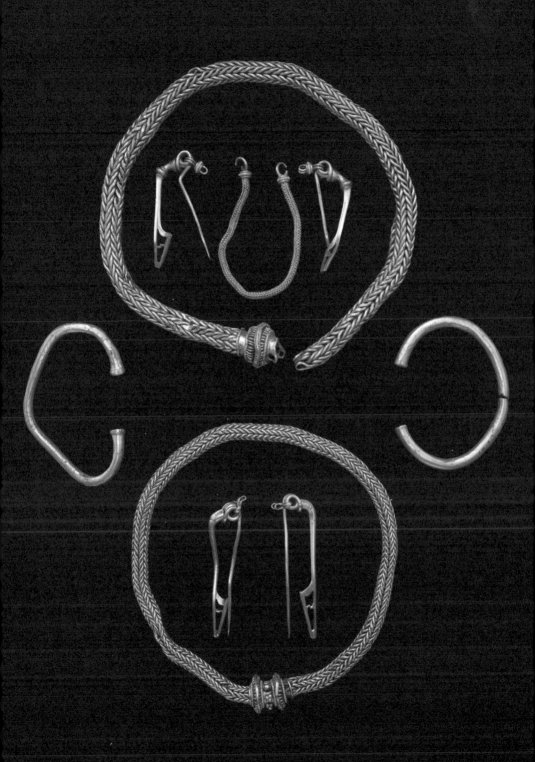

> ## "Feasting items and even imported wine amphorae turn up on burial sites, and early coins suggest that some of these leaders were proclaiming themselves 'Kings' for the first time"

They're in the style typical of the native north-west European Iron Age cultures, known as 'La Tène', and show wear patterns that indicate they were well used before being deposited.

The gold rope necklaces, however, are in a style never seen before – wires woven in interlinked rings to make a thick, flexible rope, with cylindrical clasps on each end to make a full circlet. British Iron Age gold neck ornaments were normally solid and rigid rings rather than flexible necklaces (for example see the Blair Drummond Hoard, p272, or the Sedgeford Torc, p27). Torcs were an important status symbol, worn by the leaders and chiefs, and possibly by their family members too. The Winchester torc-necklaces show evidence that they, too, were worn before being deposited.

The Winchester style of manufacture is most similar to the work that was being done in the Mediterranean at the time, and it's led researchers to suggest that either a craftsperson trained in the Mediterranean world was working local to Iron Age Hampshire, or that the key pieces in the Winchester Hoard were a special gift given by Roman dignitaries to a local leader. Some have gone as far as to suggest that the uniqueness and quality of craftsmanship means that the hoard must have been a gift from one of the great legends of Rome – Julius Caesar, Mark Antony or the Emperor Augustus.

## The people of Iron Age Winchester

The hoard has been dated to around 75–25BC, a time of significant social change in southern England. Successful Iron Age chiefs had contacts with tribal leaders on the continent and Roman commanders and ambassadors too. Feasting items and even imported wine amphorae turn up on burial sites, and early coins suggest that some of these leaders were proclaiming themselves 'Kings' for the first time. This was the time just before the Romans first began threatening invasion, although the chief leaders would certainly have known about, and perhaps even been involved with, the troubles tribespeople on the continent were having with the Roman Army.

The Iron Age British tribes did not write, and so we don't have any documents from their perspective. What we do have, though, are the Roman and Greek writers' impressions of these early Brits. They describe them as wearing brightly checked and striped woollen clothes, taking pride in their fierceness, and wearing their hair long. Men also cultivated their facial hair – Diodorus Siculus, perhaps intending to mock the barbarians with their daft fashions, wrote: 'When they are eating, the moustache becomes entangled in the food, and when they are drinking the drink passes, as it were, through a sort of strainer'. But despite their unappealing eating and drinking habits, leaders in the Winchester area were clearly important people to befriend.

Winchester was known as *Venta Belgarum* by the Romans, meaning 'town of the Belgae tribe', and shortly after the invasion in 43AD, it grew into the sixth-largest Roman town in Britannia. The Belgae were perhaps people whose relatives also lived in north France and what is now modern-day Belgium. Julius Caesar, during his campaigns in Gaul (58–51BC), described the Belgae as the bravest of the Gaulish tribes, partly because traders didn't deal with them and so they hadn't been introduced to imported goods that might weaken their fighting spirit.

Although we don't know who owned the precious items of the Winchester Hoard, we do know that they were carefully and intentionally deposited. Roman writers describe that many of the local British people's sacred shrines were in watery places – bogs, rivers and lakes – but archaeologists have also identified a pattern of deposits in dry, open places on high ground, especially of torcs.

The excavation at the find site didn't reveal any evidence of a building or man-made shrine at the top of the hill in the field. It's possible that the appeal of the site was that it was entirely open, or perhaps the focus was a natural grouping of stones or trees.

It's likely that these 'dry land hoards' were a different type of ritual offering to the water-based activities. Perhaps the watery offerings related to the earth or underworld, and hill offerings related to the sky or upper-world. We can't be sure. Further research and further finds will help us build a clearer picture of this exciting time at the end of prehistory.

**See also:**
Blair Drummond Torc Hoard
Sedgeford Torc
Hallaton Treasure

# Roman Slave Shackle

## *A dark reminder*

In 1992, a keen detectorist was searching near the line of the Roman Road that ran between *Venta Belgarum* (Winchester) and *Calleva Atrebatum* (Silchester), in modern-day Hampshire when he discovered this corroded, 357g piece of wrought iron. This troubling object is a human shackle – used to bind the ankles of a Roman slave.

Experts can't pin down its age more tightly than 200–400AD, as it was likely to have been used for many decades before it was finally lost or thrown away. This particular type of shackle, the 'Bavay' type,

> **Date:** 200–400AD, Roman
>
> **Where, when and how found:** Headbourne Worthy, near Winchester, Hampshire; 1992; metal detecting
>
> **Finder:** Anonymous
>
> **Where is it now?** Returned to finder
>
> **Visit:** Silchester Roman city walls and amphitheatre, Hampshire (site managed by English Heritage) www.english-heritage.org.uk
>
> Museum of London, London www.museumoflondon.org.uk

seems to have been used mostly in rural parts of Gaul and Britain, possibly to control slaves being transported, or to secure farm workers after a day's work. Figurines from the Roman period in Britain have been discovered showing naked men, crouched and with bound feet and hands, and similar examples of shackles have been discovered across England.

## The 'necessity' of slavery

Slaves were integral to the functioning of the Roman Empire, and attitudes to 'owning' another person were very different to our modern ideas. For Romans, slaves were one of the greatest imports from new territories; enemies captured in war were enslaved rather than killed, and the Romans traded with regions outside their control in order to meet the demand for slaves.

Experts have estimated that a quarter of all people living under Roman rule were slaves. They were the property of their owners, rather than people

in their own right – they had no rights, couldn't legally own anything and were not allowed to marry or have a legitimate family. One fragment of a slave sale guarantee discovered in London records the purchase of a slave girl: 'Vegetus ... has bought and received ... the girl Fortunata, or by whatever name she is known, from Jublains [in N. France] from Albicianus ... for 600 denarii.' The guarantee goes on to confirm 'that the girl in question is transferred in good health, that she is liable not to wander or to run away'.

Some slaves were treated relatively well, especially those who were educated and could work as musicians, doctors or teachers. Other slaves were abused and brutalised, and death was preferable to life under shackle. Slaves were sometimes used in games and tournaments held in amphitheatres, as 'bait' for wild animals, or they were trained as gladiators. Documents record that professional 'slave catchers' were at work in the Roman Empire, helping owners find and return runaways. When a runaway slave was caught, he or she would be fitted with an iron collar and sometimes branded on the forehead. Some of these inscribed iron slave collars have survived and are now held in museum collections.

There was never a feeling within Rome that slavery was intrinsically wrong. When the Emperor Constantine adopted Christianity into the Roman Empire, around the year 319, he made it illegal to kill a slave, and decreed that they could no longer be branded on the face, only on the arms and legs. But it was thought that Jesus had not preached against slavery, and so it was not really considered immoral or unchristian.

Slavery was only made illegal throughout the whole of the British Empire in 1843 – much of modern Britain was built on the backs of slaves from British colonies. People-trafficking remains a global problem today, and millions of people are forced to work as enslaved or bonded labourers in dangerous conditions and in fear for their lives. This shackle isn't just about Roman history, it's a powerful and troubling reminder that slavery is not yet in our past.

See also:
Putney 'Brothel' Token
Syston Knife Handle

# THE PEOPLE WHO FIND TREASURE

Even in the past, people finding what we now know to be stone tools made by prehistoric man thought that they were tools made by long-dead giants, or petrified lightning bolts. Stone circles, skilfully engineered by early Britons five thousand or more years ago, are described in folklore traditions as frozen giants, fairy rings, or troll circles. Although medieval people might not have had a modern, scientific understanding of what these finds were, they knew that some of them were very special. Discoveries were often made when people disturbed the ground through building or farming, but even back then people found pleasure in searching for 'treasure'.

Where we do have reports from these early treasure quests, often into burial mounds, they can be frustrating reading – we hear of workers digging though old bones, pieces of burnt pot, a few old beads to get to the 'treasure' underneath ... and often coming up empty-handed. What these tomb raiders dismissed as bits of burnt rubbish getting in the way of the good stuff, were actually the materials that can be so valuable to modern archaeology. They tell us who these people were, how they were buried, when, and in what sort of structures. Hoards aren't just about market value or the purity of the gold – they're about how the items were deposited, why, and by whom. Cutting-edge archaeological analysis means that we can put these finds into the bigger landscape, and build a picture of how people were moving about and using their environment.

Nowadays, more people go looking for treasure than ever before – either beachcombing, fieldwalking or metal detecting. Searching for finds can be immensely rewarding and there are many passionate and incredibly well-informed searchers out there. Their hobby can add enormous amounts to our understanding of Britain's past, and many detectorists and other finders are valued members of archaeological teams and projects. One of the most significant battlefields in British history was accurately located because of the efforts of skilled and committed metal detectorists (see the **Boar Badge of Richard III**, p164). Through recording these finds, the public are changing our understanding of Britain's past.

But metal detecting can also be really destructive if it's not done responsibly. All land has an owner, including roadside verges and footpaths, and permission must be obtained before you search. In Northern Ireland, using a metal detector to find archaeological objects is illegal without a professional licence.

In archaeology, context is everything – if we don't know where a find was from, or the details of how it was deposited, valuable information is lost forever. Even though only 'Treasure' finds must be reported legally (see p296), landowners should insist that detectorists searching on their land report all their finds to the local PAS Finds Liaison Officer. In Scotland, the old laws of Treasure Trove still apply, and all finds of any type must be reported to Treasure Trove Scotland.

The importance of logging finds is showcased by some of the treasures in this book – most of these aren't legally Treasure, but they are nationally important, and archaeologically priceless. Have a look at the **Get Involved** chapter (on p288) for more information on ways to explore our heritage.

# Tisbury Hoard

## *1,000 years of buried bronze with many secrets yet to be revealed*

In 2011, a metal detectorist discovered a spearhead on farmland near Salisbury in Wiltshire. He knew it was Bronze Age – so at least 2,800 years old, and he suspected that there was much more under the soil. With the utmost self-control, he stopped digging and immediately alerted his local Finds Liaison Officer, and the site was excavated and investigated by archaeologists.

The excavation revealed a staggering 114 Bronze Age and Iron Age artefacts and in the surrounding area there were later Iron Age coin deposits, and even deposits from the Roman period. Because of careful reporting by metal detectorists and others, we're establishing a new understanding of the importance of Tisbury in prehistory.

The initial Tisbury Hoard itself is still in the process of assessment, and not all the artefacts have been cleaned or fully analysed. What is known is that the hoard is a collection of bronze weapons, woodworking tools and other items dating from the early Bronze Age, around 2000BC, to the early Iron Age, around 700BC. There are sword blades, axeheads, leaf-shaped spearheads, knives, chisels, sickles, razors and a few ornaments like pins and fragments of hilts, handles and rivets.

But although the artefacts date from a range of over 1,000 years, they appear to have been buried at the same time, around 700BC. These were clearly treasured items that were either handed between generations or rediscovered while the people were digging or working the land. It's often assumed that hoards were deposited not long after the metal objects were made, but the Tisbury Hoard shows that these prehistoric people

**Date:** 2000–700BC, early Bronze Age–early Iron Age

**Where, when and how found:** Tisbury, near Wardour, Wiltshire; 2011; metal detecting

**Finder:** Anonymous

**Where is it now?** Salisbury Museum
www.salisburymuseum.org.uk

**Also visit:** Numerous prehistoric monuments in Wiltshire that were used into the Bronze Age – the most famous are Stonehenge, and the monuments around Avebury
www.english-heritage.org.uk

were interested in the past too, using already-ancient artefacts for special ceremonial purposes.

## The Bronze Age

Copper working was first introduced to Britain around 2400BC, and bronze working around 2200BC. It marks a shift from the late Stone Age, the Neolithic. The first metal artefacts were probably traded to Britain, and the first skilled metalworkers probably came from the continent. But local people soon learned these new technologies and specifically British traditions of metalwork quickly developed.

The significant aspect of bronze making is that it requires the alloying of tin and copper – but tin ore and copper ore are never found in the same place. It's likely that the tin used in the Tisbury artefacts came from Cornwall, where it was mined and traded. The copper ore might have come from south Wales. Wiltshire was already a rich and well-connected area – the monumental complexes at Stonehenge, Avebury and surrounds are testament to that – and the importance of metalworking in this area is no surprise.

By the 800s BC the technology was highly refined, and specialist metal-workers created items that were beautiful, functional and strong. Bronze weapons were both effective and prestigious. But there's also some evidence that by the late Bronze Age people were intentionally removing bronze artefacts from circulation, perhaps to increase demand and improve prestige – if an item is too easy to get hold of and everyone's got one, it inevitably loses some of its value. There have also been finds of poor-quality bronze axeheads with too much lead content – rendering them useless as axes, but possibly still useful as trading or symbolic items.

## To make a bronze sword

To make a bronze sword, a smith crushes copper and tin ores into a coarse powder and then heats them in a crucible in a super-hot fire. Scum and impurities rise up and are discarded, and the molten metal is then poured into a stone or clay mould and allowed to cool and harden. Before modern, accurate thermometers, smiths would have had to be very skilled to achieve

the correct fire temperature, otherwise the metal wouldn't cast properly. And if there had been too many impurities or the balance of metals in the alloy was incorrect, the finished blade would be too fragile or too brittle.

Once the cast metal sword blade has cooled a bit, the blackened and rough blade can be removed, plunged into water and riveted on to a carved wooden handle. Hours of hand polishing would transform the casting into a smooth, sharp and gleaming blade, deadly and beautiful.

It's quite likely that metallurgists had a special role and status in society – theirs was a magical job, turning rocks into molten liquid, and then into metal. Many folk traditions around the world single out smiths as having special and potentially dangerous powers. It has even been suggested by some folklorists that the origin of King Arthur's legendary Sword in the Stone originates from forged bronze blades being removed from stone moulds.

Some ritual deposits from the early Iron Age have shown that weapons were intentionally damaged, or 'killed' – sometimes even new blades are bent

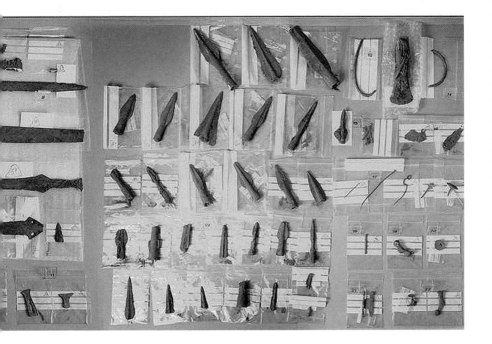

or snapped in two before being thrown into watery graves in rivers, lakes and bogs, or deposited in dry-land hoards. The weapons from Tisbury haven't undergone this ritual 'killing', and appear to have been buried in an area that was never waterlogged. Perhaps they were buried for economic reasons rather than ritual reasons, or the Tisbury Hoard was dedicated to a different set of gods that demanded a different set of rituals and offerings.

Tisbury helps us piece together the activities of our ancestors, but it also raises many questions – why was this spot special to them, what event triggered such a large deposit to be made, why did they hoard already ancient objects, and how do the deposits at this site fit with the changing technologies and ritual practices of the Iron Age?

Thanks to the discipline of the finder, every piece of evidence from the site was preserved, and every find recorded. This is the start of a long process of discovery – there's a lot more for Tisbury to teach us yet.

See also:
Milton Keynes Hoard
Near Lewes Hoard
Alnwick Sword

# Tanworth Iron Age Comb

## A unique high-status hairbrush

Some of the most intriguing finds are ones that combine beauty with function – like this little copper-alloy comb. Weighing 30g, measuring 6.4cm long and discovered in a field by a metal detector in 2006, the Tanworth comb is the only one from this period ever found in Britain.

Comparing the decoration to designs found on mirrors, spoons and horse harness rings, we can safely date the comb to the middle part of the 1st century AD, around the time of the Roman invasion of Britain (43AD). We know the comb was designed, made and used by native British Iron Age people, but we don't know whether it was made for horses, or people.

When it was new, the comb would have shone a beautiful golden bronze colour. It's decorated on both sides in the same style as a number of exquisite 2,000-year-old mirrors (see the Pegsdon Mirror, p149). The patterns would have been made with compasses, and the comb was cast by a highly skilled metalworker. It has a hole at the top, so it could be suspended or hung on a cord. We don't know whether this would have been for when it was stored, when it was used, or whether the hole is simply part of the artistic design.

> **Date:** 25–70AD, Late Iron Age
>
> **Where, when and how found:** Tanworth in Arden, Warwickshire; 2006; metal detecting
>
> **Finder:** Anonymous
>
> **Where is it now?** Private collector
>
> **Visit:** Butser Iron Age experimental farm, Hampshire www.butserancientfarm.co.uk
>
> Lindow Man bog body on display at the British Museum, London www.britishmuseum.org

## Celts

Iron Age peoples from across Britain, Ireland, France and Spain are sometimes known as Celts, but we should be careful using this term. Ancient Roman and Greek writers never referred to natives of Britain and Ireland as Celts (*Keltoi* in Greek, *Celtae* in Latin), they only used the term for the people in continental Europe.

The first use of the term 'Celt' for British and Irish societies was among scholars of linguistics in the 1600s, who linked early Gaulish languages with Irish, Scots Gaelic, Welsh, Cornish and Breton and called them all 'Celtic'.

There wasn't a shared culture over these lands, though – in the same way that Argentineans, Romanians and Italians all speak Romance languages, but have different cultures.

The population of Britain at this time was around 2–3 million. We don't know what the natives of Britain referred to themselves as - different tribes had different names, and it's likely that they didn't use a national name at all.

## A day in the life of the Dobunni

The people living in the central Midlands area around Tanworth in Arden were members of the *Dobunni* and *Cornovii* tribes. It was a rich agricultural area and everyday life was relatively unchanged since 2000BC, with small extended family groups farming the land and living in thatched roundhouses surrounded by their crops and animals. The British countryside looked quite a lot like it does now – small areas of woodland, ploughed fields and pasture land, with hedges, fences and walls to mark out different fields.

The climate was roughly similar to today's, and the Ancient Greek geographer Strabo (64BC–21AD) wrote what might feel like a familiar description:

'Their weather is more rainy than snowy; and on the days of clear sky, fog prevails so long a time that throughout a whole day the sun is to be seen for only about three or four hours'.

There were extensive trade networks across the country and to the continent, and people from distant lands sometimes travelled to and settled in the area, possibly also in marriage exchanges. Over the centuries following the Roman invasion, these native Britons took up many elements of Roman culture.

## Hairdressing and horses

From unusually preserved bodies that have been found in peat bogs, we know that some Iron Age men and women wore their hair long and women especially dressed it up in plaits and twists. Some men used lime rubbed into their hair like a form of hair gel, and they might also have used clarified animal or vegetable fat as conditioners.

> " Horses would have been status symbols and, just like today, sources of pride and pleasure. Some warriors even had horses buried in their graves with them "

Iron Age people in Britain enjoyed dressing up and looking good – the evidence includes preserved textiles, Roman written sources and numerous exquisite pieces of jewellery that have been found in Britain and abroad. The Lindow Man bog body, on display in the British Museum, had trimmed his beard with shears and had cut his fingernails. Unfortunately, a short time later he was brutally killed and thrown in a bog in Cheshire.

The Tanworth Comb could easily have been used for brushing out tangles in long hair, or as a decorative comb once a hairstyle was complete. But experts and members of the public alike have pointed out that the Tanworth Comb also looks very similar to a modern curry comb – the tool used to brush out a horse's mane and tail.

We know that Iron Age people loved their horses, so it's not impossible to imagine that a horse-grooming tool would be crafted so beautifully. Although horseback riding wasn't common, the small, sturdy native breed horses were trained to pull elaborate and richly decorated chariots as well as functional carts, in both times of peace and of battle. Horses would have been status symbols and, just like today, sources of pride and pleasure. Some warriors even had horses buried in their graves with them.

Further research, and perhaps further discoveries of artefacts, may one day reveal whether the creature having its hair brushed was human or equine. What's certain is that even if it was used for combing a horse's tail, it wasn't just a functional item – this treasure is evidence of a rich and sophisticated tribe who enjoyed beautiful things.

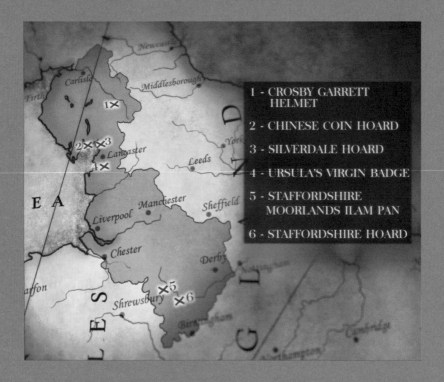

1 - CROSBY GARRETT HELMET

2 - CHINESE COIN HOARD

3 - SILVERDALE HOARD

4 - URSULA'S VIRGIN BADGE

5 - STAFFORDSHIRE MOORLANDS ILAM PAN

6 - STAFFORDSHIRE HOARD

**THE NORTH WEST** is a region of great contrasts and dramatic beauty – from the flat Cheshire plains to the high Cumbrian mountains, and from lakes to dales. It has the coldest average temperatures in England, at Cross Fell in the Pennine Hills, and the place with the highest average rainfall in England, Seathwaite in Cumbria. It has the largest body of water in England, Lake Windermere, and the highest English mountain, Scafell Pike.

The North West was at the centre of the Industrial Revolution – perfectly placed for raw materials (wool, water, coal) and a way to get the products and materials in and out across the British Empire through huge ports like Liverpool. In 1747, Liverpool overtook Bristol to become the biggest slave-trading port in Britain, at the heart of an aggressive colonial expansion strategy. Iron was first smelted in a furnace in Telford, cotton was imported in the millions of tons, and techniques and craftsmanship developed in the Staffordshire Potteries, most famously by Josiah Wedgwood, making British products desirable around the world.

The region was changed forever when cottage industries transformed into massive commercial enterprises. The toll on the environment and the population is still visible around us – in stone foundations in overgrown woods and pock-marked hillsides, in the enormous factories that have now been converted into penthouse apartments, as well as the terraced houses that still provide homes for working people.

The **Staffordshire Hoard (p212)** came out of a very ordinary field, but has enabled experts to shed more light on the so-called Dark Ages. The **Crosby Garrett Helmet (p194)** also captured people's attention, but unfortunately this stunning piece of military bling is not on permanent public display. It's now owned privately by an art collector somewhere in the country – a real secret treasure.

The **Staffordshire Moorlands Ilam Pan (p201)** captures another Roman soldier's experiences at the frontier of 'Civilisation'. It was possibly owned by a travelling soldier who came to live in the North West after long years travelling and fighting for the Empire. **Ursula's Virgin Badge (p199)** probably commemorates a very different journey that someone undertook. Thirteen hundred years later, on a spiritual pilgrimage, they might have gone all the way to Cologne, Germany, to get it. It's also possible that a significant shrine somewhere in the North West has been lost from memory and the archives, but could still be unearthed. The **Chinese Coin Hoard (p209)** found in the great steel and shipbuilding town of Barrow raises more questions than it can possibly ever answer.

Finds like these show us how willing people were to travel – for profit, for pleasure, for faith. They remind us that we shouldn't underestimate our ancestors. And they reveal that underneath the modern industrial history, there are treasures throughout the North West telling far older stories.

# Crosby Garrett Helmet

## The £2-million Treasure controversy

The finder of this artefact wishes to remain anonymous as does the private collector who now owns it. Shrouded in mystery, the Crosby Garrett Helmet has ended up at the centre of one of the most controversial heritage battles in recent memory.

A father and son who enjoyed metal detecting in Crosby Garrett parish, Cumbria, were out in May 2010 searching across a few familiar grassy fields. They'd been going over the area for years and had found some Roman coins, but nothing exceptional or particularly valuable.

When the son did get a signal that day, he thought the pieces of corroded metal he found in the soil were a Victorian ornament. Then he unearthed a large piece in the shape of a man's face. The men collected up the metal fragments and took them home. It was only after they looked online and contacted the Portable Antiquities Scheme that they realised they'd found an exceptional example of a Roman Cavalry Sports helmet.

The experts who saw the helmet were astonished: other Cavalry Sports helmets had been found, but often only the face mask section had survived. The Crosby Garrett helmet was almost complete, although in more than sixty fragile, corroded fragments. This was without doubt a find of international importance.

Sadly, because this striking 2,000-year-old helmet is made from copper alloy rather than gold or silver, it isn't legally classed as Treasure. If it were, the Crown could claim it, pay the finder and landowner a full reward and

---

**Date:** 75–250AD, Roman

**Where, when and how found:** Crosby Garrett, Cumbria; 2010; metal detecting

**Finder:** Anonymous

**Where is it now?** Acquired at auction by an anonymous private collector in 2010, its current location is within the UK but otherwise unknown. It was publicly exhibited for the first time in 2012 in the *Bronze* exhibition at the Royal Academy of Arts, London

**Visit:** Two other Roman cavalry helmets discovered in Britain can be seen in museums: The Ribchester Helmet at the British Museum, London
www.britishmuseum.org
Newstead Helmet at the National Museum of Scotland, Edinburgh
www.nms.ac.uk

the Treasure would go to a public museum. So despite it being an artefact of extraordinary importance, the finder and the landowner were entitled to dispose of the Crosby Garrett helmet in whatever way they wanted to.

## The open market

The owners instructed Christie's auction house in London to restore the helmet and prepare it for sale on the open market – anyone could bid for it and it would go to the highest bidder. This risked the helmet going to a private collector who would not allow further archaeological research or conservation, and would not allow the helmet to be displayed. It could effectively be lost all over again.

As a restorer carefully cleaned, reshaped and pieced together the 68 helmet fragments, the regional museum closest to the find site, Tullie House Museum and Art Gallery in Carlisle, launched an enormous fundraising campaign, hoping to purchase the helmet and display it publicly. They raised an astonishing £1.7 million in less than four weeks, but the finder and landowner didn't agree to sell. The helmet would go to public auction.

On the day of the auction, six bidders pushed the price past £1 million in minutes. Tullie House Museum dropped out at £1.7 million, and the hammer finally fell at £2 million. Including the buyer's premium and VAT, the helmet's new owner forked out a total of £2,330,468.75 for it.

All that is known about the helmet's new owner is that it's a man and he's a UK resident. He allowed the helmet to be exhibited in public for the first time in 2012 as part of an exhibition at the Royal Academy of Arts in London. If he ever wanted to export it from the UK, he would have to apply for a licence.

## Elite horsemen and their helmets

Dated to around 75–250AD, the Crosby Garrett helmet was owned by an elite soldier stationed on the northern frontiers of Roman Britain. Following the Roman invasion in 43AD, the Roman Army took control of Britain as far north as Hadrian's Wall. Attempts to push further north met with repeated failure, but they did hold the northern frontier until the end of the Roman occupation, around 410AD.

Soldiers sent to the remote outposts of their Empire worked hard to maintain their Roman lifestyle and military training. Mounted regiments regularly conducted cavalry tournaments, or *hippika gymnasia* ('Horse Exercises' in Greek), practising complex equestrian and military manoeuvres in parade grounds situated outside the Roman forts.

Horses and riders would wear brightly coloured tunics and harness decorations, with special display armour. Teams would demonstrate their skills with shields and weapons, and take turns to attack and defend in stylised equestrian games. These flamboyant displays improved their riding skills, but also impressed the Roman elite, and, when necessary, intimidated the locals.

The elite riders would have worn striking, polished, full-face Cavalry Sports helmets, richly decorated and embossed, with shining face mask visors with only small slits for the eyes. Coloured ribbons might have been attached to the tops of the helmets, to emphasise the speed of the riders galloping around.

Not intended for real battle, these helmets were designed to catch and hold the attention of spectators and competitors alike. They made the riders look like classical heroes or divine beings, celebrated Greek or Amazon warriors, both men and women, rather than just soldiers on horses.

A number of Cavalry Sports helmets have been recorded across countries that were part of the Roman Empire – from Algeria to Romania, Syria to Germany and Britain, but the Crosby Garrett helmet is one of the finest examples ever discovered, because of both the workmanship and its completeness. After almost 2,000 years in the ground, just two small sections of the helmet are missing – one piece of the chin, and some curls of hair from the back of the helmet.

The face mask is in the idealised 'Greek' style of a young man – clean-shaven, with luxurious, curly hair. Like other helmets of this type, the face mask hinges upwards so the helmet can be put on. A leather strap would have fastened around the rider's neck and then be secured on iron studs behind the mask's ears. The face mask is copper alloy coated with a layer of tin so when it was new it would have shone a brilliant white-silver colour.

The shape of the hat section, known as a 'Phrygian cap', is unusual, and the winged griffin crest fixed at the top is a unique survival. The hair and hat sections are a slightly different copper-based alloy, made by a skilled metallurgist to be a rich golden colour.

The griffin crest is made with 10% lead mixed into the metal, so would have stood out from the rest of the helmet. The griffin, a legendary creature with the back and legs of a lion and the wings and head of an eagle, was linked to Nemesis, the Goddess of Vengeance and Fate. It's an intimidating icon perfect for an elite cavalryman training and fighting at the edge of his empire.

Construction of Hadrian's Wall began in 122AD, and Crosby Garrett was en route to the frontier. Although the whole region would have had a significant military presence, no Roman garrisons are documented at Crosby Garrett. The burning question has yet to be answered: why did a helmet that was only ever used in equestrian parade grounds end up buried in Crosby Garrett?

Cavalry Sports helmets were part of a soldier's personal possessions, rather than issued by centralised military uniform supplies, and individual men would have bought their own helmets, or even commissioned them to their own specifications. Some sports helmets have been discovered in Roman graves, buried with their likely owners, and others seem to have been ritually buried on their own, perhaps as a particularly valuable and personal offering to the gods.

The Crosby Garrett helmet doesn't seem to have been associated with a burial, so archaeologists think it's most likely to have been buried as an offering, known as 'votive deposition', or perhaps stolen and hidden as loot which was never retrieved. Only archaeological excavation of the findspot might reveal more.

We can only speculate on what became of the owner of the Crosby Garrett helmet, fighting and performing equestrian feats at this far edge of the Roman Empire. The helmet's current resting place is also a topic for speculation, and has certainly fired up public debate on how best to protect our portable heritage, and whether the rules of the Treasure Act should be revised.

For further details of the Treasure Act, see p296.

See also:
Hadrian's Wall Coins
Cautopates Roman Figurine

# Ursula's Virgin Badge

## *A medieval badge from the cult of 11,000 virgins*

In April 2011, Paul King, a member of the South Ribble metal detecting club, was searching land he'd already gone over before. This time he was trying out a new machine, hit a very good signal, dug down and immediately knew he'd found something exciting. It was a small, thick metal badge of a young woman – 3cm across, folded in two, but otherwise in amazing condition.

> **Date:** 1500–1530, Medieval
> **Where, when and how found:** Preston, Lancashire; 2011; metal detecting
> **Finder:** Paul King
> **Official valuation:** £500
> **Where is it now?** Museum of Lancashire, Preston
> www.lancashire.gov.uk/museumoflancash

The badge is made from silver, and dates to the early-16th century, so is officially Treasure. It is thought to represent one of the companions of Ursula, a legendary saint linked to an impressively strange shrine in Cologne, Germany.

## St Ursula

There is no reliable historical evidence for St Ursula at all, and depending on the source, she's said to have lived some time between the 3rd and 7th centuries AD. The story goes that Ursula, a British princess, was sent to marry a pagan prince in France, but instead she diverted her journey (and escaped her

> ## "She travelled across Europe, gathering 11,000 virgins who wanted to travel with her"

marriage) to go on pilgrimage to Rome. She travelled across Europe, gathering 11,000 virgins who wanted to travel with her, but when the group arrived in Cologne, she and her companions were all murdered by pagan Hun tribesmen.

In the 11th century an ancient cemetery was discovered in Cologne, and the bones were declared to be evidence of the slaughter of Ursula's virgins. Her cult spread rapidly across Europe, reliquaries holding bones were distributed around the Christian world, and people began to make pilgrimage to see her shrine.

## The badge

In medieval times, badges were sold at all major pilgrimage sites. The fact that this badge is made of silver makes it rare, however, as most pilgrim badges were made from base metals like lead or copper alloy. No other badges of this design have ever been found. The young woman depicted, wearing a 'kennel-shape' headdress, loose hair and low neckline with cross pendant, dates the badge by clothing style to the early 1500s. She bears a striking resemblance to the design of a reliquary linked to St Ursula, which also probably represents one of Ursula's virgin companions. The reliquary was made in Bruges, Belgium, and is now held at the Metropolitan Museum of Art in New York, USA.

It's not clear whether this badge was intentionally folded over before it was deposited, or whether it was both accidentally bent and accidentally lost. It's possible that a lost shrine dedicated to St Ursula existed somewhere in the North of England. But the most likely explanation is that someone from Preston made the long pilgrimage to Cologne. They brought this badge back as a spiritual keepsake, infused with St Ursula's power and memories of their sacred journey.

**See also:**
Canterbury Pilgrim Badges
Hockley Pendant

# Staffordshire Moorlands Ilam Pan

## *The 1,900-year-old Roman souvenir*

The Staffordshire Moorlands are centred around the towns of Leek and Biddulph, boasting some of the most beautiful scenery in the Peak District National Park. Settled for thousands of years, this part of the country has a history as glorious as its scenery.

In 2003, Kevin Blackburn was metal detecting with friends when he discovered something he initially thought must just be a Coke can. But when he unearthed it, he realised the brightly coloured metal, 10cm across and weighing around 130g, was clearly very old and very precious. The friends immediately contacted their Finds Liaison Officer, Jane Stewart.

> **Date:** 100–200AD, Roman
>
> **Where, when and how found:** Ilam, Staffordshire; 2003; metal detecting
>
> **Finder:** Kevin Blackburn
>
> **Where is it now?** Acquired jointly and on display at Tullie House Museum, Carlisle, Cumbria (April 2013–April 2015); The Potteries Museum, Stoke-on-Trent (April 2015–April 2017); British Museum, London (April 2017–April 2019)
> www.tulliehouse.co.uk
> www.stokemuseums.org.uk
>
> **Also visit:** Hadrian's Wall, a UNESCO World Heritage Site
> www.visithadrianswall.co.uk

Kevin had found a gaudy, enamelled bronze dish, intricately decorated with a coiling enamelled 'Celtic' pattern and a Latin inscription around the rim. Originally it would have had a flat bow-tie-shaped handle (the scar where it was soldered on is still visible), and a flat, circular base. It was made in Roman times for drinking special liquids. Others like it have been found linked with the Roman baths in the city of *Aquae Sulis* (the modern-day city of Bath), and they may have been designed to scoop up and drink healing spring waters.

The Roman term for the item would have either been *trulla,* a pan with a handle, or *patera*, a shallow dish that normally doesn't have a handle. Experts disagree on its correct Roman name, but all accept the term 'pan', despite the modern-day association with functional kitchen equipment.

The pattern on the pan is a 'curvilinear scrollwork' design, with eight round sections (roundels) with curving whirligig patterns inside them with blue, turquoise and red inlaid enamel. The enamel-inlaid inscription that runs around the whole pan without a break is the detail that really gets archaeologists fascinated. It's because it links this treasure to the greatest Roman structure in Britain – Hadrian's Wall.

## The Wall

The Emperor Hadrian ordered construction to begin on the Wall in around 122AD, an unparalleled military fortification of turf banks and stone walls, 72 miles from west coast to east coast, separating the Romans from the northern 'Barbarian' tribes.

Like modern frontiers, it would have controlled access between the two regions, ensuring that only authorised and unarmed people travelled into the Roman province, and it would have prevented raiding on rural settlements near to the Wall. It was also a military base from which to police, protect and tax the native British communities, and to continue surveillance of the tribal leaders north of the Wall.

Incredibly, we don't actually know what the Romans called Hadrian's Wall themselves, but this little pan gives us our most intriguing clue to the puzzle. The inscription around the rim of the dish says:

### MAIS COGGABATA VXELODVNVM CAMMOGLANNA RIGORE VALI AELI DRACONIS

These are clearly the names of four forts along the western sector of Hadrian's Wall – *Maius* (Bowness-on-Solway), *Coggabata* (Drumburgh), *Uxelodunum* (Stanwix) and *Camboglanna* (Castlesteads), but the section **RIGORE VALI AELI DRACONIS** is harder to decipher, and experts have established a number of possibilities.

*Rigore* means 'on the line of' or 'in order of'. *Vali* means 'of the Wall' or 'of the Rampart' (*Vallum* means 'Rampart' or 'Wall'); *Aeli* is the family name of, amongst others, Emperor Hadrian.

So **RIGORE VALI AELI** could be the first direct archaeological reference to Hadrian's Wall – 'On the line of the Aelian Rampart'.

The alternative explanation is that *Aeli* refers to the family name of the person who owned the pan, rather than the emperor who built the Wall. *Draconis* is the personal name Draco or Dracon, so the owner of this bowl may well have been called Aelius Draco. That might mean the whole inscription reads 'Aelius Draco at Maius, Coggabata, Uxelodunum and Camboglanna in their order along the Wall'.

"Draco isn't a common Roman or British name, its origin is Greek – so it's possible that this man was very far from home"

Draco isn't a common Roman or British name, its origin is Greek – so it's possible that this man was very far from home, either co-opted into the military or serving as a slave, and posted to the far northern frontier. The most popular theory is that this veteran soldier, Draco, was either

> " Quite how the pan ended up 200 miles south [of Hadrian's Wall], in north Staffordshire, is a mystery "

awarded his enamelled dish as a keepsake after long years of good service, or he commissioned it himself as a memento of his time on the Wall.

This pan is somewhere between a tourist souvenir, a 'places I've been' piece of tour memorabilia, and an inscribed retirement gift. Today, our 21st-century soldiers serving in distant conflict zones regularly bring back local artefacts to commemorate their time on the front line, and it's clearly a habit that's been going on for millennia.

Quite how the pan ended up 200 miles south, in north Staffordshire, is a mystery. Perhaps Draco got a taste for British living and settled down with a local Romano-British lady. Roman soldiers weren't officially allowed to marry until they had completed twenty-five years of military service and been discharged, although many had 'unofficial' families living in civilian settlements just outside Roman Forts. Just like collecting souvenirs, going out with the local ladies is also something soldiers have been doing for generations.

The Staffordshire Moorlands Ilam Pan was purchased by three museums working in partnership, so that as many people as possible get a chance to see it. The Potteries Museum in Stoke-on-Trent is the regional museum closest to the findspot, the British Museum in London entered the partnership because the pan is of national importance, and the Tullie House Museum in Carlisle links the pan with the physical site of Hadrian's Wall.

See also:
Hadrian's Wall Coins
Crosby Garrett Helmet
Billingford Amulet

# Silverdale Hoard

## *The unknown chief from a Viking hoard*

The Silverdale Hoard is the third biggest Viking hoard ever discovered in the UK. Two hundred and one silver objects and coins were found in a crude sheet-lead container, including arm rings, ingots and the coin of a previously unrecorded ruler.

Finder Darren Webster stopped at the field, one of his regular sites, with a few hours to burn. When his detector gave off a signal he imagined it would be a coin, but then he saw fragments of lead. He realised the lead was a rough sheet folded in on itself, and when he picked it out of the ground, silver coins tumbled out of the bottom. He rang his wife to tell her that he had found Treasure.

**Date:** 900–910AD, Viking

**Where, when and how found:** Silverdale area, Lancashire; 2011; metal detecting

**Finder:** Darren Webster

**Official valuation:** £109,815

**Where is it now?** Lancashire Museums
www.lancashire.gov.uk/museums

When Darren got home, he called the landowner and the following morning he reported his incredible discovery to local Finds Liaison Officer, Dot Boughton, who arranged for the site to be excavated archaeologically.

In Viking times, the value of the hoard would have been huge: Gareth Williams, an expert at the British Museum, estimates that the hoard, totalling more than a kilo of silver, would easily have bought a whole herd of cattle – just one arm ring would be worth an ox.

## The importance of the hoard

The artefacts and coins in the hoard show the wide trading and cultural contacts of the Vikings – spanning Ireland to Russia and across the Islamic world. The hoard had been carefully deposited, and three highly decorated arm rings were placed carefully inside one another. One of the rings has unusual terminals in the form of animal heads. These fancy rings were possibly given as rewards from leaders to loyal high-ranking warriors. Far from being feminine jewellery, these solid arm rings were worn by military men on their sword arms, indicating their allegiance and prowess in battle: The more rings you had, the more military and social power you possessed.

The plainer rings and fragments are 'bullion-rings', rather than jewellery items. In a mixed economy, Vikings used pieces of solid silver as bullion currency. These arm rings appear to have been cast in multiples of the Viking 'ounce', equivalent to around 25 modern grams. They could then be cut into pieces, or melted and recast to a different weight.

A number of pieces in the Silverdale hoard show evidence of cuts made into the solid metal. These cut marks show where the quality of the metal has been tested. Before the invention of technology that could digitally measure the proportions of different metals in an alloy, and in many parts of the world still today, skilled metal smiths and traders could judge the purity of precious metal from its feel and softness. By cutting a testing nick into a solid ingot or ring, you can check that you aren't being swindled with fake ingots with a silver coating, or silver mixed with a base metal like lead or copper. If silver was mixed with a cheaper metal it would feel wrong under the knife.

The coins date the hoard to the years around 900–910AD. This was a time when the Anglo-Saxon King Edward the Elder, son of King Alfred 'the

Great', was pushing northwards, reclaiming territory from Vikings who had settled across the kingdom of Northumbria. The boundary of their territory, known later as the Danelaw, established in a treaty between Alfred and the Viking leader Guthrum, was overstepped, and the Danes fled or submitted to their new English overlords. Vikings were also expelled from Dublin around this time, by the native Irish tribes. Some of the artefacts in the Silverdale Hoard show artistic links with pieces that were being created and traded around the Irish Sea – it's possible that the Silverdale treasures have something to do with the persecuted Dublin Vikings.

Despite the Viking decline in the early 900s, their influence is still with us – including in our flesh and blood. Viking-origin surnames like Rigby, Thompson and Robinson are more common in areas that were under Viking control 1,000 years ago, and researchers at the University of Leicester have shown that many people also carry genetic markers that indicate a strong Norse heritage. Viking men are known to have married native women, but genetic material on the Y-Chromosome, passed down from father to son, retains an unbroken link to a Viking past. Up to 50% of old Lancashire families have Norse ancestry.

## Lost in translation

Two coins from the Silverdale Hoard are particularly interesting. The first is a contemporary forgery of a Frankish coin, which is plated with silver, but with a base metal core. Surprisingly, it wasn't weeded out by its Viking owner with a test cut.

The second is a coin bearing the mysterious name 'Airdeconut'. Not recorded in any documentary sources, this Viking ruler, with enough power to commission coins to be struck in his name, was previously lost to history. Experts have speculated that Airdeconut is a local interpretation of the Danish name, Harthacnut, which literally means 'Hard Knot'. It's possible that the person creating the die to stamp the coins was Anglo-Saxon, and couldn't fully catch the foreign-sounding name.

A later Harthacnut ruled England from 1040–1042, but the ruler on the Silverdale Hoard coin was alive and minting coins 120 years earlier. Perhaps more finds will shed light on this mystery ruler, his exploits and his fate. Despite the length and importance of the Viking reign in Britain, in many regards, we know surprisingly little about them.

On the other side of the coin is **DNS** (standing for Dominus) and **REX** (king), arranged in a cross.

Viking leaders readily adopted Christianity when they began to permanently settle in Britain, from the 860s onwards. Conversion meant that their Anglo-Saxon counterparts in the south were more willing to engage in trading activities and alliances with them. It seems that the Viking settlers kept their connection to the Norse gods and goddesses like Thor, Odin and Freyja, but also incorporated Christian imagery and characters into their lives and goods.

We don't know why the person or people who buried the hoard never returned for it. This was an incredibly dynamic period, where threats might have come from other Viking settlers as much as advancing Anglo-Saxon forces from the south. We don't have many written sources that document these centuries from the Viking perspective, so we rely heavily on the accidental discovery and archaeological recovery of artefacts like these at Silverdale. Numerous hoards are likely to have been buried at this time, but only the ones that were never retrieved are left, waiting for someone to discover them. Someone's loss 1,000 years ago is very much our gain today.

See also:
Chalgrove Hoard
Vale of York Viking Hoard
West Yorkshire Ring Hoard

# Chinese Coin Hoard

## *107 coins from the time of the Opium Wars*

This intriguing find was discovered by Dave Taylor on farmland in Barrow-in-Furness – 107 circular copper-alloy coins with square holes and traces of a thread which once strung the coins together. All the coins had what appeared to be Chinese characters stamped into them. Dave reported his discovery to his local Finds Liaison

**Date:** Around 1659–1850, Post Medieval

**Where, when and how found:** Barrow-in-Furness, Cumbria; 2011; metal detecting

**Finder:** Dave Taylor

**Where is it now?** Hoard was donated to The Dock Museum, Barrow
www.dockmuseum.org.uk

Officer, Dot Boughton, and the coins were identified as 'cash coins' of east Asia, mostly China. All but three of them are from the Chinese Qing dynasty, which ruled from 1644 to 1911.

The coins are all of the same denomination, 1-cash (like a 'one-pound' coin). The inscriptions indicate when the coins were issued. But the majority of the coins appear to be underweight forgeries – only eight coins are probably official issues.

The fact that they're fakes means it's quite difficult to determine when exactly most of the coins were cast. According to their inscriptions, the coins range in date from 1659 to 1850. The earliest coin was probably cast between 1659 and 1661, and the obverse (front side) has the character inscription **Shunzhi tongbao** – 'Shunzhi' is the name of the emperor, 'tongbao' literally means 'circulating treasure'. The majority of the coins (56) have the inscriptions **Daoguang tongbao** and were probably cast in the Daoguang reign period (1821–1850) or later. They're probably the latest coins in the hoard. What we know for certain is that among the eight official coins, the earliest date to between 1736–1795. Two coins in the hoard are from Vietnam and date to the 18th–19th century.

Stringing coins together was a common practice in China and other countries in east Asia, and it's not that unusual to find some Vietnamese coins amongst Chinese issues. But why were these coins buried in Barrow-in-Furness?

## Why Barrow-in-Furness?

The findspot offered no clues for why the coins had been buried there. We don't know if they were buried permanently, or intended to be retrieved. What's certain is that these coins wouldn't have had any monetary value in Cumbria, except as novel, exotic trinkets. Perhaps that's why they were buried or dumped – without any monetary value, the owner lost interest in keeping hold of them.

It's also possible that they were buried temporarily, and the owner was planning on taking the coins back to China, where they would have had monetary value. In the 1850s the coins, if accepted as authentic, would have bought you around two kilos of rice in China. Which leads us to the most intriguing question in this Chinese Coin mystery story – who actually brought the coins to Barrow in the first place?

## Whodunnit?

In 1839 an aggressive and brutal conflict known as the First Opium War began between China and the British Empire. The British had introduced the habit of smoking opium with tobacco to China in the late 1700s, and throughout the 1800s they increased production of opium in India and sold it for increasingly vast sums to now-addicted Chinese buyers.

Chinese officials led by the Daoguang emperor were outraged, and tried to stop the trade that was turning their people into junkies. The British responded with a brutal and barbaric series of attacks on Chinese communities along the coast, finally forcing the Emperor to agree to a 'peace' treaty in 1842. The bullying tactics of the British colonial leaders won the day – they secured a large sum of compensation, and the rights to sell opium to the Chinese with even greater impunity, fixed taxation and the territory of Hong Kong, a colony Britain kept until 1997. A young MP in England, William Gladstone (later Prime Minister), challenged the morality of the Opium War in Parliament, declaring that 'a War more unjust in its origin, a War more calculated to cover this country with permanent disgrace, I do not know.'

> " In 1839 an aggressive and brutal conflict known as the First Opium War began between China and the British Empire "

The flow of merchants, missionaries, soldiers and diplomats between the two countries accelerated after the First Opium War, and throughout the vast global networks of the British Empire. Barrow was a thriving and prosperous port, and would have been a very cosmopolitan place. New railways, steel works and shipbuilding yards may have attracted labourers from overseas, and it's possible that a Chinese worker or servant travelled to Barrow with the coins and failed to retrieve them before heading home. Perhaps they never went home, and instead settled in Cumbria permanently.

This isn't the only hoard of Chinese coins found in Britain, but they are rare, especially outside London. This mysterious treasure was generously donated by Dave Taylor to the Dock Museum in Barrow – hopefully further study will shed more light on the relationship between Cumbria and China 150 years ago.

See also:
French Forgery Hoard
Spanish-American Gold
  Doubloons

# Staffordshire Hoard

## *The hoard that captured the public's heart*

Terry Herbert is an experienced metal detectorist and a member of his local detecting club. Over the years he'd reported various finds to his local Finds Liaison Officer, but he hadn't found anything that had rewritten the history books. Then, in July 2009, while detecting in a ploughed field in Staffordshire, his machine gave the signal that would change his life.

Over five days of detecting, Terry found thousands of pieces of Anglo-Saxon gold, silver and jewels mixed up in the loose plough-soil. In total, the field contained more than 3,500 pieces of treasure, made from 5.1kg of gold and 1.8kg of silver. Terry reported his discovery to his local Finds Liaison Officer, the Coroner was informed and an immediate security clampdown on the site was imposed. This find was too significant to risk illegal detectorists hearing about it and raiding the site.

An excavation confirmed that the hoard had been scattered by ploughing and that there was no obvious focus to the deposit. A geophysical survey failed to find any features in the field that could relate to the hoard – the site was a mystery. When the field was ploughed again in November 2012 a metal detector survey was carried out by an experienced team of detectorists who had taken part in surveys of battlefield sites. They found hundreds of pieces of metal of which eighty-one, found in the area of the original discovery, were deemed part of the original hoard. Most of the new finds were small, but there were some significant discoveries, including the matching partner to a helmet cheek-piece found by Terry.

> **Date:** probably 640–700AD, Anglo-Saxon
>
> **Where, when and how found:** Staffordshire; 2009; metal detecting. A further 81 associated pieces found in 2012 during a metal detecting survey.
>
> **Finder:** Terry Herbert
>
> **Official valuation:** £3,285,000
>
> **Where is it now?** Star finds on display at Birmingham Museum and Art Gallery and the Potteries Museum, Stoke-on-Trent www.staffordshirehoard.org.uk
>
> **Help:** Fundraising to pay for the cleaning, conservation and study of the hoard is ongoing www.staffordshirehoard.org.uk/donate

## Weapons and Warfare: the contents of the hoard

The strange thing about the Staffordshire Hoard is that it's almost entirely made up of 'war-gear' – items associated with warriors. Pieces of helmet, sword hilts and fittings, pommel caps from swords and seaxes (short single-edged swords), often with garnets inlaid into gold, as well as many items that haven't yet been identified. Hardly any items are complete – the sword fittings are there, but there's no evidence of the actual iron blades.

Other Anglo-Saxon prestige items are conspicuous by their absence: there are no feminine dress fittings, pins, brooches or pendants, which are normally common finds compared to sword fittings. The material in the hoard had been carefully selected.

Most of the art-work is in a 7th-century style; interlaced, ribbon-like animals cross over each other and their own bodies, biting their tails or each other. The Anglo-Saxons loved patterns which wove these ambiguous animals into complicated knots, and the different designs and animals probably had specific, important meanings. One of the best examples of these animal patterns is on the pair of helmet cheek-pieces. The main part is decorated with bands of biting animals and down the edges there are interlaced snakes. These cheek-pieces are masterpieces of early medieval art and design.

In addition to the war-gear the hoard contains two (possibly three) Christian crosses, and an intriguing strip of silver. All the crosses had been damaged before burial – the arms of the large cross had been folded together, one limb of the cross-pendant had been broken off and the inscribed strip was probably ripped off a larger object. It's not known if the crosses were deliberately desecrated or just broken and folded for ease of packing. On each of the two faces of one particular item, an inscribed strip, is a line from the Bible written in Latin (Numbers 10:35) which translates as:

**'Rise up, O Lord, and may thy enemies be scattered and those who hate thee be driven from thy face.'**

A precious stone would have been set into one end of the strip, and rivet holes show that it was once attached to something else – perhaps a reliquary box for sacred remains, a bible or a cross.

## Who buried these treasures?

The archaeological evidence doesn't suggest this hoard was part of a grave or burial, but it may have been deposited in some kind of ritual offering to the gods, or people may have buried the treasures for safekeeping in troubled times, and for some reason never retrieved them. Whether an offering or a safety deposit, it's unlikely that all these items came from one original owner. It's more likely that they were trophies of war, or tribute given to a particular leader or group of elite warriors.

Around the time the hoard was buried, Staffordshire was part of the kingdom of Mercia – controlled by some of the Anglo-Saxons who had initially come to Britain from modern-day Denmark and Germany after the Romans left around 410AD. These warrior chieftains had control of most of England, living in tribal tensions with other chiefs and fighting with the native Britons and Welsh.

This was well before the first Vikings arrived – instead, the focus of aggression was towards other Anglo-Saxon kings, and towards suppressing the 'natives'. In the middle of the 7th century, the time the Staffordshire Hoard was probably deposited, Kings Penda (633–655), Wulfhere (658–675) and Aethelred (675–704) fought numerous ferocious battles with the East Anglian, Northumbrian and Wessex kings, wrestling for power, wealth and territory.

Penda was the last pagan King of Mercia, and he defeated and killed three Christian kings. The Mercians converted to Christianity around this time and the presence of the folded crosses and inscription strip in the hoard raise intriguing questions about the faith of the people who buried them.

Splendid as it is, the Staffordshire Hoard doesn't give us a balanced picture of early medieval royalty. The great ship-burial found at Sutton Hoo in Suffolk in 1939 reveals many of the other treasures an Anglo-Saxon king would have used – fine dress fittings, personal jewellery, cups and bowls for feasting, cooking vessels, a lyre to provide music and, at least if you were near water, a ship. The textiles and organic items have been lost, but it's clear that these were not primitive barbarians, but members of sophisticated societies that appreciated artistic skill as much as they did the art of war.

## The public response

When news of the Staffordshire Hoard broke, the public response was unprecedented. The website built by the PAS received 10 million hits in a week. Temporary displays in Birmingham and Stoke-on-Trent were seen by more than 100,000 people. People flew in from around the world to see the treasures, queues went around the block and the museums extended their opening hours to meet visitor demand.

People were instantly struck by the quality and quantity of the treasures as well as by the romance of the story of a discovery from a long and forgotten age. The Treasure Valuation Committee, based on the best advice available, valued the hoard at £3.285 million, an astonishing sum that was shared by Terry and the farmer who owned the land. Almost a million pounds was donated by the public to help the Birmingham Museum and Art Gallery and the Potteries Museum, Stoke-on-Trent, acquire the hoard and keep it in the public museums forever.

The hoard pieces are still being cleaned and analysed, work that will continue for years. This extraordinary treasure from Staffordshire has, without doubt, shed a brilliant light on what were once known as the Dark Ages.

See also:
North West Essex Ring
Holderness Cross

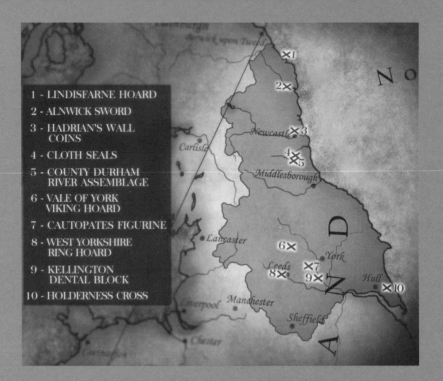

1 - LINDISFARNE HOARD

2 - ALNWICK SWORD

3 - HADRIAN'S WALL COINS

4 - CLOTH SEALS

5 - COUNTY DURHAM RIVER ASSEMBLAGE

6 - VALE OF YORK VIKING HOARD

7 - CAUTOPATES FIGURINE

8 - WEST YORKSHIRE RING HOARD

9 - KELLINGTON DENTAL BLOCK

10 - HOLDERNESS CROSS

**MORE THAN ANY OTHER REGION**, the treasures from the North East make you imagine moments of battle and defence. Wild country breeds strong people, and there are over 500 buildings with fortifications in Northumberland alone. In an area bordered by exposed and windswept coastline, the gritstone hills of the Pennines, and the deep-rooted cultural border between England and Scotland, the raiders, invaders and adventurers of the North East have left us a fantastic legacy of both buildings and artefacts.

Highlights include the Roman forts along Hadrian's Wall, the early Christian coastal settlements like Jarrow and Holy Island (Lindisfarne), the industrial and maritime heritage around Hartlepool, the medieval cathedral city of Durham and the Viking capital, York.

The area was always a prime target for the Vikings, first lured by the undefended riches in the remote coastal monasteries, and then by the farmland and high peaks, and excellent harbours. The wealth of the Anglo-Scandinavian networks is exquisitely demonstrated by the **Vale of York Viking Hoard (p234)**. But rich and creative cultures thrived across the region for centuries before that. The **County Durham River Assemblage (p244)** and the **Cautopates Figurine (p227)** perfectly demonstrate the ways by which Romans brought their religious practices to newly occupied territories.

From more unsettled times, the **Hadrian's Wall Coins (p239)** come from the dangerous and exciting frontier at the end of the Roman Empire; the **Alnwick Sword (p218)** was part of the ceremonial death rites of a high-status warrior; the **West Yorkshire Ring Hoard (p252)** captures a moment of fear, or panic, or triumph, that put four precious rings in the ground never to be retrieved.

# Alnwick Sword

## *The ritual killing of a warrior's sword*

The finder of this sword is a local man who discovered a series of Anglo-Saxon artefacts in a field near Alnwick, in Northumberland. He had permission from the landowner to search, and every time he found something, he carefully recorded it with the local Finds Liaison Officer, Rob Collins.

Most of his initial finds were made of bronze, but looking at the emerging pattern, Rob suggested that the finder keep his eyes out for iron artefacts too – he might be detecting a site that was once an Anglo-Saxon cemetery, and any weapons buried in graves would have been made from iron rather than bronze.

In August 2012, the finder made a spectacular discovery, even though to the untrained eye, it just looks like a lump of rusty metal. In fact this assemblage of iron artefacts, fused together with rust, reveals the surprising, and intriguing, funeral activities of people around 500–650AD.

> **Date:** 500–650AD, Anglo-Saxon, Early Medieval
>
> **Where, when and how found:** Near Alnwick, Northumberland; 2012; metal detecting
>
> **Finder:** Anonymous
>
> **Where is it now?** Finds donated to the Great North Museum, Newcastle upon Tyne
> www.twmuseums.org.uk

## Anglo-Saxons in the north

In the period following the collapse of the Western Roman Empire, Britain fragmented into a number of smaller kingdoms. Germanic and Scandinavian peoples – the Anglo-Saxons – colonised southern and eastern Britain, but there were always areas in the north and west under the control of native Britons.

It has always been thought that north England did not have a large Anglo-Saxon population, and the people who were here might not have been the wealthiest or most fashionable. The archaeology of the kingdom of Northumbria is a mix of Anglo-Saxon, native British and Irish traditions – but the finds from this site are forcing the experts to reconsider the importance of the Anglo-Saxons.

This period in Britain is often called the Dark Ages – after the Western Roman Empire, technological innovation seems to have slowed in some aspects, and economies shrank to more local production and trade. No more Roman villas – instead, round houses, defensive hill forts and smaller, tribal kingdoms. Archaeological evidence shows 're-fortification' of certain sites, where lots of effort was put into improving the defensive structures with new fences and palisades, bigger and higher earth banks, and populations moving into these defended areas from the surrounding countryside.

## The finds

The main item in the corroded lump is a double-edged iron sword – 37cm of the blade, folded in half so the two broken ends are touching each other. We only have the middle section of the blade – the tang (the section that goes into the handle), the handle and the tip are missing.

Other iron objects have been pushed into the crease of the folded sword – a short knife in its sheath, another blade or tool higher up, and two other iron fittings have fused to the edges of the blade, suggesting that they were purposely placed alongside the sword when it was deposited.

As well as rusty iron, the other material present at the findspot was fragmented bone – this was clearly a human burial, even though the acidic soil had eaten away most of the skeleton. The presence of the weapons in the grave, as well as shield fittings found in the area, suggests that this was a high-status, male Anglo-Saxon warrior.

X-ray analysis of the sword shows that it was made with a technique called 'pattern-welding', and probably made of four strands. Anglo-Saxon swords were beautiful things – expert smiths would hammer a 'plait' of metal strands into one another in a specific pattern. Heating, hammering,

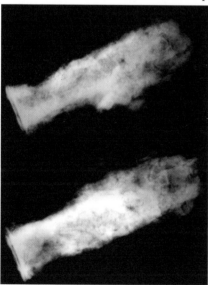

twisting and reheating, the core of the sword would be strong and flexible, and the edges of the sword would stay sharp and straight. That way, you'd have the sharpest and deadliest blade possible, that was the least likely to snap. Pattern-welding also produces a sword blade with amazing swirls in the metal – beautiful, but also symbolically powerful.

To fold a sword blade in half like this would have required careful but forceful hammering or reheating in a forge. Normally swords found in Anglo-Saxon graves haven't been destroyed or bent, but just laid with the body. The reason the Alnwick Sword was folded is unclear, but it's likely to have been a way of ritually 'killing' the sword, ensuring it couldn't be used by anyone else, and sending it to the Afterlife with the warrior.

## Warriors' weapons

The early Anglo-Saxon era was a time when weapons were much more than just functional killing-equipment.

There are many legendary swords from this time, or a little later – an ancient Irish sword carried by legendary heroes, known as *Caladbolg*; the Norse sword *Gram*, used by the hero Sigurd, even the French Emperor Charlemagne supposedly had the legendary sword *Joyeuse* which is still at the Louvre in Paris.

If a historical King Arthur ever existed, it was around this time – the earliest mentions of him in Welsh describe him carrying a special spear, a shield, and a sword, *Caledfwlch*, which means something like 'battle-breach'. *Caledfwlch* became the Latin *Caliburnus* which turned into the name we now recognise – *Excalibur*. Excalibur was said to be able to cut iron as well as it could cut wood, and the sword's sheath would keep the person wearing it safe from death.

The relationship between this warrior and his sword was an important one – one that would continue on into the Afterlife, and one that was clearly demonstrated for the whole community to see at the time of the grand funeral. With his sword 'killed' and his body laid out, the warrior's power and importance was celebrated in death, and by association, his family and friends would benefit too.

Further excavations will hopefully reveal more information about the warrior and his grave site, as well as the wider landscape. The finder has generously donated the objects he's found to the Great North Museum so that they can be studied and appreciated by all.

See also:
Hadrian's Wall Coins
Tamlaght Hoard
Staffordshire Hoard

# Durham Cloth Seals

### *Quality control from the 16th and 17th centuries*

Gary Bankhead is a professional fire-fighter and keen underwater archaeologist. His long hours of training using breathing apparatus in smoke-filled buildings have prepared him perfectly for the long hours using scuba gear in the freezing cold, low-visibility, River Wear, in County Durham.

Gary has scoured the ancient riverbed for years, and amassed an extraordinary collection of over 3,000 items, including toys, coins, pipes and pistols. One set of items in Gary's unique collection tells an intriguing story about trade 400 years ago, and it's so important that he's now begun a post-graduate research project at Durham University Archaeology Department to investigate them further.

These cloth seals are simple lead tags that were attached to pieces of cloth to prove their quality and provenance. The seals may have accidentally fallen off individual pieces of cloth that were being rinsed after dyeing in riverside mills, or they may have been thrown away as litter when they were no longer needed. Gary has found 290 of them so far.

Cloth seals were part of a sophisticated control process similar to a kitemark, or the sales tag on a new piece of clothing today. They allowed purchasers to confirm the origin of the fabric, its quality and size, and whether the correct tax had been paid on it. Some carried the marks of weavers (who spun the wool and weaved it into cloth), fullers (who processed

| |
|---|
| **Date:** 1550–1650, Post Medieval |
| **Where, when and how found:** River Wear, Durham; ongoing; scuba diving |
| **Finder:** Gary Bankhead |
| **Where is it now?** Collection held at Durham University Archaeology Department www.dur.ac.uk/archaeology |
| **Get involved:** Nautical Archaeology Society www.nauticalarchaeologysociety.org British Sub Aqua Club www.bsac.com |

the freshly woven wool cloth to get the grease out and knit the fibres together), dyers (who coloured the cloth) and clothiers (who bought and sold the finished cloth).

Most seals were originally made with two or four lead alloy discs connected by a thin strip that would be fixed together over the edge of the cloth, and then stamped with relevant information about the fabric. Some seals have been stamped with letters indicating that the cloth has been woven narrower than the stipulated width, and others have the legend, 'too shorte'.

Cloth-making and trading textiles have been incredibly important since medieval times. In the 16th and 17th centuries Britain was famed for its wool, and port towns sent thousands of tonnes of unfinished wool and woven cloth across Europe. Continental textiles were also imported – cloth was a global commodity. Despite periods of political and religious instability at home, this was a time of imperial expansion, exploration of the new worlds and complex agreements that privileged trade with our neighbours. Under the reigns of Elizabeth I, James I and Charles I, cloth accounted for around 90% of British exports.

Gary's 290 seals come from cloth traded around Britain and from the continent. Durham had a fulling mill, so some of the cloth might have come to the city to be finished, dyed and sold on. Some of the seals come from Norwich, showing the three-towered castle that was the mark of the city, others are from the Low Countries, like Holland. Once the cloth had arrived in Durham and been sold, buyers would presumably rip off the seals and chuck them away, or they would have come off while the cloth was being processed. Gary's scuba searches clearly confirm the old saying that 'archaeology is rubbish'. Our ancestors' littering is sometimes to the historian's benefit.

See also:
Rosemarkie Trade Weights
Holy Island Mason Hoard

# Holderness Cross

## *Anglo-Saxon treasure in a farmer's sideboard*

This lovely garnet and gold cross was found in 1968 in the mud of a Yorkshire pig farm as Ron Wray was walking through one of his fields. There were no other items, and Ron assumed that the pigs must have rooted it up from the soil, perhaps where it had been dropped by its original owner some time in the past. He took it back home, washed the mud off, and slipped it into the drawer of his kitchen sideboard.

It sat there for three decades, undisturbed. On a whim in March 1998, Ron's daughter suggested they take it down to a local finds identification day at Hull Museum. The Wrays were astounded to discover that their little cross was almost 1,400 years old and made of solid gold and precious stones.

> **Date:** 620–660AD, Anglo-Saxon, Early Medieval
>
> **Where, when and how found:** Holderness, East Riding of Yorkshire; Found around 1968, but only identified in 1998
>
> **Finder:** Ronald Wray
>
> **Where is it now?** Ashmolean Museum, Oxford www.ashmolean.org
>
> **Also visit:** All Hallow's Church, Goodmanham, East Riding of Yorkshire
>
> *Bede's World* historic site, Wearmouth-Jarrow, Northumbria www.bedesworld.co.uk

Before the Treasure Act 1996, a precious metal object had to be buried with the intention of recovery in order to be legally considered 'Treasure Trove'. That meant that if an object had been lost or buried accidentally or was from an ancient grave, it belonged to the finder. Nowadays, however a precious item was initially deposited, it's still potential Treasure and needs to be properly reported.

When the Holderness Cross resurfaced in 1998, it needed to be assessed against the legislation that had been legal at the time it was first found, to determine whether it was or wasn't Treasure Trove. A Coroner's Court deliberated upon the find, decided that it hadn't been buried with intention of recovery, and was therefore not Treasure Trove. They thought it had been deliberately put into the ground as part of a burial.

> ## "We know of just three other pectoral crosses from the same period – these are incredibly rare pieces"

The Holderness Cross is known as a 'pectoral cross', meaning that it would have been worn in the centre of the chest, over the heart, normally hanging from a cord around the neck. These large, square crosses are now only usually worn by priests and other clergymen, but in the early medieval period lay people would have worn them as well.

The Holderness Cross is about 5cm square, making it quite large compared with others from the 600s AD. It's made from 77% gold and 22% silver and was originally inlaid with 95 garnets. The quality of the gold and jewels indicates that this was no ordinary lay person's cross. If it didn't belong to a wealthy priest, it belonged to a high-status, secular leader instead. We know of just three other pectoral crosses from the same period – these are incredibly rare pieces.

One slightly later cross, known as St Cuthbert's Cross, was discovered inside the saint's coffin, and two others (from Ixworth and Trumpington) were buried with women. We therefore don't know if the person who owned the Holderness Cross was a man or a woman, and the bones in the grave have since rotted away, so there is no way of knowing. What is certain, is that they were an elite Anglo-Saxon follower of the new Christian faith.

## The new faith

Missionaries were sent by Pope Gregory in the late 590s, to convert the pagan Anglo-Saxons who had lived in Britain since the collapse of Roman rule in around 410AD.

The first missionary to arrive was St Augustine, in 597AD in Kent. The new faith spread north, and eventually all the major English kingdoms converted. Many old shrines and temple sites were destroyed and churches were built in their place. One significant event near to the findspot at Holderness is mentioned by the medieval historian and monk, Bede.

Bede describes that when King Edwin of the kingdom of Northumbria converted to Christianity around 627AD, the pagan High Priest Coifi rode to a pagan shrine in the village now known as Goodmanham, in the East Riding of Yorkshire. Coifi addressed the gathered crowd, scorning the old religion: 'there is nothing in this religion that we have professed ... the more I sought the truth of it the less I found ... I advise that ... we set fire to those temples and altars which we have consecrated!'

Coifi took a war horse and a spear (both traditionally forbidden to him as a priest) and galloped towards the inner sanctuary of the temple. He lifted his spear, and threw it into the sacred place, desecrating the temple and shaming the gods. The crowd waited to see what would happen to him ... and when they saw that Coifi was unharmed, they followed their priest's lead and burned the rest of the sacred enclosure and the temple to the ground. A church was built on the pagan site, and a later Norman church, surrounded by ancient ditch and earthworks, still stands on the site in Goodmanham today.

We won't ever know enough about the context that the Holderness Cross was buried in to link it more closely to Coifi's dramatic act and the conversion of the north kingdom, but certainly the dating places the cross firmly in these tumultuous decades of religious upheaval, decades that laid the foundations of Christian faith in this country.

See also:
North West Essex Ring
Staffordshire Hoard

# Cautopates Roman Figurine

## *A man who brings darkness to a mysterious Roman cult*

This compelling, cloaked figure was found by a metal detectorist searching cultivated land in November 2007 in the Selby district of North Yorkshire. It is a copper-alloy figurine of Cautopates, a torch-bearer and servant of the Roman god, Mithras, and is at least 1,700 years old.

Cautopates is dressed in Persian (Ancient Iranian) clothes, and on his

**Date:** Around 43–313AD, Roman

**Where, when and how found:** Newton Kyme, North Yorkshire; 2007; metal detecting

**Finder:** Anonymous

**Where is it now?** Privately owned

**Visit:** Remains of Temples of Mithras are exposed at Walbrook, in the City of London, and at Carrawburgh, Northumberland, on Hadrian's Wall

head he's wearing what is known as a Phrygian cap. In his right hand he's holding a flaming torch upside down. His legendary companion, Cautes, is always depicted holding a flaming torch the right way up. Cautes represents sunrise, light and new life. Cautopates represents sunset, darkness and death – the extinguishing of light.

The copper-alloy figurine doesn't stand up on its own, but there's no clear evidence that it was ever attached to a base or a bracket. We don't know quite how this item was used, but it would have been very important to worshippers of Mithras. Theirs was a Roman 'mystery religion' that kept all the details of their faith and rituals secret to outsiders.

Because of this secrecy, and because there are few surviving written accounts of the religion, we

> "A number of the mysterious underground temples survive, including one in London and a number along Hadrian's Wall"

don't entirely understand the way Mithras and the other gods in the cult were worshipped. Based on surviving stone carvings, the central features of Mithras' story appear to be that he was born out of a rock, he made water magically appear from a stone he shot with an arrow, he slayed a sacred bull, and he dined with Sol, the Sun god, in a cave before ascending to Heaven in a chariot.

Cult members built temples underground to replicate Mithras' cave. There were seven grades of initiation which worshippers had to undergo before they were full members. The initiations involved trials of heat, cold and danger, and some surviving temples have an 'ordeal pit' in the centre of the floor. Rituals included feasting and animal sacrifice.

The cult of Mithras was very popular with Roman soldiers in the 1st to 4th centuries AD, and members used a special handshake to identify themselves; women were forbidden from worshipping Mithras.

A number of the mysterious underground temples survive, including one in London and a number along Hadrian's Wall. A particularly good example is in Carrawburgh, in Northumberland.

The cult of Mithras died out in the early 300s, when the new cult of Christianity began to spread across the Roman Empire from around 313AD onwards. The Cautopates figurine was found less than 1km from the site of a Roman fort, but the find site hasn't revealed any further archaeological context that could explain why the figurine was where it was. It's certainly possible that it was used by Roman soldiers, but whether it was lost, deposited or thrown away when the new religion arrived, we will never know.

See also:
Crosby Garrett Helmet (another Roman figure wearing a Phrygian Cap)
Syston Knife Handle
Carlton Knight

# Kellington Dental Block

## *A denture device from the turn of the century*

This odd treasure is a dental swaging block (pronounced *sway-jing*) – a solid copper-alloy form that would have enabled a dentist to make a bespoke set of dentures. It dates from the late 1800s or early 1900s, and was discovered in a field in Kellington, North Yorkshire, by a local metal detectorist.

Nowadays a dentist will use a special rubbery dental putty to take an impression of your gums and teeth, and that impression will then be filled with Plaster of Paris, so that a model of your mouth is achieved. The process is repeated again, making the model more accurate. Dentists then use special dental wax to establish the way your bottom and top teeth bite together, and dental laboratory technicians will position shape-matched

**Date:** Around 1890–1930, Modern

**Where, when and how found:** Kellington, North Yorkshire; 2011; metal detecting

**Finder:** Alan Mort

**Where is it now?** Returned to finder

**Also visit:** Dental Museum, London
www.bda.org/museum

Beamish Living Museum of the North, Co Durham
www.beamish.org.uk

Hunterian Museum, Royal College of Surgeons, London
www.rcseng.ac.uk/museums

Other medical museums listed at
www.medicalmuseums.org

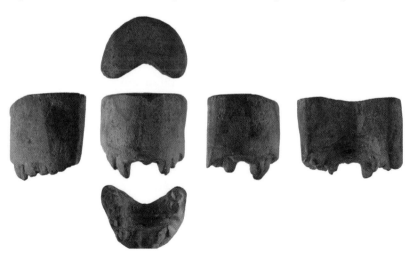

and colour-matched porcelain, acrylic or metal teeth into a shaded pink plastic so that the denture looks as natural as possible and feels comfortable and well-fitting.

Although the process is infinitely more refined now, the basic principle wasn't so different 100-odd years ago. The dentist who used this swaging block would have used softened beeswax to take an initial impression from the patient's mouth, an interim substance to make a mould, and then molten copper-alloy to make this solid block in the shape of the patient's mouth. Once cooled and hardened, the block would have been used as the form over which to make the dentures themselves. The swaging block would be fixed down and a dental plate 'blank' would be forced over the block under high pressure, so it took on the exact shape of the patient's mouth. Metal blanks, celluloid and the hard rubber, Vulcanite, which had been developed by the Goodyear tyre company in the 1840s and first used for dentures in 1851, were all used to make affordable and better-fitting, lightweight dentures.

Full sets of upper dentures now stay in place because of suction created between the well-fitting dental plate and the roof of your mouth. Previously people struggled to keep their false teeth in place, and had to put up with the effects on their speech, eating, and comfort – some false teeth were in fact intended to be removed when you ate, and worn only to look nice in public. Sets of upper and lower teeth were sometimes jointed together and held apart by little springs at the back of the mouth - probably both uncomfortable and comical.

In the 16th, 17th and 18th centuries, it was common to use carved bone, ivory or wood as the tooth inserts, but because the 'teeth' were organic but didn't have enamel, they'd soon begin to rot and cause as many problems as the teeth they'd replaced. An improvement (in some ways) was to use either animal teeth, find a desperately poor person who was willing to sell their living teeth, or acquire fresh teeth from a dead body. There is evidence that graves were robbed for teeth, but more common in the 19th century was to use dead soldiers' teeth sent back from the European battlefields. The teeth

"Porcelain or gold teeth were considered the best, but were expensive and not available to most people"

would be extracted from the mouths of the dead men, packed into barrels and sold in London and other cities to the new and fashionable dentistry professionals. Porcelain or gold teeth were considered the best, but were expensive and not available to most people.

## The rise of the dentist

The Dental Hospital of London was established in 1858, and the National Dental Hospital the following year. Before that there was no official training or control of dentists, and trainees would have learned the trade through apprenticeship. For centuries, tooth extractions had been performed by blacksmiths, apothecaries and barber-surgeons, or roving 'toothdrawers' who plied their trade at fairs and markets. Many people suffered at the hands of ill-trained and negligent 'dentists' – some people even lost their lives.

By the mid-19th century, there was increasing pressure to professionalise, and The Dentists' Act of 1878 required that anyone who wanted to call themselves a dentist needed to complete official training. The impact was that unqualified practitioners simply didn't use the label 'dentist', and carried on regardless. It was only in 1921 that laws were introduced to restrict practising any dentistry to qualified people only.

Perhaps the person who made and used this swaging block was a qualified dentist, perhaps not. It seems surprising that it was lost or dumped, rather than melted down so that the copper-alloy could be reused to make a different model.

The block is a model of an upper set of teeth from an adult who was missing the right canine, and left lateral and central incisors. It has been dated to between 1890 and 1930, which means that the patient might have benefitted from laughing gas, ether or cocaine for pain relief, and cutting-edge treatment with a pedal drill (much quicker and less painful than hand-drilling). Improved techniques for swaging dental plates and slightly more comfortable materials were available. Although early dentures were hard to clean and often made your mouth sore, they were much more affordable than everything that had come before. Middle-class people could afford well-fitting and functional false teeth for the first time in history.

See also:
Beddingham Nose
Daventry Visard Mask
Pegsdon Mirror

# THE BIRTH OF ENGLAND

In the mid-9th century, there were four main kingdoms in Britain – Northumbria, East Anglia, Mercia and the West Saxon kingdom, Wessex. Viking leaders first conquered the East Anglians, then forced them to support Viking attacks on York (866AD) and southern Northumbria (867AD). The warrior Hálfdan conquered the Kingdom of Mercia in 874AD, and some of Wessex in 878AD, supposedly forcing King Alfred – later Alfred the Great – to hide in a Somerset marsh to save his own life.

Rural Anglian populations in the conquered lands weren't necessarily brutalised or killed, although the Viking immigrants may well have reallocated land and resources to themselves and their favourites, forcing people to relocate and pay tribute and tax.

Modern English words that have a Scandinavian origin are quite telling – many are everyday words – egg, sister, husband, skin, sky, knife and cake, for example. It indicates that local people adopted Viking ways and speech into their everyday lives, and that it wasn't just the language of a high-class elite, or the language only used to govern or police the country. The Vikings weren't invaders, but colonists.

The north and west areas under Viking control later became known as the Danelaw, and the frontier between Angles and Saxons (who had been in Britain since the 400s AD) and the new Viking colonies ran roughly from London to Chester, following a series of rivers and Roman roads. Parts of the modern A5 still follow the divide.

The Viking influence over these areas can be traced in place names (for example, a place name ending in –by means settlement, e.g. Derby, -thorpe means secondary settlement, e.g. Scunthorpe, –wick, means bay, e.g. Berwick), as well as in the genetic makeup of the modern population, where a significant proportion of men from families that haven't recently moved to the area share DNA with men in Norway and Denmark, the so-called 'Viking genes'.

The extent of Viking control was huge, and many Anglo-Saxon rulers capitulated to the powerful Viking leaders, paying tribute taxes and providing support during military offensives. But the battered Kingdom of Wessex would not be beaten. Conducting a war of resistance for more than twenty years, King Alfred ultimately defended his lands against the Viking colonists. After Alfred's death in 899AD, his son Edward the Elder conquered territory from the Scandinavian settlers, all the while building on a grand new idea – a single Kingdom of the English, united under one English king. This had never existed before.

Edward's son Athelstan came to power in 925AD and began a concerted drive for power and territory. He forced submission from local rulers in parts of Cornwall, Wales and Scotland in quick succession, and took control of the Kingdom of Northumbria in 927AD. Occupying York, he was declared 'King of All Britain'.

Athelstan defeated a coalition army of Vikings, Welsh and Scots at the Battle of Brunaburh in 937AD, a devastating conflict which took the lives of many thousands on both sides, and was known as 'The Great Battle'. Athelstan's victory further strengthened his position as the king of a united land. But when Athelstan died in 939AD aged around 45, the men of York immediately declared the Viking leader Olaf Guthfrithsson as their king. Athelstan's half-brother Edmund, who became King Edmund I (reigned 939–946AD), and his younger brother, the succeeding king, Eadred (reigned 946–955AD), were again forced into battle to try and regain control of the north.

Eric Bloodaxe, the last Viking King of Northumbria, was expelled from the region in 954AD, and the people of Northumbria declared their loyalty to King Eadred. Although the Vikings continued to thrive in parts of what are now Scotland, Cumbria, Ireland, North Wales and the Isle of Man, the Kingdom of England was definitively united once again.

# Vale of York Viking Hoard

## *The Viking world in one vessel*

Father and son, David and Andrew Whelan, had been metal detecting for years when they made the discovery of a lifetime. They were searching a field that had never revealed anything more interesting than a Victorian button before, but it had recently been ploughed and the men decided it was worth a search. After ten minutes, David got a signal. As he dug down, he unearthed fragments of lead, then a round thing tumbled out of the loosened soil. About 12cm in diameter, covered in thick mud, David thought he'd found an old bit of toilet ballcock.

**Date:** Around 928AD, Viking

**Where, when and how found:** Vale of York near Harrogate, North Yorkshire; 2007; Metal detecting

**Finders:** David and Andrew Whelan

**Official valuation:** £1,082,800

**Where is it now?** Acquired by British Museum and York Museums Trust
www.britishmuseum.org
www.yorkmuseumtrust.org.uk

**Visit:** Jorvik Viking Centre, York; Danelaw Living History Centre, Murton Park, Yorkshire
www.jorvik-viking-centre.co.uk
www.murtonpark.co.uk

When he put his glasses on, however, he immediately realised that this 'ballcock' was engraved all over, and that the loose items on top of it were coins. David recognised some of the coins – they were from rulers more than one thousand years ago, including a distinctive silver penny from King Edward the Elder, who reigned from 899–924AD. Judging by its weight, it was clearly full of metal. David and Andrew found more fragments of sheet lead and some bigger chunks of silver in the surrounding soil, then they carefully noted the findspot and refilled the hole. Importantly, and despite the obvious appeal, they didn't empty the cup. They knew they'd found something very special, and they knew that archaeologists would be able to unpack the cup forensically so that all the information it held could be recorded and analysed. They promptly notified the British Museum of their discovery and reported it to the local coroner –they had found Treasure.

## Forensic cup work

The cup was brought to the British Museum, X-rayed and then carefully excavated in 1cm layers in a process that took a whole week.

Altogether, it was revealed that the hoard comprised a gold arm ring, around 65 pieces of silver including arm rings, ingots and jewellery fragments, 617 silver coins, the fragments of lead that had probably once been a makeshift cover on the top of the cup, and the cup itself – exquisitely decorated silver with a thin covering of bright gold.

The coins and jewellery came from places spanning the Viking world, from Ireland to the Middle East, and the coins date the hoard to around 928AD. As a whole, the Vale of York Hoard tells of the incredible rise and fall of Viking power in England.

## Raiders, traders and settlers

The popular image of the Vikings is of shaggy-haired, axe-wielding barbarians arriving on British shores for a bit of beserker frenzy, slave-taking and the plunder of undefended monasteries, before sailing back east with their loot.

Although in the early period, around the 790s and 800s AD, this was mostly accurate, by the 860s and 870s AD the Vikings had changed their focus from hit-and-run raiding, to permanent settlement and military

> "By the 900s AD, the Anglo-Saxon kings were seeking to unite England under one king, something which had never been done before"

control. Still feared and violent, they nonetheless adopted local customs and the local religion, Christianity, and maintained trading links with the equally violent Anglo-Saxon kings in the south, the Irish Sea Vikings in the north-west of Britain and in Ireland, as well as links across continental Europe and to the Middle East.

By the 900s AD, the Anglo-Saxon kings were seeking to unite England under one king, something which had never been done before. King Athelstan, the grandson of Alfred the Great, began a great and brutal campaign to oust the Vikings, unite the smaller kingdoms and seize ultimate control of all England.

## Burying the hoard

This dynamic political and military landscape is the backdrop to the moment when someone took their valuables into a field and buried them. That person never came back for them, and we can only speculate on the reasons why.

Unlike some other hoards in this book, it's very unlikely that the Vale of York treasure was meant to stay in the ground – there's no evidence of Viking traditions for making ritual deposits or offerings of precious metals. Much more likely is that it was hidden for safekeeping and its hiding place was lost or forgotten, or the person planning to retrieve it fled the area, or was killed.

The area around the findspot was excavated, and the surrounding field was surveyed, but there's no evidence of further activity or buildings that could help explain why the burial spot was chosen.

The remaining pieces of the unsolvable puzzle come from the contents of the hoard itself.

## The cup

At 9.2cm high and weighing 371g, the cup is engraved solid silver, thinly coated with gold inside and out, a process known as 'gilding'. It was most likely the spoil of a raiding party. It dates to the mid-800s AD, which means that the cup was almost 100 years old when it was buried. It may have been used to hold consecrated bread during a mass – if so, it would originally have had a lid. A cup very similar to the Vale of York cup was found in a Viking hoard at Halton Moor in Lancashire in 1815. That hoard was dated to the 1020s, so that means the Halton Moor cup was almost two hundred years old when it was buried. Clearly these were treasured artefacts, rather than just raided for their precious metal.

The decoration includes six 'roundel' shapes, with a single animal inside each – a lion, a big cat, a deer, a stag, a form of antelope and a horse or wild ass. All the animals are running, but the predators are leaping forwards and the prey species are fleeing, heads turned back. The animal roundels bear a striking resemblance to metalwork and textiles from Persia. Between the roundels are leaf designs typical of Frankish Empire craftsmen, from an area that's now mainly in France and west Germany. The cup represents the transfer of ideas and artefacts from the Near East artists to Frankish metalworkers to Viking settlers in what's now Yorkshire – a global network of influence and contact.

## The coins and silver

The silver pieces in the hoard are ingots, fragments of jewellery used as currency ('hack-silver'), and arm- and neck-rings. One neck-ring fragment is probably from north Russia, where men traditionally made rings to a specific weight from melted-down coins and gave them to their wives. Another arm ring is not more than a crudely curved rod, again made to deliberate weight. These arm rings are known as 'bullion-rings', and they're thought to have been used as tokens of loyalty from leaders to their subjects, cast from a specific weight of silver that could then be used for exchange.

> "Most of the 617 coins in the hoard are Anglo-Saxon silver pennies struck in England, but there were also four Frankish *deniers* and fifteen Islamic *dirhams*"

Most of the 617 coins in the hoard are Anglo-Saxon silver pennies struck in England, but there were also four Frankish *deniers* and fifteen Islamic *dirhams* from both the Middle East and Afghanistan.

The Anglo-Saxon coins are from the reigns of Alfred the Great (r. 871–899), his son Edward the Elder (r. 899–924) and Edward's son Athelstan (r. 924–939).

The hoard also contains several Anglo-Viking coins. Some of these show a Viking sword as the main design. They were issued in the name of St Peter, the patron saint of York, but include the hammer of the Viking god Thor as the final 'T' in Petri ('Peter'). This is clear evidence for the hybrid culture of British Vikings – combining new and old religious symbols.

One single coin in the hoard declares Athelstan as 'King of All Britain' (**REX TOTIUS BRITANNIAE**), pictured, and was struck in late 927 or 928AD. The fact that there is only one coin of this type and age, and that it isn't worn, leads experts to believe that the hoard was buried when this coin was very new. The fact that this timing links with Athelstan's conquest of Northumbria is notable. Anglo-Saxon sources imply that Athelstan ruled peacefully in the years immediately following his conquest, but history books are never neutral. It's quite possible that this incredibly precious hoard is the sum of a Viking warrior's wealth buried in a time of continued discord and fear.

See also:
Llanbedrgoch Viking Treasure
West Yorkshire Ring Hoard
Saltfleetby Spindle Whorl

# Hadrian's Wall Coins

## *A dropped purse that redefines Roman Britain*

These eight bronze Roman coins, discovered by metal detectorist Barry Seger in 2007, have changed our understanding of Roman activity in the north of Britain, giving us more information about the twilight years of the Roman occupation of Britain.

Roman Britain began to change noticeably in the later 300s AD: The archaeological record shows towns declining, activity dispersing into the countryside, and no new villas being built. There was increased military pressure as Angles and Saxons from the continent, Picts from Scotland, and Scotti and Irish from Ireland began raiding in greater numbers. These peoples wanted precious goods, livestock and land, and Britannia's coastal communities had plenty of everything.

**Date:** 406–408AD, Roman

**Where, when and how found:** Great Whittington, Northumberland; 2007; metal detecting

**Finder:** Barry Seger

**Where is it now?** Returned to finder

**Visit:** Hadrian's Wall, a UNESCO World Heritage Site
www.visithadrianswall.co.uk

Birdoswald Fort, managed by English Heritage
www.english-heritage.org.uk

The slow but inevitable decline of the wider Roman Empire continued – economically, it was teetering – tax collection systems were failing, and food supplies in the large cities were insecure. The eastern and western empires split in the 390s, and in 405AD, 'Barbarian' attacks on the north of Italy forced troops to be withdrawn from the far provinces, including Britannia, and mobilised to defend the core territories and the Eternal City itself, Rome.

It's often said that the official end of Roman Britain was when the Romanised Britons petitioned Rome for assistance against their attackers in 409-410AD, but instead of help and reinforcement troops, Emperor Honorious sent letters to the cities of Britain saying no back-up would be coming, and urged them to defend themselves. These letters are known as the *Rescript of Honorious*, although recent controversial scholarship has suggested that they were never sent to Britannia, a distant and relatively unimportant province, and are more likely to have been sent to *Brettia*, in southern Italy. The scribe recording the events may have made a simple error in his writing.

It's quite possible that the influence of Rome at Hadrian's Wall came to an end before 409AD – particularly if soldiers were no longer being paid or drilled by their commanders. Some of them may well have switched to working for local communities as hired security or mercenaries, extorted protection money from other locals, or simply sought work labouring and trading alongside the natives.

## The coins

This background makes Barry's find intriguing. Of the eight coins he discovered, the latest one is a type only issued between 406-408AD. It was struck in one of the eastern mints of the Roman Empire, possibly Constantinople, Cyzicus, Antioch or Alexandria, cities which are in modern-day Turkey and Egypt. Although these coins are common finds in the east Mediterranean, only one other has ever been discovered in Britain. The final, and most startling, detail is that the coins were found north of Hadrian's Wall.

The coins were found close together, and not in conjunction with any pottery. There are only eight of them, so they're likely to have been a lost coin purse made from cloth or leather that has long-since rotted away, rather than a hoard or intentional deposit.

The coins don't appear to be worn enough to have travelled such a long distance through normal monetary exchanges, so they probably arrived with a soldier or a trader who had travelled from the Mediterranean to the edge of the crumbling Roman Empire. This suggests that military and trade networks were continuing to function until much later than previously thought and it clearly shows that the area around Hadrian's Wall hadn't been abandoned. At least as late as 406AD, Northumberland had a distinct Roman presence – not just local Roman soldiers, but incomers travelling from the Mediterranean who were willing to go north of the Wall.

"When Romans had greater control over the area, local people may have been forced to accept Roman Coinage, but by 406AD, the balance of power shifted"

But as the Empire was failing, local people might not have accepted these coins as 'legal' tender anymore. Made from bronze, rather than precious metal, the coins had negligible value in themselves. When Romans had greater control over the area, local people may have been forced to accept Roman coinage, but by 406AD, the balance of power had shifted. These exotic coins may well have been worthless – a small consolation to the person who dropped his or her purse 1,600 years ago.

See also:
Crosby Garrett Helmet
Staffordshire Moorlands Ilam Pan
Hallaton Treasure

# County Durham River Assemblage

## Over 5,000 artefacts at a Roman river crossing

Bob Middlemass and Rolfe Mitchinson have spent the last thirty years diving along a river that seems to be full of archaeological finds. They've recovered over 5,000 artefacts, and believe there are still more to discover. Each find is carefully reported, and Bob and Rolfe's commitment is helping us build a rich picture of life and belief in ancient County Durham.

The majority of the finds date from Roman Britain, from around 90AD to 400AD, and are likely to have been offerings or sacrifices. The items shown here are an 8cm-high copper-alloy cupid figurine, popular along the northern frontier, and an elaborate gold and glass finger ring. Brooches and coins are also present, as well as more everyday items like fragments of Roman pottery, which may have been lost or rubbish tossed in the river.

Rivers have always been significant to people – as a source of fresh water and food, as a means to travel easily, as well as a way to defend and control your borders. But rivers are also rich with symbolic and spiritual power, and have been associated with the supernatural across cultures and throughout history.

**Date/period:** 90–400AD, Roman

**Where, when and how found:** River Tees, County Durham; 1985–present; underwater visual searching and metal detecting

**Finders:** Bob Middlemass and Rolfe Mitchinson

**Where are they now?** Currently being catalogued as a potential Treasure case. It is hoped that they will be acquired by a museum in the North East

**Visit:** Piercebridge Roman Bridge and Roman Fort sites, Piercebridge, near Darlington, County Durham www.english-heritage.org.uk

Other Piercebridge finds at Bowes Museum, Barnard Castle www.thebowesmuseum.org.uk

**Get involved:** The Nautical Archaeology Society holds talks, events and practical skills training for underwater and foreshore archaeology www.nauticalarchaeologysociety.org

## Supernatural rivers

Native British Iron Age people often worshipped at watery places, making offerings at lakes, bogs and rivers. When the Romans invaded Britain in

43AD, they adopted many of the local customs, and incorporated local deities into the Roman pantheon (see, for example, the link between the goddesses Minerva and Senuna in the Ashwell Hoard, p50). Worship at native shrines often continued, although practices adapted over time. Water was important in Roman belief, too – for its healing properties, in connection with fertility, and in the link between life and death.

The divide between the living human world and the underworld perhaps seemed more blurred in rivers – they might have been thought of as gateways, or portals, to the realm of the gods. Whether it was the importance of water for life, something about the perpetual motion of fresh running water, or something about the magical semi-transparency of deep water that caught their attention, we can't be sure. What's certain is that offerings were made at river sites and particularly at river crossings.

## Roman Piercebridge

The areas in which Bob and Rolfe dive are around the site of a series of ancient bridges that crossed the River Tees along the route of the *Via Principalis,* also known as Dere Street, a major Roman Road linking York with Corbridge, near Hadrian's Wall.

The modern village of Piercebridge is mostly inside the site of an original Roman fort on Dere Street, and you can still see some of the earthworks hidden under the village green. There would also have been an extended *vicus* (civilian settlement) by the fort, and there's evidence of a villa, bath

houses and other grand buildings in the local area. Burials outside the fort and walls are also apparent.

Research suggests that there was a pre-Roman bridge over the river that was then rebuilt as the Romans arrived in the area around 70AD, pushing northwards (it took just under thirty years for the Romans to reach this far north, following the invasion into southern Britain in 43AD). The river was wider in Roman times, and the extended stone foundations of a later Roman bridge are now around 90m south of the modern river course, sitting stranded in a field.

It's possible that some of the artefacts Bob and Rolfe have recovered were accidental losses that fell from people's hands when they were crossing the river. But the quantity and quality of the deposits means that these are more than just the outcome of Roman clumsiness. Soldiers may have made offerings before entering the town, or before beginning a journey to another site, or north, to the frontier. Permanent residents may also have made regular offerings to the gods at the river.

Research by *Time Team* in 2010 suggested that there may have been a small island in the middle of the river. It's possible that shrines were built on the island, and people placed their offerings there. Over time, the island eroded away, leaving the offerings sitting at the bottom of the river. It's also possible that people were throwing offerings directly into the water.

The Romans didn't distinguish between the sacred and the secular in the way most of us do now – all aspects of life would have been infused with prayers, and people would have carried talismans and charms to stay safe,

> **"** It's possible that some of the artefacts Bob and Rolfe have recovered were accidental losses that fell from people's hands when they were crossing the river **"**

be well and bring fortune. As well as ceremonies in temples, there would also have been roadside shrines and household shrines, as well as chance opportunities for offerings at rivers and other natural features like groves of trees.

Rivers and springs are still considered sacred around the world – from the River Ganges in India, to the Holy Well at Holywell, in Flintshire, North Wales. Every time we throw a penny into a fountain or river, we echo an ancient practice linking life, belief and water. Thanks to hours of careful searching by Bob and Rolfe, we have more than 5,000 compelling artefacts that give us an insight into the everyday offerings from Roman Piercebridge.

**See also:**
Billingford Amulet
Ashwell Hoard and the Goddess Senuna
Canterbury Pilgrim Badges
Langstone Tankard

# Holy Island Mason Hoard

## *Seventeen secret coins in a little brown jug*

Richard Mason, a Northumberland builder, has the distinct honour of having his hoard discovery named after him. In 2003, while he was underpinning the extension on a modern house on Lindisfarne, also known as Holy Island, off the coast of Northumberland, he stumbled across a small brown jug nestled alongside a 1960s drainage pipe. Keen to complete the job, Richard popped the jug in his van and continued with his work. It then went into his garage and was forgotten about for years.

**Date:** In, or soon after 1562, Post Medieval

**Where, when and how found:** Lindisfarne, Northumberland; 2003; discovered during building work

**Finder:** Richard Mason

**Where is it now?** Stored at British Museum, London, until Treasure process completed. 1962 hoard at Great North Museum, Newcastle upon Tyne, which hopes to acquire the new discovery
www.twmuseums.org.uk

It was only in 2011, when he was having a clear out, that Richard actually examined the jug and discovered seventeen gold and silver coins inside. He alerted the authorities and the 'Mason Hoard' is now mid-way through assessment and inquest to determine whether it is legally classed as Treasure.

## The coins

The vessel the coins were in is a common type known as a 'Bartmann Jug' or 'Bellarmine Jug'. It dates to the mid-1500s, and was made in Germany. 'Bartmann' means 'bearded man' in German, and some jugs of this type have the decoration of a bearded man's face fixed to the outside surface. These functional stoneware vessels have been found right across Europe, and were originally for food and drink – they were like the Tupperware of the 16th and 17th centuries.

Inside the jug, there were ten gold and seven silver coins. The earliest is from the late 1420s or early 1430s, minted by Henry VI (r. 1422–60), and the latest is a silver penny minted in 1562 by Elizabeth I (r. 1551–1603). The majority of the coins are more than 90% pure gold or silver. The coins

minted by Henry VIII and Edward VI are from a period known as the 'Great Debasement', when less precious metal was put into gold and silver coinage – they're around 80% pure.

The hoard contains six foreign coins, from France, Saxony (Germany), the Netherlands and the Papal States. In the early 1560s, Elizabeth I tried to ban the use of foreign coinage, but it's likely that gold coins continued to be widely accepted across the country, regardless of where and when they were issued. Nonetheless, it makes the presence of the six foreign coins an interesting detail in this hoard.

The value of the coins would have been around £6 in the 1560s, a significant sum in a time when a working man would earn around £10 per year, and £40 would fund a gentleman's lifestyle. A couple of the half-Sovereigns weigh more than 6g, but the really impressive – and unusual – coin is the silver *Thaler* (pronounced 'tal-er'), weighing 28.48g (a modern £2 coin weighs 12g). Thalers were used for more than 400 years, and are the predecessors of 'Dollars' – still the name of more than twenty different currencies around the world.

## The 1962 hoard

Incredibly, in 1962, when another builder, Alan Short, was putting the pipe at the Lindisfarne house *in*, he had found another, almost identical jug containing fifty silver sixpences and groats (four-pences). It must have been inches away from the Mason Hoard jug, but Alan didn't see the other one in the soil. The latest of the coins in Alan's jug was from Elizabeth I, dated to 1562 – the same as the Mason Hoard coin – so it's likely that the two jugs were buried around the same time as one another.

Although the 1962 hoard has a different mix of coins, it seems like it was buried for the same reason – safekeeping. We can't be sure why the jugs were never retrieved, but the likelihood is that these coins were buried as household or business savings. Perhaps the house was owned by a merchant, and the Mason Hoard was for international and high-value exchanges, where the foreign coins would be accepted, and the 1962 hoard was for local, day-to-day trading.

The 1560s were a time of great trade and Imperial expansion, but also a time of political and religious instability, particularly between England and Scotland, the Protestants and the Catholics. Raiding and fighting would almost certainly have affected people on Lindisfarne island, and it's entirely understandable that in times of risk, the safest place for your cash was under the floorboards, in a hole in the garden, or buried in a field somewhere nearby.

We don't know what the findspot land was used for in the 1560s – further research may begin to paint a richer picture of what happened to the people who buried their little brown jugs and never came back for them.

**See also:**
*Girona* Wreck Cameo
Raglan Ring
Daventry Visard Mask

# HOW DO TREASURES GET BURIED?

People sometimes say that archaeology is rubbish – and often they're right. Archaeological finds are often in 'midden' layers (old rubbish heaps) or cesspits, or have been thrown away randomly because they're no longer of use – broken pottery, old animal bone, belts and buckles, and possibly also items like the **Chinese Coin Hoard** (p209) and the **Kellington Dental Block** (p229).

Other items aren't intentionally thrown away, but lost accidentally. Some treasures might have been keenly missed, like the **Mourning Ring** from Shropshire (p137), while other items, like the **Durham Cloth Seals** (p222), were entirely ignored.

The third group of finds are of items that were intentionally deposited. Some were buried with the intention of retrieving them at a later date, like the **Nether Stowey Hoard** (p100) and the **Holy Island Mason Hoard** (p246). In other rare, and more recent cases, like the **Hackney WWII Hoard** (p68), we can piece together the specific story behind the treasure.

A famous example of 'safekeeping' gone wrong is from Samuel Pepys, the diary-writer of the 1600s. In 1667, fearful that the Dutch were going to attack London, Pepys sent his father and wife Elizabeth to bury all their gold coins in the garden. When the danger of war had passed, Pepys returned to collect the coins but couldn't locate the spot. When he finally did, he found himself almost thirty coins short. He records in his diary how furious he is about the whole episode.

Other intentional deposits are deliberate and permanent – making offerings with absolutely no intention of retrieving them. Either in a burial, or a ritual deposit that we can often only guess at, these items were sacrifices to the gods, ceremonially discarded because of a belief system, or 'killed' at the end of their owners' lives. The **Langstone Tankard** (p126), the **Frome Hoard** (p108), the **Canterbury Pilgrim Badges** (p86), **Tamlaght Hoard** (p266) and the **Ringlemere Cup** (p54) are great examples of intentional deposits.

# HOW ARTEFACTS ARE DATED, ANALYSED & CONSERVED

There are a number of ways that finds can be dated. When an artefact is first examined, its shape and style, the method of manufacture, and any decorations can be used to put it into a well-known dating pattern for that type of object. The **Marcus Aurelius Bust** (p157) was confirmed as genuine partly because his glass eyes had been coloured by a distinctly Roman method.

Although there will always be finds that don't exactly fit the expected design or 'typology' (the **Kirkcaldy Heart Brooch** on p256 is a good example), the general trend of fashions and styles holds true. Sometimes a find is so significant that it demands that the typologies are reassessed, like in the case of the **Staffordshire Hoard** (p212).

Finds can sometimes be linked, albeit tentatively, to a historically documented person (like the **Hawking Vervel**, p18 or the **Baldehildis Seal**, p21), which can give a good date. Other times a find can be linked with historical details that have been documented elsewhere – for example, by dating the uniform styles of the **Fort George Toy Soldiers** (p278), or the stamps on the **Durham Cloth Seals** (p222).

Coins can help date other artefacts very closely – if a piece of jewellery is found with a coin, the date on the coin can help pin down the date of the jewellery. Pottery can also help date structures and artefacts based on typologies.

One of the most familiar tools in the archaeologist's arsenal is Radiocarbon Dating. Carbon naturally occurs in various forms, including the isotope (a chemical form of the element) called Carbon-14 ($^{14}$C). Every living organism absorbs carbon from its food and the atmosphere, and when it dies, it stops absorbing new carbon. The $^{14}$C in the cells also starts to break down chemically – the longer ago something died, the more $^{14}$C is broken down.

By mapping the pattern of the $^{14}$C isotope in any sample, a 'fingerprint' can be determined that will show how old the organic materials are. Radiocarbon Dating can tell us when, for example, an oak tree was cut down in order to produce the **Carpow Logboat** (p285), or when the pigs at Hallaton (p159) were killed.

New techniques using isotopes of other chemical elements are revealing some very interesting results. Along with carbon, we also absorb strontium, oxygen, nitrogen and sulphur isotopes from our food, and they're laid down in our body tissues. Different geographical areas have different amounts of each form of the elements, and patterns in the elements can show what people ate, as well as where they grew up. Human remains can be used to build a much more detailed picture of who the person was, when they breathed their last, and how they're linked to the treasures people discover. The context is an essential part of the 'story' of every find – without knowing exactly where a find came from, and how it went into the ground, we will never know very much about it.

Finds are conserved so that they don't get damaged or destroyed by environmental factors. They're often stored in controlled environments, and protected by sterile and non-reactive paper, foam or plastic. Reconstructing or repairing ancient finds is a balancing act between representing what was really found in the ground, with the wider responsibility to show the find at its best. Some people felt that the **Crosby Garrett Helmet** (p194) was *over* reconstructed and made to look almost new. Other finds, like the **Frome Hoard** and its 52,503 coins may never all be cleaned (p108); the **Tamlaght Hoard** cup pieces were protected by the outer bowl but there simply isn't enough of the cup left for it to be restored or displayed (p266).

Some of the most challenging items to conserve are those made from organic materials – like the **Carpow Bronze Age Logboat** and the **Langstone Tankard** (p126). Quick thinking from curators saved the tankard from almost-certain damage before it was conserved. The experts know that the cutting-edge techniques we have now may be considered far from ideal in the future, as our technology and understanding improves. The goal now is to always opt for conservation techniques that are reversible and to use techniques that are non-destructive to date and analyse finds, if at all possible. Once a treasure has been found, it's the conservators' job to ensure that it's preserved for future generations to enjoy.

# West Yorkshire Ring Hoard

## Anglo-Saxon hidden treasure

Frank Andrusyk was metal detecting a field in west Yorkshire when he got a pretty ordinary sounding signal. He thought his machine had picked up a piece of lead, but when he dug up the earth he was surprised to see a bright, shining golden chunk – part of an ingot of gold.

He returned the next day and picked up another signal a foot away from the first – it was a gold finger ring. Scattered across the immediate area were two more rings and a fragment of a brooch.

> **Date:** 900–1000AD, Medieval
>
> **Where, when and how found:** West Yorkshire; 2008 & 2009; metal detecting
>
> **Finder:** Frank Andrusyk
>
> **Official valuation:** £171,310
>
> **Where is it now?** Leeds City Museum
> www.leeds.gov.uk/
> museumsandgalleries/
>
> **Also visit:** Jorvik Viking Centre, York
> www.jorvik-viking-centre.co.uk

Frank recorded the findspots and informed his local Finds Liaison Officer, Amy Downes. She organised a survey of the field to record any crucial clues about why the rings might have been buried or lost in that particular field. There weren't any conclusive results, but Frank still felt that there might be more secrets in that field. He wasn't wrong.

Six months later, Frank found a fourth ring, 30g of almost pure gold, and a small lead spindle whorl, a weight used for spinning thread.

## A mystery

The find site has not revealed any evidence of why the rings might have been deposited where they were. Archaeologists don't think that they were part of a burial, so the most likely explanation is that they were either buried for safekeeping during a time of conflict, or stashed as the proceeds of a robbery, and no one ever returned to retrieve them.

The dating of the items raises another interesting mystery – the brooch fragment is of a style seen in the 600s AD, like in the Staffordshire Hoard (p212) or Holderness Cross (p224). The finger rings seem to date from

between 800 and 1000AD, but all the pieces were buried together at the same time. The brooch fragment would have been an antique when it went into the ground.

The ring set with a central garnet is decorated with filigree gold wire and 'granulation', raised dots of gold in the pattern. It's similar to another ring discovered in North Yorkshire, another in Hertfordshire, and one in the Inner Hebrides. The decoration style is typically Anglo-Saxon, which gives us insight into the activity in the area at this time.

Unlike the valuables in the Vale of York Hoard, which are clearly Viking possessions, the west Yorkshire rings are not. The current theory is that these rings were the stashed proceeds of a robbery, rather than a family's heirlooms buried for safekeeping. We won't ever know what happened to the people who buried them, or whether they were Vikings or Anglo-Saxons. They could have been innocents swept up in the panic and chaos of war, or common criminals who fled, were apprehended or killed. Perhaps they did return and simply couldn't find the hiding spot again.

It's a compelling window into Yorkshire's tumultuous history. Leeds City Museum worked hard to raise the funds to acquire the Ring Hoard, and these treasures will now rightly stay in the region.

See also:
Vale of York Hoard
Saltfleetby Spindle Whorl
Holderness Cross

1 - ROSEMARKIE TRADE WEIGHTS
2 - FORT GEORGE TOY SOLDIERS
3 - INVERNESS SHOULDER-BELT
    PLATE
4 - CARPOW BRONZE AGE
    LOGBOAT
5 - BLAIR DRUMMOND HOARD
6 - KIRKCALDY HEART BROOCH
7 - GIRONA WRECK CAMEO
8 - NEWTON STEWART DOG LEAD
9 - HORNS AND CROTAL
    MUSICAL INSTRUMENTS
10 - CLONMORE SHRINE
11 - TAMLAGHT HOARD

**NORTHERN IRELAND** is a region where you're never much more than 30 minutes' drive from the sea coast. That coastline can be unforgiving; plenty of ships and men have met their end in the treacherous waters. The incredible tale of the *Girona* **Wreck Cameo (p281)** is one tiny piece of the story of the Spanish Armada.

The land can be hard too. The Sperrin Mountains, the Antrim Hills and the Mountains of Mourne have always been wild territories, but have offered places of protection and defence. The Mournes give you views of Strangford Lough to the north-east and across the Irish Sea to the Isle of Man.

The historic cities of Belfast, Derry-Londonderry and Armagh are rich with modern and ancient political and religious history that has impacted the whole country and beyond. St Patrick and the early Church in Armagh is beautifully represented by the **Clonmore Shrine (p258)**.

And then there is the mix of land and water, the half-wet, half-dry edges that the prehistoric peoples of Ireland appear to have worshipped at, just like the people around the rest of the British Isles. The watery inland could be as important as the magnificent coastline, and Northern Ireland has both. The **Horns and Crotal Musical Instruments (p275)** are fascinatingly odd finds from bogs.

**SCOTLAND** boasts equally varied landscape, from the barren, snow-scalded Cairngorm mountains high above the tree line, to the gentle, fertile border country that's protected from the worst excesses of the weather.

The borders have long been a target for visitors and invaders witnessing wave after wave of rebellion, territorial battles, raids and disputes. The Highlands appear to be a natural, pristine landscape, but they're strongly shaped by humans. Deforestation began in prehistory, and our ancestors' skilled use of timber is revealed in exquisite glory with the **Carpow Logboat (p285)**.

Aristocratic pursuits like hunting transformed the countryside. On many large Scottish estates, land management is still focused on developing the best 'wilderness' to maintain prestige sports. Finds like the **Newton Stewart Dog Lead (p261)** give us a tiny hint of the grandeur and importance these activities have had for centuries.

Determinedly independent, Scottish communities often focused their economic, social and political attentions out across the sea. From the very earliest times, people in Scotland weren't inward-looking. The **Blair Drummond Torc Hoard (p272)** is evidence that they were part of a powerful and far-reaching network. Items like the **Rosemarkie Trade Weights (p264)** demonstrate the smart, entrepreneurial approaches to trade and commerce in busy port areas.

Scotland and Northern Ireland have different rules regarding Treasure. In Northern Ireland, metal detecting for archaeological artefacts is illegal unless professionally licensed. In Scotland and Northern Ireland, all archaeological finds need to be reported to the appropriate authorities. Local museum staff will take you through the appropriate steps of how to report a find.

# Kirkcaldy Heart Brooch

## *A talisman to protect from violent death*

Karl Driske was metal detecting in Kirkcaldy when he struck a series of signals that revealed a range of artefacts. Amongst the medieval coins, musket balls and buttons, there were two rings and this striking silver heart-shaped brooch.

**Date:** Around 1350, Medieval

**Where, when and how found:** Kirkcaldy, Fife; 2012; metal detecting

**Finder:** Karl Driske

**Where is it now?** Fife Museum www.fifedirect.org/museums

**Also visit:** National Museum of Scotland, Edinburgh www.nms.ac.uk

The brooch has some intriguing features: Firstly, the front is plain, and the back is inscribed. The inscription has been carefully engraved in a style known as 'Lombardic lettering' and reads: '**+ ihesus nazaren**', a short form for the popular inscription '**IHESUS NAZARENUS REX IUDEORUM**', meaning 'Jesus of Nazareth, King of the Jews'.

It was a common phrase to have engraved on to jewellery throughout Europe in the 1300s, even though many people couldn't read. Often, even the person engraving the badge wouldn't be able to read, they'd simply copy the shapes of the letters. What was important was that you knew the phrase was on the badge, not whether you could read it.

Many medieval people thought that wearing Jesus' name would act as a talisman, hopefully protecting you against illness, disease and accidents. It's likely that someone in 14th-century Fife bought this brooch for a loved one to wear.

It's estimated that at least one in three children didn't survive childhood, and if they did, average life expectancy was between forty and fifty years old. Common illnesses like measles, infected water and food, virulent pandemics like the plague, household and occupational accidents, and for women, childbirth, all massively increased the risk of dying young and dying badly. Belief in the supernatural infused everyday life, and miracles, marvels and evil spirits were a part of the natural order of things. Christian belief, magic and superstition weren't separate – God controlled all things, so charms and

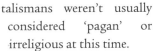

talismans weren't usually considered 'pagan' or irreligious at this time.

Putting an inscription on the back of a brooch is a more common practice with obviously 'amatory' (romantic) messages, often written in Norman French – that way, a casual observer wouldn't see your lover's words, but you could keep them close to your heart. 'Jesus of Nazareth' inscriptions were more often on the front, visible to all. Using the Jesus of Nazareth phrase is unusual for a romantic gift, but it possibly shows that this badge was both a love token and a talisman for good fortune, all rolled into one.

Together with the style of the brooch pin and the form of the lettering, experts have dated this brooch to the mid-1300s, much earlier than most other examples of heart-shaped brooches. Heart brooches are relatively rare until the 15th century, but recently a similar heart-shaped badge inscribed with '+ **ihesus nazaren**' was discovered in Dumfries and Galloway. Based on the rarity of the design from this period and the identical shapes in the engraved lettering, it's likely that both badges were made by the same fashion-forward jeweller.

**See also:**
Rochester Cufflink
Hockley Pendant
Mourning Ring

# Clonmore Shrine

## *The earliest Christian metalwork in Ireland*

Before the River Blackwater reaches Lough Neagh, the largest inland body of water in Ireland, it runs past several fields in the townland of Clonmore in County Armagh. In the 1970s and late 1980s, attempts to reduce the risk of the River Blackwater flooding saw tonnes of river silt dredged and dumped in the fields bordering the Blackwater riverbanks.

It was in one of these fields that Eamon McCurry and James Walshe discovered the first four pieces of this incredible 8cm by 3cm by 8cm long tomb-shaped shrine. Further parts of the shrine were uncovered periodically in systematic searches organised

Date: 650–700AD, Early Medieval

Where, when and how found: Dredged river silt, Clonmore, County Armagh; 1990, 1991, 2000 & 2001; metal detecting (1990) and systematic search organised by Ulster Museum

Finders: Eamon McCurry & James Walshe (1990); Ulster Museum staff

Where is it now? Ulster Museum, Belfast
www.nmni.com/um

Also visit: Armagh Cathedral, Armagh City
www.stpatricks-cathedral.org

Armagh County Museum
www.nmni.com/acm

later by the Ulster Museum. These included a hinge to allow the shrine to be opened; a locking mechanism and part of a carrying attachment. Conservators have carefully put the shrine back together, now almost complete. It turns out to be the earliest example of Christian metalwork ever found in Ireland – over 1,400 years old and dating to the 600s AD.

The Clonmore Shrine was designed to hold the relics of a saint inside. The surfaces have swirling designs all over them, and there would have been a dramatic colour contrast between the silvery tinned sections and the golden parts of the pattern. The decoration is influenced by earlier Iron Age 'Celtic' patterns but is combined with new design ideas that had become popular in religious manuscripts from the 600s AD. The combination of these artistic traditions, as well as the exquisite level of craftsmanship, reveals just how well-connected and wealthy the early Irish Church was.

## The importance of Armagh

Armagh was an important early Christian power base – St Patrick is said to have ordered a church to be built on a hill known as *Druim Saileach* ('Sallow Ridge') in 455AD, which is now the site of the current Church of Ireland Cathedral. Armagh's religious community grew up around St Patrick's church, and Armagh became a destination for scholars, priests, pilgrims and craft workers. The Clonmore Shrine is likely to have been made in Armagh itself.

> "The fact that the Clonmore Shrine survived at the bottom of the Blackwater for hundreds if not a thousand years, is close to a miracle in itself"

A key historical manuscript, *The Book of Armagh*, was written around 807AD by the educated, literate monks and scholars living in the city. It explains that one reason why Armagh is so important is because of the relics it holds of St Peter, St Paul, and the linen shroud of Jesus Christ. These were thought to be incredibly potent items, infused with the Holy Spirit and the power of the saints. Armagh became an important pilgrimage site in Ireland, and devoted Christians travelled a long way to worship in the city.

*The Book of Armagh* also reports the parading of relics around the streets of Armagh, and it's possible that the Clonmore Shrine was used in these processions. Such a beautiful artefact would have reflected the importance of the items inside. The design of the Clonmore Shrine means it both celebrates and conceals the relics inside, all at the same time.

The Clonmore shrine is very similar to another reliquary shrine known as the Bobbio Shrine. Bobbio, a town in northern Italy, was founded by the Irish monk St Columbanus, who died there in 615AD. The similarity of the Bobbio and Clonmore shrines suggests that they were both made in Armagh, and close links between the Irish and the north Italians must have continued for generations after St Columbanus' death.

We don't know how the Clonmore Shrine ended up in the Blackwater River, some miles from Armagh. It could have been lost in the early medieval period itself – an entry in the Annals of Ulster in the year 1118 records a priest falling into the River Blackwater with fine church metalwork, but we have no way of knowing whether the entry is describing this little shrine. The fact that the Clonmore Shrine survived at the bottom of the Blackwater for hundreds if not a thousand years, is close to a miracle in itself.

**See also:**
Holderness Cross
North West Essex Ring
Hockley Pendant

# Newton Stewart Dog Lead

## *A stylish medieval accessory for man's best friends*

We've always been a nation who loves our dogs, and that was never more true than when hunting was a sport of nobles, and man's best friend could give you a leg up the social ladder.

This is a bronze swivel ring attachment for joining two dog leads to a central point, so that one handler could hold and release two hunting dogs easily. It dates to the 12th–13th centuries, a time when cultural attitudes across Scotland, England and the whole of western Europe were shifting. Previously, a nobleman's status and power came primarily from his ability and willingness to raise armies and fight with, and for, other lords. Loyalty and obligation was the glue that stuck the social system together. Lords would provide protection and support to the people living on their land, and in exchange, workers and labourers were expected to support their nobles in conflicts and battles, and pay their dues.

Date: 1100–1200, Medieval

Where, when and how found: Newton Stewart, Galloway; 2010; metal detecting

Finder: J. A. Spencer

Where is it now? Stranraer Museum, Stranraer www.dumfriesmuseum.demon.co.uk/stranmuse.html

Also visit: The Dog Collar Museum, Leeds Castle, Kent www.leeds-castle.com

But increasingly, an aristocrat's social etiquette and chivalry was just as important as his prowess in battle. Off the battlefield, getting ahead in elite Scottish society depended on demonstrating your manliness and your skill in other physical pursuits – and there was no better arena to show off than during the hunt.

## Medieval hunting

Hunting was an incredibly important activity in a medieval nobleman's life. It wasn't just an entertaining pastime, but was a way to demonstrate your charm, your prowess and your understanding of the finer details of courtly etiquette and chivalry. This was an age when your fortunes, and even your life, depended on finding favour with the people in charge. If you were a noblewoman hoping to marry well, your fate would be determined to a great extent by how well your father, brothers and uncles could carry themselves at court, in battle and during 'the Chase'.

Dogs would have been trained by servants as well as perhaps by their owners. A man's prestige was demonstrated by his horses, his hounds and his hawks – how good they were at working, and how well turned-out they were on the hunting field.

There are many rituals associated with medieval hunting, including butchering the hunted prey in the forest in a formalised and ritual manner. It was another opportunity to demonstrate your nobility – you could show that you knew the correct terms for the different stages and the different parts of the animal, and were good at the skilled butchery process. The first hunting manuals are written in the 1100s, helping the upwardly thrusting young noble to do his homework and get a headstart. The allocation of meat from hunts was also a way to demonstrate your social status – the modern phrase to eat 'humble pie' originates from the medieval English word for offal – *umbles*. If you were eating 'umbles pie', it showed that you were lowly and at the bottom of the pecking order.

## The medieval dog

The dog lead found in Newton Stewart is finely crafted, and shows how much people invested in their hunting equipment. The swivel ring section is shaped like a clenched human fist gripping the larger oval, and the loop and dog lead attachment plates are engraved with little patterns around the borders and rivets. The practice of working hunting dogs as a pair, known as a 'couple', was common across Europe.

> " There are many rituals associated with medieval hunting, including butchering the hunted prey in the forest in a formalised and ritual manner "

This lead would have been used to clip a couple of hunting dogs to a huntsman's wrist. The actual leather of the leads has survived in part, and its thickness suggests that this was a lead for a pair of small- to medium-sized dogs which would have been used for scenting out prey or hunting smaller game like hares. At the appropriate time in the hunting field, the huntsman would 'loose' the dogs and they would be able to run out and work.

Dog breeds as we know them now didn't exist in medieval times – but an intelligent, athletic hunting bitch would be mated with an intelligent, athletic hunting dog, in the hopes that the puppies would also be good hunters. The trend towards a particular type of coat, shape of ear or muzzle would have led from this, but 'show' breeds were only invented in Victorian times. In medieval times, regardless of what a dog looked like, if it couldn't chase down a hare or follow a scent, it was pretty useless.

See also:
Carlton Knight
Hawking Vervel

# Rosemarkie Trade Weights

## *Illegal weights from a cosmopolitan coastal village*

Sometimes the most functional of items can give us an evocative insight into the lives of our ancestors. This set of nested weights was discovered by Robert Brown at Rosemarkie, a small village overlooking the Moray Firth, twelve miles north-east of Inverness.

Known as 'Trade Weights', they would have been used by merchants to measure their goods. The Rosemarkie set measures in 'troy ounces' (1 troy ounce is about 31 grams), a measure traditionally used for precious metals and gemstones.

**Date:** 1707–1725, Post Medieval
**Where, when and how found:** Rosemarkie, Highlands; 2011; metal detecting
**Finder:** Robert Brown
**Where is it now?** Groam House Museum, Rosemarkie
www.groamhouse.org.uk

Maker's marks on the set reveal that it was made in Nuremburg, Germany, by a founder named Hans Leonhard Abend, between 1707 and 1725. Given Rosemarkie's relative isolation from the main centres of trade in Britain, it's possible that locals had easier access to imported continental items than items from southern Scotland or England. Metal detectorists in Scotland have found a number of knives, toys and dress accessories made in Germany and Holland, and each find is drawing a clearer picture of 1600s and 1700s east-coast Scotland being more cosmopolitan than we'd previously thought.

Law makers attempted to control and standardise trade weights, protecting buyer, seller and their own tax revenues. The Rosemarkie set has authentication marks from the city of Emden, a sea port in modern Germany. Rosemarkie itself never had a harbour – instead, mariners came to nearby Fortrose and goods and coinage would have been traded out from there.

The Rosemarkie weights would certainly not have been considered legal in Scotland or England, but it's very likely that in the north-east, coastal

> "Maker's marks on the set reveal that it was made in Nuremburg, Germany, by a founder named Hans Leonhard Abend, between 1707 and 1725"

communities' attitudes to trade were a little freer, and people exercised a degree of discretion that wouldn't have been tolerated elsewhere. The national economy was floundering in the early 1700s, and Scotland was badly hit. It's quite likely that local people depended on European trade and exchange for their economic wellbeing.

The Rosemarkie weights might have been buried because they were illegal and someone didn't want to get caught with them in their possession, and for some reason were never able to recover them. We can't be sure, but the idea of illicit trading in cosmopolitan 18th-century Rosemarkie is an intriguing one.

See also:
French Forgery Hoard
Chinese Coin Hoard

# Tamlaght Hoard

## A sword, bowl, cup and ring from Bronze Age Armagh

Sean McGirr discovered this hoard in the townland of Tamlaght, County Armagh, in 2004. Alongside pieces of what looked like a bronze sword, there was a battered metal bowl with hundreds of tiny metal fragments sitting inside it. Sean immediately realised the significance of his discovery, and carefully retaining the soil around and within the bowl, he took the items to Armagh County Museum. An excavation at the site unearthed more fragments and conservators began the long process of cleaning and restoring them.

### The hoard items

The Tamlaght Hoard dates to around 1000BC, and comprises a bronze sword, bowl, cup and

ring. The items had been carefully buried in what had then been a marshy area. The cup had been placed inside the bowl, and as it had begun to break apart, the cup pieces had collected inside the bowl. Specialists were able to use some of the patterns preserved in the peat around the finds to help reconstruct the cup – and the results were intriguing.

The cup had been richly decorated with raised circular bosses, ribbed designs and punched dots. The handle was ornate, and based on analysis of the shape and design, it appears to have been made in Central Europe, around the modern Czech Republic. Cups like this have been found in Central Europe before, but Sean's find is unique for Britain and Ireland. The bowl is of a plainer design, wide and shallow, and had likely been made in the south-east of Germany. Both items had clearly travelled a long way, probably passing through many dozens of hands in a long exchange network. Perhaps

> **Date:** 1050–950BC, Late Bronze Age
>
> **Where, when and how found:** Tamlaght, County Armagh, Northern Ireland; 2004; metal detecting
>
> **Finder:** Sean McGirr
>
> **Where is it now?** Ulster Museum www.nmni.com/um
>
> **Also visit:** Armagh County Museum www.nmni.com/acm
>
> Emain Macha, Navan Visitor Centre & Fort, Armagh www.armagh.co.uk/place/navan-centre-fort
>
> **Get involved:** With a local group, like the Armagh History Group www.armaghhistorygroup.com

they had been given as diplomatic gifts, in marriage exchanges, as payment to a chief or warrior, or simply bartered for other local valuables.

The sword is a more typical item from Ireland in the Late Bronze Age: the blade would have been cast in a clay mould, and then fitted with a bone or wooden handle which has since rotted away. These were often functional weapons, but close analysis of the surfaces of some swords show that they have never been used – either they were made solely for ritual offerings, or they were 'dress' swords – for display rather than battle.

## Bronze Age Armagh

Most people in the Bronze Age were small-scale farmers, living in round houses surrounded by their animals and fields. This wasn't always a peaceful rural idyll though – there was probably inter-tribal violence between local groups, and tribes may well have raided each other's territories for valuables and livestock as well as taking live prisoners as slaves. We also know that there were sophisticated trading networks across western Europe, and along the coasts of the British Isles (see for example the Ringlemere Cup, p54).

People could travel long distances with relative ease – they were proficient sailors, knowledgeable about the coast and the sea and river systems.

But the end of the Bronze Age saw a change in climate across much of Europe, and there's some evidence pointing to living standards getting worse. There's also a definite shift in social organisation.

Not all the experts agree, but many think that the explosion of bladed weapons towards the end of the Bronze Age is partly linked to the change in climate. There's also evidence for people digging ditches and building fences around their settlements, which might mean people felt the need to defend their homes, or perhaps tribes were building these fortifications for show – competing in a regional my-ditches-are-better-than-your-ditches power struggle.

It's possible that a new 'breed' of warrior elites also arose at this time – gaining power and influence because they were able to fight, defend and protect their people. Perhaps the owner of the Tamlaght Hoard was one of these warrior elites. What we do know is that the location of the hoard is close to some other very important sites.

## Haughey's Fort and the ritual pool

Nothing can been seen above ground any more of the enormous late Bronze Age defensive hillfort known as Haughey's Fort, not far from the Tamlaght Hoard site and dating to the same era. Haughey's Fort had three concentric rings of ditches and banks forming a rough circle round the summit of a natural hill, and the enclosed area in the centre was about 150m in diameter. When there was a threat, people would have brought their families, livestock and valuables into the hillfort, and the men would have taken up arms and faced the enemy.

Hillforts are more normally associated with the later period, the Iron Age, but hillfort-building in Ireland starts earlier than

> "We don't know whether the Tamlaght items were offerings made by their warrior owner, or were perhaps deposited after he died"

anywhere else in Britain. The more famous Navan 'Fort', or Emain Macha, was built nearby, but a thousand years later. Excavations have revealed that Navan was never really a defensive fort, but instead a sophisticated ritual site. When people were living at Haughey's Fort, around 1000BC, it appears that their main ritual site was a mystical pool 300m to the north-west, at the bottom of the hill.

The pool is known as 'The King's Stables', because it's said to be the place that the legendary Kings of Ulster watered their horses. This strange little pond is a bit special. About 25m in diameter and 3.5m deep, it was intentionally dug around 1000BC, and surrounded by a low earth bank.

Excavated in the 1970s, archaeologists found rich evidence of ritual deposits in the depths of the pool: clay moulds for making bronze swords like the one in the Tamlaght Hoard, the bones of sacrificed animals including dogs and deer, and most gruesome of all, a young human skull that had been severed from its body before being cast into the waters.

It seems likely that the Tamlaght Hoard site, Haughey's Fort, and the King's Stables pool, are linked parts of a complex landscape full of spiritual significance. We don't know whether the Tamlaght items were offerings made by their warrior owner, or were perhaps deposited after he died. What's certain is that the power of bronze objects, especially bronze swords, wasn't just in their strength and value in battle. These were ritually and probably spiritually powerful items, and the act of placing or throwing them into a watery 'grave' was a very potent act.

Intriguingly, local place names suggest that the site of Haughey's Fort was also known as *Rath Glaise Cuilg* – the 'Fort of the Sword-Stream'. Perhaps Sean's finds are the last of dozens of discoveries in this special landscape.

See also:
Tisbury Hoard
Carpow Logboat
Ringlemere Cup

# Inverness Shoulder-belt Plate

## Uniform embellishment from the original 'Dad's Army'

Jack Mackay was metal detecting in a field near Inverness when he started to discover a series of finds from the same period – musket balls, coins, and this striking uniform decoration. The Inverness Shoulder-belt Plate is copper alloy with traces of silver coating. It measures 6.5cm by 5cm, and has a distinctive thistle and crown design and the words *Fort William Volunteers* around the edge – a regiment that we know was active between the years 1794 and 1816.

**Date:** Between 1794 and 1816, Early Modern

**Where, when and how found:** Inverness; 2012; metal detecting

**Finder:** Jack Mackay

**Where is it now?** Inverness Museum www.inverness.highland.museum

**Also visit:** National War Museum, Edinburgh Castle, Edinburgh www.nms.ac.uk/our_museums/war_museum.aspx

Shoulder-belt plates were worn in the centre of the chest by British officers and soldiers alike, a striking and decorative part of their uniform that was designed to buckle their leather shoulder-belts together. Fixed with studs to one end of the leather, a hook on the back of the belt plate would enable the soldier to quickly fasten, adjust or unhook the other end of his belt. This plate has scars on the back where the metal studs and hook fastenings have come away.

Often officers' shoulder-belt plates were made from silver, and regular soldiers' would have been polished bronze. Volunteer regiments like the Fort William Volunteers had to pay for their own uniforms, unlike the regular army soldiers, which may explain why this belt plate was crafted in silver-gilt (base metal with a thin plating of silver) instead of solid silver. Nonetheless, when it was new it would have shone beautifully, and been a bright, silvery colour. Every regiment had their own design of shoulder-belt plate, and officers and men wore their belt plates with pride.

## The Fort William Volunteers

In the late 1700s, the regular British Army was stretched to breaking point. Many men had been needed to fight wars in America, continental Europe and in the Indian colonies. After the French Revolution in 1789, hostilities across Europe led to brutal waves of Revolutionary Wars (1793–1802) and then almost without break, Britain was thrown into twelve years of Napoleonic Wars, from 1803–1815.

Volunteer regiments were assembled in Britain to provide security on the home front, and to man coastal defences in case of a French attack. Volunteer Corps were locally focused and often organised and funded by local gentry 'doing their bit'. Part-time and under-drilled, the British Volunteer Corps were somewhere between the Territorial Army and Dad's Army, and at the peak, over 340,000 men had subscribed across the country.

The British Volunteer Corps found themselves the butt of satirical jokes right from the start, suggesting they were badly drilled, unfit and lacking in military skills and sense. The Fort William Volunteers regiment is likely to have trained at Fort William itself, as well as at Fort George, near Inverness. Because the plate was found in Inverness, it's been suggested that a luckless volunteer lost it during a training session or camp.

See also:
Fort George Toy Soldiers
Boar Badge of Richard III

# Blair Drummond Torc Hoard

## *The gold jewellery that rewrites Scotland's ancient history*

These extraordinary gold treasures come with an extraordinary story to match. David Booth was in Stirling on his first outing with his metal detector – he'd previously got as far as practising his detection skills on knives and forks in his own garden. On the day in September 2009, he asked the landowner permission to search, parked his car, turned

Date: 300–100BC, Iron Age
Where, when and how found: Blair Drummond, Stirling; 2009; metal detecting
Finder: David Booth
Where is it now? National Museum of Scotland, Edinburgh
www.nms.ac.uk

on the machine, took seven steps ... and discovered one of the greatest treasures ever found in Scotland.

When Dr Fraser Hunter at the National Museum of Scotland received photos of the hoard items lying on David's kitchen table the next morning, he was flabbergasted, and archaeologists were immediately sent to the find site.

David had unearthed a stash of four gold neck collars known as 'torcs' that are more than 2,000 years old. Torcs were worn by elite members of a tribe as high-status, highly decorated jewellery, which would rest at the base of the wearer's neck.

Two of the torcs are 'ribbon torcs', a familiar style in Scotland and Ireland, where a fine strip of gold is hammered into a spiral.

Only half of the third torc was buried, broken into two pieces. When complete, it would have formed a full circle necklet, with a clasp to join the ends together. The unusual style suggests that it was made by craftspeople in south-west France.

The fourth torc rewrites the history books. The main body of the piece is crafted from eight strands of braided gold wire, a common technique and shape used in British torcs. But the end terminals have a pattern of decoration never seen before in the British Isles. Made from hooped and braided gold wires filled with tiny gold beads, delicate gold wire and a very fine fastening chain, the work indicates that the jewellery maker learned his or her skills from Ancient Greek or Roman jewellers – and then combined it with the traditional

British style. Either the jeweller or the torc made an extraordinary journey, from the Mediterranean to the heart of Scotland. And whoever received and wore this exotic piece would have been very important indeed.

The fact that this piece, and the craft skills to make it, travelled such a great distance, reveals that the people living near Stirling 2,000 years ago were much more powerful and well-connected than we had ever previously thought. Archaeologists had thought that Iron Age tribes in Scotland were quite isolated and inward-looking. They thought that the British Isles was a cultural backwater, compared to the flourishing societies in continental Europe. But the Blair Drummond torcs prove that these Stirlingshire people were also rich and powerful, and well connected to the cultural flows across prehistoric Europe.

Once the find was reported, archaeologists began excavating, to recover valuable information about how the hoard was originally deposited. The neckrings had been put in a shallow hole inside what had once been a circular timber-framed building. The wood and thatch had long since rotted away, but the 'footprint' of the structure remains in the ground.

In Iron Age times this would have been an isolated and boggy site and it's unlikely that this was just a normal house – but was it some kind of ritual place where the torcs were buried as an offering to the gods? Or was the building a much older structure, with the torcs buried in a place linked to the ancestors? Iron Age people across north-western Europe made offerings of valuable metal artefacts in semi-watery places like bogs and marshes, and human 'Bog Bodies' reveal that people were also sometimes sacrificed in rites we don't fully understand. We don't know the details of who or what the Iron Age people were worshipping, but the value of the offerings proves that this was a very important activity that communities invested a lot of resources in.

Further research will ultimately reveal more about the early peoples of Scotland, and their rich and sophisticated cultures.

**See also:**
Winchester Hoard
Langstone Tankard

# Horns and Crotal Musical Instruments

## Potent instruments inspired by cattle

During the Bronze Age in Ireland many astonishing bronze artefacts were deposited in bogs, rivers and lakes. Clearly an important part of our ancestors' ritual lives was to make offerings of precious objects at watery places in the landscape. These horns were found in an ancient bog; the crotal was discovered in an ancient ditch. Almost three thousand years old, these musical instruments can still make incredible music.

**Date:** Around 800BC, Late Bronze Age

**Where, when and how found:**
**Horns:** Drumbest, County Antrim; 1840; peat cutting in a bog
**Crotal:** Calhame 'Fort', County Antrim; 1887; discovered in an ancient ditch

**Finder:** Mr Thompson (Horns), Mr McLean (Crotal)

**Where are they now?** Two of the horns from the Drumbest Hoard are on display at the Ulster Museum, Belfast
www.amni.com/um

The Crotal is on display at Armagh County Museum, Armagh City
www.amni.com/acm

**Listen:** Simon O'Dwyer playing the original Drumbest horns at Ulster Museum
www.bagofbees.co.uk/26treasures/#

More info at
www.ancientmusicireland.com

## The Horns

More than one hundred Bronze Age horns have been found in Ireland – more than anywhere else in Europe. There are two types of horn – a 'side blow' horn with the hole towards the narrow closed end and an 'end blow' horn which is more trumpet-shaped. For a long time no one was sure about how to get a clear sound from these ancient horns, until the parallel with the native Australian didgeridoo was identified. Musicians suggested that these horns weren't supposed to be blown into like a trumpet – instead, if you use circular breathing and loose, vibrating lips, a deep, rhythmic, musical sound is produced.

The two types of horns (end and side blow) are often found in pairs, perhaps because they were intended to be played together. The end blow

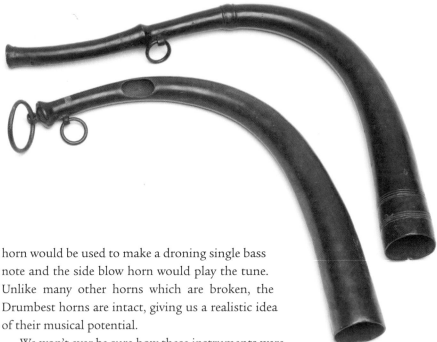

horn would be used to make a droning single bass note and the side blow horn would play the tune. Unlike many other horns which are broken, the Drumbest horns are intact, giving us a realistic idea of their musical potential.

We won't ever be sure how these instruments were played, how they sounded, or even whether they were used to make 'music' or whether they made sounds for a different purpose – summoning the gods, marking the passing of time or a specific event, perhaps. Modern specialist musicians can create some very sophisticated sounds and tunes with the horns, played separately and in pairs, but it's always possible that they're making them sound more 'musical' than our ancestors ever did.

## The Crotal

The Crotal is a cast and welded hollow bronze bell. About the size of a pear, most have a stone or piece of metal inside to create a rolling or rattling sound. Because they make this sound, experts think they are probably some kind of percussion instrument for ritual music-making – like an ancient maraca.

They're also similar to traditional cow, horse and cat bells, but the effort and skill used to make these Bronze Age

"Bronze Age people in Ireland certainly raised cattle, and it's not hard to imagine that prized animals inspired these valuable bronze instruments"

artefacts, and the nature of their deposition in bogs suggests that crotals were much more than just functional. Bells are used across the world in ritual and religious ceremonies, and it's quite possible that our ancestors used crotals in ritual practices too.

## Holy cows

The horns and crotals could be strong evidence indicating that Bronze Age people in Ireland had a society focused around cattle. Like pastoral, cattle-focused communities in modern East Africa, such as the Nuer and Dinka peoples of South Sudan and Ethiopia, cattle can be a functional source of milk and meat, wealth on-the-hoof, as well as treasured possessions with deep spiritual and ritual importance. Nuer people are so devoted to their cattle that men and women take a cow or bull's name as well as their birth name, favourite cows will be groomed, stroked and sung to, and all important ceremonies will be marked by a cattle sacrifice. Bronze Age people in Ireland certainly raised cattle, and it's not hard to imagine that prized animals inspired these valuable bronze instruments.

The horns look like cows' horns simply enough, and it's been pointed out that crotal bells are shaped like the testicles of a bull – a source of potency in many cultures. Even now, modern slang reveals the great legacy linking balls with power, strength, bravery and family lineage. It's possible that the shape of the crotal was as important and as potent as the noise it made for its Bronze Age owners.

**See also:**
Pegsdon Mirror
Nesscliffe Ritual Spoons
Hallaton Treasure

# Fort George Toy Soldiers

## 18th-century toys from a Highland fortress

Eric Soane was given a metal detector a decade ago, but it didn't immediately grab his interest and it spent a few years languishing in his shed. Then he found some back issues of a metal detecting magazine in a charity shop, and his interest was fired. Once he started detecting, he didn't look back – he's now logged more than 20,000 finds from the Ardersier area with the Treasure Trove Unit in Scotland, as he's required to do under Scottish law.

**Date:** 1748–1768, Post Medieval

**Where, when and how found:** Fort George, Ardersier, Inverness; 2005 & 2006; metal detecting

**Finder:** Eric Soane

**Where is it now:** Held in collections at Inverness Museum www.inverness.highland.museum

**Visit:** Fort George, Ardersier, Inverness www.historic-scotland.gov.uk

Eric found these cast-lead toy soldiers near Fort George, an enormous military base built by King George II to quash Jacobite Rebellions led by Bonnie Prince Charlie in the 1700s. It's still a working army base, and is considered to be the best artillery fortification ever built in Britain.

## Fort George

In 1746, Bonnie Prince Charlie was defeated by the forces of King George II at the Battle of Culloden. To prevent further rebellions, King George ordered the building of the biggest, most sophisticated defence fortress ever conceived. In today's money, Fort George cost around £1 billion to build, and it took the best part of twenty years to complete.

It was built on a defendable promontory looking out into the Moray Firth, and was bristling with 80 guns and stores of 2,500 barrels of gunpowder, and staffed by officers, an artillery detachment and 1,600 infantry troops armed with swords and muskets. Before Fort George was completed, British soldiers camped at the site, ensuring the construction wasn't attacked, and conducting regular patrols in the region. They were well-drilled, well-armed, and would have been an intimidating presence to the rebels.

Fort George was completed in 1769, well over-budget and well behind schedule, and by that time, the rebellious forces fighting against King George in the Highlands had been subdued. It meant a shot was never fired in anger from Fort George, and its defences have never been tested. Its true build quality is revealed by the fact that it's still used as a working army barracks now, virtually unchanged.

Eighteenth-century life in the Highlands was hard, but clearly the soldiers known as 'Red Coats' had at least elements of domestic life and social time – enough to make toys and trinkets.

## The Toy Soldiers

Around 3cm high, these two soldiers were found on separate occasions but are clearly from the same mould. The two halves of the mould are slightly misaligned, and the lead is probably from melted-down musket balls, which suggests that these little figures were made locally by non-specialists using materials they had to hand.

> **"Interestingly, soldiers' coat skirts were always hooked back for parade or other duties, and left hanging in front when on campaign, so these soldiers look ready for action"**

Each toy soldier is dressed in a knee-length coat with a flaring skirt, a cap, shoulder belt but no waist belt, and a musket over the left shoulder. Based on the style of coat, experts have been able to date the soldiers – waist belts were worn over the coat until 1748, and the skirted style of coat was worn by the soldiers until 1768, when it was replaced by a slightly differently tailored coat. So, by deduction, these soldiers date from between 1748 and 1768.

Interestingly, soldiers' coat skirts were always hooked back for parade or other duties, and left hanging in front when on campaign, so these soldiers look ready for action.

For some, the building of Fort George was a threat, for others it was an opportunity. So many soldiers posted far from home needed servicing – and the local economies around Fort George and her sister fort at Fort William, boomed. Some soldiers may have had families living outside the fort but close by, a few families might have lived within the fort itself, and other soldiers inevitably found their company elsewhere, in the local community. We don't know who the toy soldiers were made for, but it's likely that men were crafting little toys and trinkets for the kids in their lives.

**See also:**
Pitminster Toy Cannon
Inverness Shoulder-belt Plate
Prisoner of War Farthing Pendant

# *Girona* Wreck Cameo

## *A missing piece from an Armada tragedy*

In the 1960s a team of commercial divers discovered the historic wreck of *La Girona*, close to the Giant's Causeway off the coast of County Antrim, Northern Ireland. Among the wreckage, they found eleven 4cm high lapis lazuli cameos – oval pieces of jewellery with a profile portrait in the middle of an ornate frame. The portraits were of Roman emperors and the frames were solid gold, with enamelling and two strings of pearls threaded along each side.

**Date:** Shipwrecked in 1588, Post Medieval

**Where, when and how found:** Wreck of *La Girona*, Lacada Point, County Antrim; 1998; chance find by an authorised diver

**Finder:** Frank Madden

**Where is it now?** Ulster Museum, Belfast
www.nmni.com

**Also visit:** The area of the Causeway Coast
www.causewaycoastandglens.com

Glenarm Castle, Ballymena, County Antrim
www.glenarmcastle.com

The divers suspected there should have been twelve cameos, and that they would have been strung together to make a magnificent chain, a bit like a Town Mayor's chain of office now.

The 1960s divers never found the twelfth cameo, despite a thorough search, although they did bring up many other staggering and precious treasures including rings, a tiny reliquary, pendants, weapons and hundreds of gold and silver coins. The fact that the wreck was giving up such precious treasures was not surprising, given the circumstances of her loss.

## The wrecking of *La Girona*

*La Girona* was one of the ships of the Spanish Armada of 1588, a force of around 130 ships sent by Philip II of Spain to invade England. The Armada fleet was defeated at the naval Battle of Gravelines in the English Channel, but managed to get into formation and sail away. The surviving Spanish ships were forced into the North Sea, off the east coast of Britain, and it was decided that they should sail up over the top of the British Isles, down the west coast of Ireland and then continue south to get back to Spain. It was certainly the long way round, but infinitely safer than running the gauntlet back through the English Channel.

The navigators of the fleet didn't have any of the benefits of modern, or even traditional, equipment to help fix their positions. They didn't have chronometers or sextants and they didn't even have accurate maps of the coastline. They were also unaware of the effect of the Gulf Stream current, so every time they estimated their position, they thought that they'd travelled much further than they actually had. Instead of passing to the north of the Shetland Islands, they passed between Orkney and Fair Isle, much closer to dangerous rocky shores than they realised. They miscalculated again when they started to move south along the west coast of Scotland and then around Ireland.

By this time, many of the ships were low on supplies and fresh water, many men were injured or sick, and the ships themselves were leaking and damaged – they'd lost masts, yard arms, sails and anchors, and repairs couldn't be done unless they sailed closer to the coast to find sheltered waters. Added to that were weeks and weeks of poor visibility and gale-force conditions, that meant the fleet was sailing 'blind'.

Most of the eighty-odd remaining ships kept west, didn't stop to re-supply, and managed to avoid the Irish coastline and make landfall on the Spanish coast – despite the cripplingly poor condition of the sailors and soldiers on board.

*La Girona* was one of the ships that decided to take refuge closer in to the Irish coast, so that her rudder could be repaired – the crew landed at Killybegs, where the locals were sympathetic and willingly provided supplies and stores. While *La Girona* was being repaired at Killybegs, a plan was made that she would take the surviving crews from two other wrecked Armada ships that had foundered nearby, sail everyone to Scotland to recuperate, before journeying back south to reach Spain. All in all, when she set off again, *La Girona* was laden down with thirteen hundred men, extra cannon, stores and supplies. She had been built to carry 550 people.

Soon afterwards, another fierce gale blew up. The rowers on board could make no headway and the sails were useless; the anchors were lost, and

eventually the helpless, overloaded *Girona* was driven in total darkness on to the rocks of Lacada Point.

No one can be quite sure, but the local story is that only five people out of 1,300 survived the wreck on that stormy, ferocious night. *La Girona* was one of around twenty-five Armada ships wrecked on the west coast of Ireland in just a few days in October 1588, and she holds the dubious record for the greatest loss of life. Human bones washed on to the shore for years afterwards, and the local harbour still remembers the *Girona* shipwreck – it's called *Port na Spaniagh*, 'Spanish Port'.

Salvage of valuables from the wreck began almost immediately – bronze cannon were recovered, and one of the wooden chests at Glenarm Castle is from *La Girona*. It's said that the pockets of the drowned sailors washed up ashore were also checked – any gold was good gold.

Most of the treasures of *La Girona* were lost under the waves, though, and were only retrieved when divers rediscovered the wreck in 1968. The incredible collection of Armada gold at the Ulster Museum, Belfast, is truly breathtaking. Although they unearthed so many treasures, the twelfth cameo in the set eluded the 1960s team.

## The twelfth cameo

It was only in 1998, when the authorised diver Frank Madden was diving the *Girona* wreck, that he found a small, golden oval amongst the debris and mud – it was the near-legendary twelfth cameo. Incredibly, it was in excellent condition, despite the fact that it had been on the seabed for thirty years longer than the other eleven. We don't know which of the emperors the lapis lazuli portrait represents, but it's clear that it was part of the ornate chain that was probably worn by one of the leaders of the Armada on board *La Girona*.

*La Girona* is now a protected wreck, so taking anything from the site would be illegal. The dive community saying – leave nothing but bubbles, take nothing but pictures – holds especially true for this incredible, and tragic, site. Despite our appreciation of the beauty of the *Girona* gold and treasures, it can't be forgotten that this is also a war grave.

See also:
HMS *Colossus* Shipwreck
Marcus Aurelius Bust

# Carpow Bronze Age Logboat

## An ancient oak boat resting in the River Tay for 3,000 years

In 2000 and 2001, a number of people had noticed what looked like an old tree eroding out of the tidal riverbed at Carpow. Twice a day the 'tree' was covered by water, and each time the tide went out, a bit more of it was exposed. Local men Scott McGuckin, Robert Fotheringham and Martin Brookes each realised it wasn't just a 'tree', but an ancient logboat. The incredible find was reported to local archaeologists and a team from Perth and Kinross Heritage Trust confirmed that it was indeed an ancient oak logboat – hollowed out from a single tree trunk around 3,000 years ago, dating to the late Bronze Age. They began to assess the site – to take the boat out of the riverbed could risk it breaking up, and conserving it out of the water would certainly be very expensive. If the logboat could be made safe in situ, then it could stay there – it had already survived more than 3,000 years.

**Date:** Around 1130–970BC, Late Bronze Age

**Where, when and how found:** River Tay, Carpow, Perth and Kinross; 2001; discovered on riverbed

**Finders:** Scott McGuckin, Robert Fotheringham, Martin Brookes

**Where is it now?** Part of the Museums Collection of Perth and Kinross Council, but the boat will be at Glasgow Museums Resource Centre from 2013 to 2018 for further research. Not on full public display – viewings by appointment, as well as a programme of public talks and events www.glasgowlife.org.uk/museums/our-museums/glasgow-museum-resource-centre/

**Also visit:** Scottish Crannog Centre, Loch Tay, Perthshire www.crannog.co.uk

**Get involved:** Perth and Kinross Heritage Trust outreach and community programme www.pkht.org.uk

The boat itself was incredibly well preserved and had survived to almost its full length of 9 metres. In 2006 the logboat was finally excavated; and with teams racing against the tide each day, they managed to record,

sample, survey and lift the boat in seven days. Sediments from inside the boat revealed fragments of hazelnut shells and worked wood – the litter of a Bronze Age boatman. Once the logboat was clear of its muddy resting place, it was refloated and slowly paddled downriver to a place where it could safely be lifted out. Hundreds of local people came to watch the precarious but successful mission, and the boat was taken to the National Museums Scotland conservation lab near Edinburgh. The specialists couldn't allow the logboat to dry out – if it did, the wood would shrink, crack and disintegrate. They carefully soaked the whole of the logboat in a chemical bath that replaced the water in the wood cells with Polyethylene glycol (a substance that's also used in laxative treatments and experimental medicines for spinal injuries). The final step was to freeze-dry the remaining water out of the timber in an industrial freezer oven. The whole conservation process took more than five years, dozens of experts, and hundreds of thousands of pounds. When the Carpow Logboat was put on display in 2012 at the Perth Museum, more than 82,000 people came to see it.

## Logboat technology

Building a picture from the tool marks in the wood of the Carpow Logboat, from tools that have been discovered, and from modern experimental archaeology, we can tell that making a logboat could involve a whole community – people used bronze axes to chop down a large, straight mature oak tree, and then a series of specialised bronze woodworking tools to shape, hollow out and smooth the trunk into a canoe-shape. The bow (front) end was shaped to a point in the wood itself, and the stern (back) was sealed with a transom board – a flat vertical board snugly fitted into the log shape to make the end watertight. When it was completed, it would have been paddled along with wooden paddles, and been able to safely carry up to a tonne of cargo, or around fourteen people.

During the Bronze Age the Tayside area was mostly wooded, with fertile, well-draining pasture and fields cleared amongst the trees. People would have lived surrounded by their fields, animals and small workshop areas and enclosures, like a modern smallholding or croft. But the Carpow Logboat reveals that these smallholders were also capable sailors and decent fishermen.

It looks like the Carpow boat gave many good years of service to its builders – perhaps up to three decades – for fishing, hunting and ferrying people, livestock, grain and building material like timber and stone along the rivers and across the estuary. Larger, more stable plank boats were also being constructed in the Bronze Age to make journeys across the open sea – we know that Bronze Age people were well connected to each other up and down the British and Irish coasts, as well as with communities across the North Sea and into France, Spain and Portugal.

The bottom of the hull of the Carpow boat had a split that was repaired seven times with oil-saturated plant glue and moss caulking, and the transom had an additional board shaped and fitted, perhaps to help prevent water seeping in. Perhaps these splits and leaks eventually meant the boat was 'retired' from service and abandoned in the river, where it sat for 3,000 years. A treasure of national importance, spotted by eagle-eyed and passionate members of the public, and preserved for us all by a committed team of professionals.

See also:
Milton Keynes Hoard
Horns and Crotal Musical
  Instruments
HMS *Colossus* Shipwreck

# Get Involved

## *Michael Lewis, Portable Antiquities Scheme*

Seen the series, read the book ... now want to get involved in archaeology?

Archaeology is for all. It doesn't matter if you have only just been inspired or you have a long-term interest in the past. There are lots of ways and opportunities to get involved. You don't necessarily need qualifications or lots of experience to 'do archaeology', and it doesn't matter how old you are either. Britain is a country rich in archaeology and history, so you can live anywhere in these isles – city, town, village or hamlet – and still play a part. All you really need is enthusiasm, and perhaps some patience. It helps if you don't mind getting dirty, but even that is not absolutely necessary.

Archaeology is the study of the human past through the 'material culture' (stuff) people left behind, whether that is their buildings, the objects they made and used or the things they ate. Although most archaeology is below ground (buried) that is not always the case. Therefore archaeology isn't just about digging, and you don't have to dig to get involved and learn more about the rich history of your country. Archaeology is all around us – both beneath and above ground – you just need to know where to go to find out more.

So, how can you get involved?

## Museums and heritage sites

An excellent way to learn about archaeology is to visit your local museum. Most people visit museums when on holiday or out for the day, but surprisingly few have visited their most local museum, which may even be in the town where they live. Museums vary tremendously in subject matter and size. Some may be run by the local council, a private institution, or even by volunteers. Some have excellent archaeological collections, and most will offer events and activities for adults and children alike. It has got to be your first stop if you want to get involved in archaeology, so see www.museums.co.uk for details of museums near you.

Few museums rival the collections of the British nationals. The British Museum (www.britishmuseum.org) has one of the best archaeological collections in the world, and it's FREE. No wonder it is the most visited tourist attraction in the UK. If you are in Edinburgh check out the National Museum of Scotland (www.nms.ac.uk), or in Cardiff, the National Museum Wales (www.museumwales.ac.uk), or in Belfast, the Ulster Museum (www.nmni.com). There are also major collections that can't be ignored in other major British cities.

Britain's best archaeological sites – think of Stonehenge, Hadrian's Wall and Dover Castle – are maintained by English Heritage (www.english-heritage.org.uk) in England, Historic Scotland (www.historic-scotland.gov.uk) in Scotland, or Cadw (www.cadw.wales.gov.uk) in Wales. Being a member of one of these organisations (for less than £1 a week) entitles you to FREE access to all sites in their care; there are also reciprocal agreements with the other home country organisations, offering free or discounted entry. In Northern Ireland many sites are maintained by the Northern Ireland Environment Agency (www.doeni.gov.uk).

Another important organisation caring for archaeological sites that you can visit is the National Trust (www.nationaltrust.org.uk). Again members of this organisation get FREE access to sites across the county.

There are also many archaeological sites on private land which can be visited. Your local council's Historic Environment Record (sometimes known as Sites and Monuments Record) will have a list of all sites near where you live, and have a duty of care towards them. You can actually find out a lot about the archaeology of your local area by Googling the place where you live. You may be surprised to learn what you can see or visit on your doorstep.

## Archaeological and heritage groups

If visiting museums and archaeological sites seems a bit passive, you could think about joining a local heritage or archaeological group. Most are keen for new members, and are very friendly and welcoming. They won't presume you have great knowledge, just an interest in the past. Most groups will normally have regular meetings at which people will give interesting talks about the archaeology and history of your local area, and there is normally some tea and biscuits for sustenance. These groups will probably also organise archaeological activities, such as heritage walks, field-walking and (possibly) excavation. During the Festival for British Archaeology (see overleaf) many groups will do something in the local community, which is a great way to find out if your local group might be for you. For more details about archaeological and heritage groups in your area, contact the Council for British Archaeology (www.archaeology.uk.org).

## Archaeology for Children

The Young Archaeologists Club (www.yac-uk.org) is aimed at children and amongst the benefits are a quarterly magazine and a 'YAC Pass' that gets members FREE or discounted entrance to 180 heritage sites across Britain. It is also possible to join a local YAC branch (for those aged 8 and above), which organise a fantastic array of archaeological-based activities for children from craft-related workshops to digging proper.

## Festival of British Archaeology

For two weeks every July more than 1,000 events and activities are organised to celebrate the Festival of British Archaeology (www.festival.britarch.ac.uk), showcasing the very best of British Archaeology. These events are organised and hosted by museums, heritage organisations, universities and local groups, etc. right across the UK, and many are free. You don't have to be an archaeologist to get involved, and the festival aims to give everyone the opportunity to learn about their local heritage, see archaeology in action (though it can be quite slow) and get hands on with history.

## Go digging

If you want to dig (and don't mind getting dirty and wet, and spending your day on your knees) it is probably best to enrol on a Community Archaeological Excavation. These normally take place in the summer, and may be organised by a local authority, university or college, local society or others. Sometimes you have to pay (or at least cover your board and lodgings – a tent), but they are an ideal way to learn many of the skills you need to be an archaeologist. If you get the bug for archaeology really badly, then you could enrol on an evening course, or even study at university. But be prepared for a life on the bread-line, as archaeologists don't get paid very well ...

Most of the finds featured in *Britain's Secret Treasures* have been found by everyday people, not archaeologists (who aren't really normal at all), and it is through these finds – if recorded – that the history of our island is being transformed. Many of these finds have been uncovered by metal detectorists. In the past relations between archaeologists and metal detectorists was poor (to put it mildly), but thanks to both sides understanding the other a little more through the work of the Portable Antiquities Scheme (see p295) relations have improved significantly.

## How to find out who owns the land/when can you dig on it?

In order to search for archaeological objects it is very important you have the permission of the landowner; to search without permission is a civil offence (trespass). Even beaches, local parks and common land will have an owner, be it an individual or local authority or suchlike. Most people search on farmland and therefore approach the farmer, but it is possible they are only a tenant, not the owner, so it is important to check. All finds found on the land are (normally) owned by the landowner, so it is a criminal offence to remove these without his/her consent. So be sure you have an agreement (written is best) as to what happens to any found objects. Many finders will show these to the landowner once they have finished searching. To keep any objects not belonging to you is theft, and you could be prosecuted. The landowner should know if any parts of the land you wish to search on are protected (such as scheduled monument) or out-of-bounds for any other reason (such as a Site of Special Scientific Interest, for wildlife), but you have the duty to be certain: English Heritage and Natural England, or your local Historic Environment Record can be contacted if you have any doubts about the status of ownership of any land.

# Metal detecting

## How metal detectors work

Modern metal detectors are sophisticated bits of kit, and some are capable of detecting very small targets under the ground. The general principle is that the metal detector emits a magnetic field from the coil at the bottom of the machine, which penetrates the ground around it. The coil picks up the magnetic signals that are bounced back, and the electronics program in the machine analyses the signal and translates it into an audio signal (or, beep).

The metal detectorist can set the controls to pick up signals from either ferrous metals (mostly iron ), or non-ferrous metals (like gold, silver or bronze), or both. Many ferrous metal signals are considered to be 'junk' – ring pulls from drinks cans, bits of machinery – so many people filter these signals out, preventing the machine making a 'beep' when it detects one. But sometimes the ferrous finds are the real treasures (for example, see the Alnwick Sword, p218).

It takes a lot of skill and patience to use a metal detector well. Practice and understanding are needed to set the machine correctly to pick up the kinds of targets you're looking for, and experience is needed to decide where to look. Anyone who plans to get the machine out of the box, turn it on and find treasure is going to be disappointed. Beginners can learn a lot about their new hobby and equipment by joining a club of responsible, like-minded individuals.

The most responsible way to enjoy metal detecting is to work on already-disturbed land, like ploughed fields, or somewhere where finds aren't in a 'closed' context. Sometimes the only surviving evidence of a site is through the finds themselves – which help archaeologists map a site no one knew about before.

If you dig below the plough soil level you may dislodge finds from their original context which is important not to do. If in doubt, stop, and call your local Finds Liaison Officer or museum curator for advice. In all the cases in this book, when finders have called in the archaeologists and an excavation has begun, finders and their family and friends stay involved and share the thrill of unearthing the discoveries. The more archaeologists and metal detectorists can work together, the more they'll understand and appreciate each other's disciplines. Good and respectful relationships between amateurs and professionals are key to protecting heritage for us all to enjoy.

People can have fun in their gardens or on the beach with a cheap metal detector (which are aimed at kids), but those serious about taking up metal detecting will invest quite a lot of money buying a decent machine (several hundred pounds at least) and require lots of patience.

Metal detecting can be both useful to archaeology and also very damaging, so it is important that anyone new to the hobby seeks good advice and makes themselves aware of the dos and don'ts before they even buy a metal detector. An essential starting place is the *Code of Practice for Responsible Metal Detecting* (which is endorsed by the main archaeological, metal detecting and landowner's organisations).

# Code of Practice for Responsible Metal Detecting

## *Being responsible means:*

### Before you go metal detecting

1. Not trespassing; before you start detecting, obtain permission to search from the landowner/occupier, regardless of the status, or perceived status, of the

land. Remember that all land has an owner. To avoid subsequent disputes it is always advisable to get permission and agreement in writing first regarding the ownership of any finds subsequently discovered (the Country Land & Business Association (www.cla.org.uk) and the National Farmers' Union (www.nfuonline.com) can provide advice to their members).

2. Adhering to the laws concerning protected sites (e.g. those defined as Scheduled Monuments or Sites of Special Scientific Interest: you can obtain details of these from the landowner/occupier, Finds Liaison Officer, Historic Environment Record or at www.magic.gov.uk). Take extra care when detecting near protected sites: for example, it is not always clear where the boundaries lie on the ground.

3. You are strongly recommended to join a metal detecting club or association that encourages co-operation and responsive exchanges with other responsible heritage groups. Details of metal detecting organisations can be found at www.ncmd.co.uk / www.fid.newbury.net.

4. Familiarising yourself with and following current conservation advice on the handling, care and storage of archaeological objects (see www.finds.org.uk).

## While you are metal detecting

5. Wherever possible, working on ground that has already been disturbed (such as ploughed land or that which has formerly been ploughed), and only within the depth of ploughing. If detecting takes place on undisturbed pasture, be careful to ensure that no damage is done to the archaeological value of the land, including earthworks.

6. Minimising any ground disturbance through the use of suitable tools and by reinstating any excavated material as neatly as possible. Endeavour not to damage stratified archaeological deposits.

7. Recording findspots as accurately as possible for all finds (i.e. to at least a one-hundred-metre square, using an Ordnance Survey map or hand-held Global Positioning Systems (GPS) device) whilst in the field. Bag finds individually and record the National Grid Reference (NGR) on the bag. Findspot information should not be passed on to other parties without the agreement of the landowner/occupier (see also Clause 9).

8. Respecting the Country Code (leave gates and property as you find them and do not damage crops, frighten animals, or disturb ground-nesting birds, and dispose properly of litter: see www.countrysideaccess.gov.uk).

## After you have been metal detecting

9. Reporting any finds to the relevant landowner/occupier; and (with the agreement of the landowner/occupier) to the Portable Antiquities Scheme, so the information can pass into the local Historic Environment Record. Both the Country Land and Business Association and the National Farmers' Union support the reporting of finds. Details of your local Finds Liaison Officer can be found at www.finds.org.uk/contacts, email: info@finds.org.uk, phone: 0207 323 8611.

10. Abiding by the provisions of the Treasure Act and Treasure Act Code of Practice, wreck law (www.mcga.gov.uk) and export licensing (www.artscouncil.org.uk). If you need advice your local Finds Liaison Officer will be able to help you.

11. Seeking expert help if you discover something large below the ploughsoil, or a concentration of finds or unusual material, or wreck remains, and ensuring that the landowner/occupier's permission is obtained to do so. Your local Finds Liaison Officer may be able to help or will be able to advise of an appropriate person. Reporting the find does not change your rights of discovery, but will result in far more archaeological evidence being discovered.

12. Calling the police, and notifying the landowner/occupier, if you find any traces of human remains.

13. Calling the police or HM Coastguard, and notifying the landowner/occupier, if you find anything that may be a live explosive: do not use a metal detector or mobile phone nearby as this might trigger an explosion. Do not attempt to move or interfere with any such explosives.

Also popular is searching on beaches and river foreshores. Anyone wishing to dig or metal detect on the River Thames foreshore requires a Port of London 'foreshore permit' to do so (http://www.pla.co.uk/display_fixedpage.cfm/id/4018). If you want to search the foreshore or beaches elsewhere in the UK you need permission from the Crown Estate (http://www.thecrownestate.co.uk/coastal/metal-detecting). It is best only to go onto river foreshores with someone who has local knowledge of the foreshores, and its dangers – don't go alone. See the PLA website for more information on being safe on river foreshores. Why not volunteer with the Thames Discovery Project's Foreshore Recording and Observation Group (FROG)? This organises trips to the River Thames foreshore in order to learn more about London's past: see http://thamesdiscovery.org/about/the_frog.

As it says in the *Code of Practice for Responsible Metal Detecting*, it is very important to know what to do if you find something. All archaeological finds, no matter if they are heavily corroded, broken or incomplete, have the potential to rewrite history, but can only do so if they are recorded. It is therefore important that you show any of your discoveries to an archaeologist.

## Illicit metal detecting

Although most people obey the law and report their discoveries, some do not, thus depriving us all of knowledge of the past. These people venture onto archaeological sites and areas renowned for their archaeological interest without permission in order to steal antiquities. They have no interest in the past and are nothing but common criminals. In recent times there has been a concerted effort to confront illegal metal detecting and those seeking to steal archaeology. Increasingly the police are pursuing criminal prosecutions, and a number of people have been arrested and punished. In the past some people have found themselves in trouble by unwittingly breaking the law, and therefore it is particularly important that anyone metal detecting ensures they follow the Code of Practice (above). Likewise, anyone spotting people illegally searching should immediately call the police.

## The Portable Antiquities Scheme

The Portable Antiquities Scheme (PAS) was established in 1997 to record archaeological objects found by the public in England and Wales (see www.finds. org.uk). Before this time people may have taken interesting finds to their local museum for museum curators to see, but there existed no systematic mechanism for recording these finds for archaeological benefit. The PAS was first set up as pilot projects in just a few areas. Then in 2003, thanks to Heritage Lottery Fund funding, the scheme was extended to the whole of England and Wales. Nowadays the PAS is principally funded by the Department for Culture, Media and Sport, and managed by the British Museum. Funded through the PAS are 40 locally based Finds Liaison Officers (FLOs) whose job it is to record finds submitted for identification and recording. They also organise outreach events and activities to encourage more people to record their discoveries. It is by this mechanism that public finds add to archaeological knowledge, so it is important that anyone finding archaeology records it with their local FLO.

All finds recorded by the PAS are added on to its online database (www. finds.org.uk/database). This is publicly available so that *all* can learn about the past, although precise findspot information and personal details are restricted. Most finds added to the database are photographed, measured and weighed. By logging onto the database you can see descriptions and images of finds recorded, and can discover more about the past by searching for finds from your area, or for types of finds you are interested in. For example, if you have seen a find in this book that interests you, you can learn more about it by logging onto the database (using the PAS find number) or discover finds found nearby or of a similar type. To date the PAS database provides access to over 900,000 finds, of which more finds are being recorded and logged every day. Besides appealing to people with an interest in archaeology and history, the data is now a powerful research tool being used by academics and researchers. The data is beginning to rewrite the history of this country. But amazingly this data is not generated by professional archaeologists, but ordinary members of the public.

To learn more about how you can contribute to one of the largest archaeology projects in the world, visit www.finds.org.uk/getinvolved.

## Scotland, Northern Ireland and UK dependencies

In Scotland and Northern Ireland there is a legal obligation to report ALL archaeological finds, as is the case in most UK dependencies (such as the Channel Islands and the Isle of Man). If you find archaeology then the simplest thing to do is take it to your local museum and say you wish to record it. They will then advise you on what to do next. There are important restrictions relating to the use of metal detecting devices in Northern Ireland.

## The Treasure Act 1996

Recording with the PAS is voluntary, but there is a legal requirement to report all finds of Treasure. In England and Wales (and Northern Ireland) finders of Treasure are required to report such discoveries to the coroner in the district in which the find was found within 14 days. In practice many (if they live in England or Wales) will contact their local FLO who will report the find on their behalf.

The Treasure Act 1996 allows museums in England, Wales and Northern Ireland to acquire Treasure finds. If this happens a reward, equal to the full market value of the find, is normally split equally between the finder/s and landowner/s. The find is valued by a committee of independent experts known as the Treasure Valuation Committee, though any interested party may wish to commission his/her own valuation for the committee to consider. The acquiring museum then has to raise the money to pay for the reward. Increasingly some finders/landowners are waiving their right to a reward, so that museums can acquire Treasure at no or reduced cost, thus saving the public purse. If a museum does not want to acquire a find then it is disclaimed (by the Crown) and returned to finder/landowner.

## Summary definition of Treasure

The following finds are Treasure under the Act, if found after 24 September 1997 (or, in the case of Category 2, if found after 1 January 2003):

1. Any metallic object, other than a coin, provided that at least 10 per cent by weight of metal is precious metal (that is, gold or silver) and that it is at least 300 years old when found. If the object is of prehistoric date it will be Treasure provided any part of it is precious metal.

2. Any group of two or more metallic objects of any composition of prehistoric date that come from the same find (see below).

3. Two or more coins from the same find provided they are at least 300 years old when found and contain 10 per cent gold or silver (if the coins contain less than 10 per cent of gold or silver there must be at least ten of them). Only the following groups of coins will normally be regarded as coming from the same find: hoards that have been deliberately hidden; smaller groups of coins, such as the contents of purses, that may been dropped or lost; votive or ritual deposits.

4. Any object, whatever it is made of, that is found in the same place as, or had previously been together with, another object that is Treasure.

5. Any object that would previously have been treasure trove, but does not fall within the specific categories given above. Only objects that are less than 300 years old, that are made substantially of gold or silver, that have been deliberately hidden with the intention of recovery and whose owners or heirs are unknown will come into this category.

6. An object or coin is part of the 'same find' as another object or coin if it is found in the same place as, or had previously been together with, the other object. Finds may have become scattered since they were originally deposited in the ground.

## Scotland and UK dependencies

Scotland and UK dependencies (such as the Channel Islands and the Isle of Man) maintain the Common Law of Treasure Trove. In essence most (if not all) archaeological finds in those places needed to be reported by law and therefore finders there should notify their local museum of any archaeological discoveries.

## Portable Antiquities Scheme database numbers for featured artefacts

*Find out more at www.finds.org.uk/database, and type in the database number in the search box.*

### EAST
*Lincolnshire, Nottinghamshire, Rutland, Cambridgeshire, Norfolk, Suffolk*
Happisburgh Handaxe, Norfolk, NMS-ECAA52
Billingford Amulet, Norfolk, NMS-7BEED8
Sedgeford Hoard, Norfolk, PAS-B1F065
Sedgeford Torc, Norfolk, PAS-F070D5
Baldehildis Seal, Norfolk, PAS-8709C3
Saltfleetby Spindle Whorl, Lincs, LIN-D92A22
Carlton Knight, Notts, SWYOR-D37EE5
Navenby Witch Bottle, Lincs, LIN-49FC12
Spanish-American Gold Doubloons, Lincs,
   LIN-55BFE7
Hawking Vervel, Norfolk, NMS-82AD63
Syston Knife Handle, Lincs, LIN-536F87

### SOUTH EAST
*Hertfordshire, Essex, London, Kent, Surrey, Sussex*
Ringlemere Cup, Kent, PAS-BE40C2
Near Lewes Hoard, E Sussex, SUSS-C5D042
Anarevitos Stater, Kent, FASAM-FCD3A2
Rochester Cufflink, Kent, BM-CAA2C7
Putney 'Brothel' Token, London, LON-E98F21
Hockley Pendant, Essex, ESS-2C4836
Canterbury Pilgrim Badges, Kent, PAS-B1BD65
Seal Matrix of Stone Priory, Surrey, SUR-B74173
Beddingham Nose, Sussex, SUSS-05BC17
Hackney WWII Hoard, London, PAS-867115
Epsom Horse Harness Boss, Surrey, SUR-23EF78
George Humber's Distinguished Conduct Medal,
   Surrey, SUR-5ADA50
Helmet Cremation Burial, Kent, KENT-FA8E56
North West Essex Ring, Essex, ESS-E396B1
Ashwell Hoard and the Goddess Senuna, Herts,
   PAS-9708E3

### SOUTH WEST & BORDERS
*Cornwall, Devon, Somerset, Dorset, Hereford, Shropshire, Wales*
Frome Hoard, Somerset, SOM-5B9453
Llanbedrgogh Viking Treasure, Anglesey, Wales,
   NMGW-C5EE45
Pitminster Toy Cannon, Somerset, SOM-
   D20D91
Nether Stowey Hoard, Somerset, SOM-849CA3
Leopard Cup, Monmouthshire, S Wales, NMGW-
   9A9D16
Langstone Tankard, Newport, S Wales, NMGW-
   9C0216
Nesscliffe Ritual Spoons, Shrops, HESH-9A4B83
Mourning Ring, Shrops, HESH-E35784
Dartmoor Sword, Devon, DEV-BB4AF7
Prisoner of War Farthing Pendant, Shrops,
   HESH-40E833

### CENTRAL & SOUTH
*Hampshire, Wiltshire, Berkshire, Gloucestershire, Oxfordshire, Buckinghamshire, Bedfordshire, Northamptonshire, Warwickshire, Worcestershire, Leicestershire*
Milton Keynes Hoard, Bucks, PAS-833958
Tisbury Hoard, Wilts, WILT-E8DA70
Hallaton Treasure, Leics, PAS-984616
Marcus Aurelius Bust, Northants, BERK-E24C84
Chalgrove Hoard and Coin of Domitianus,
   Oxfordshire, PAS-879F02
Tanworth Comb, Warwickshire, WAW-250340
Boar Badge of Richard III, Leics, LEIC-A6C834
Winchester Gold Hoard, Hampshire, PAS-845331
Roman Slave Shackle, Hampshire,
   HAMP-C45106
French Forgery Hoard, Hampshire, HAMP-
   E4E185
Isle of Wight Axehead, IoW, IOW-E579D4
Pegsdon Mirror, Beds, reported before PAS
Daventry Visard Mask, Northants, NARC-
   151A67
Bentley Miniature Book, Hampshire, HAMP527

### NORTH WEST
*Staffordshire, Derbyshire, Cheshire, Lancashire, Cumbria*
Staffordshire Moorlands Ilam Pan, Staffs,
   WMID-3FE965
Crosby Garrett Helmet, Cumbria, LANCUM-
   E48D73
Silverdale Hoard, Lancashire, LANCUM-65C1B4
Staffordshire Hoard, Staffs, WMID-0B5416
Chinese Coin Hoard, Barrow in Furness,
   LANCUM-0095B8
Ursula's Virgin Badge, Preston, LANCUM-
   61F133

### NORTH EAST
*Yorkshire, Durham, Northumberland*
County Durham River Assemblage, Durham,
   NCL-2C40A4; FAPJW-AB59E5 (sample)
Cautopates Roman Figurine, Yorks, SWYOR-
   9FCBB3
Vale of York Viking Hoard, Yorks, SWYOR-
   AECB53
Holderness Cross, Yorks, YORYM214
West Yorkshire Ring Hoard, Yorks, SWYOR-
   F86A02; SWYOR-3B5652 (sample)
Durham Cloth Seals, Durham, PUBLIC-9B0430
Kellington Dental Block, Yorks, LVPL-85A4D6
Hadrian's Wall Coins, Northumberland, NCL-
   EE2655 (sample)
Alnwick Sword, Northumberland, NCL-7EF795
Holy Island Mason Hoard, Northumberland,
   NCL-B02245

BRITAIN'S SECRET TREASURES

Only finds from England and Wales are recorded by the PAS

# Further Reading

## Prehistory

Chris Stringer; *Homo Britannicus* (Penguin)

Jill Cook; *Ice Age Art: arrival of the modern mind* (British Museum Press)

Barry Cunliffe; *Europe Between the Oceans 9000BC–AD1000* (Yale University Press)

Francis Pryor; *Britain BC* (Harper Perennial)

Mike Parker Pearson; *Stonehenge: Exploring the Greatest Stone Age Mystery* (Simon and Schuster)

## Roman Britain

Sam Moorhead and David Stuttard; *The Romans who Shaped Britain* (Thames & Hudson)

Guy de la Bedoyère; *Roman Britain: A New History* (Thames & Hudson)

Richard Hobbs and Ralph Jackson; *Roman Britain* (British Museum Press)

## Early Medieval

Robin Fleming; *Britain after Rome* (Penguin)

Nicholas Higham and Martin Ryan; *The Anglo-Saxon World* (Yale)

Sally Crawford; *Anglo-Saxon England* (Shire)

Michael Wood; *In Search of the Dark Ages* (BBC Books)

Neil Oliver; *Vikings: A History* (BBC Books)

## Medieval

Ian Mortimer; *The Time Traveller's Guide to Medieval England* (Vintage)

Marc Morris; *Castle: A History of the Buildings that Shaped Medieval Britain* (Windmill)

Paul Hindle; *Medieval Roads and Tracks* (Shire)

## Post Medieval & Modern

Chris Skidmore; *Bosworth: The birth of the Tudors* (Weidenfeld & Nicolson)

Ellis Wasson; *A History of Modern Britain: 1714 to the present* (Wiley-Blackwell)

Emma Griffin; *Liberty's Dawn: A People's History of the Industrial Revolution* (Yale)

Andrew Marr; *The Making of Modern Britain* (Macmillan)

Gabriel Moshenska; *The Archaeology of the Second World War: Uncovering Britain's Wartime Heritage* (Pen and Sword)

## General

Ruth Brocklehurst; *The Usborne History of Britain* (Usborne)

David Ross; *Scotland: History of a Nation* (Lomond)

Simon Jenkins; *A Short History of England* (Profile Books)

Jon Gower; *The Story of Wales* (BBC Books)

W. G. Hoskins; *The Making of the English Landscape* (Little Toller)

Oliver Rackman; *The History of the Countryside* (Phoenix)

Lucy Worsley; *If Walls Could Talk: An Intimate History of the Home* (Faber and Faber)

Paul Bahn; *Archaeology: A very short introduction* (Oxford University Press)

Portable Antiquities Scheme and Treasure Annual Reports (British Museum)

## BM objects in focus

Kevin Leahy and Roger Bland; *The Staffordshire Hoard*

Sam Moorhead and Anna Booth; *The Frome Hoard*

Gareth Williams and Barry Ager; *The Vale of York Hoard*

# Index

# Picture Credits

For further information about the British Museum and its collection, go to britishmuseum.org

## Acknowledgements from Mary-Ann Ochota

Sarah Emsley and Richard Roper at Headline
Ed Taylor, Michael Kelpie, Katy Thorogood and Shirley Patton at ITV
Antony Topping at Greene & Heaton
Alex and Sophieclaire Armitage at Noel Gay
Jane Compton
Andrew Lord and the graphics team at Flipbook
The ever-delightful Kate Jarvis for her invaluable research assistance
Roger Bland, Ian Richardson, and the network of Finds Liaison Officers and
National Finds Advisors at the PAS, and the curators and staff at the British
Museum, National Museums Scotland, National Museums Northern Ireland
and Amgueddfa Cymru National Museum Wales, for their guidance and
expertise.

Special thanks to Michael Lewis, Deputy Head of the Portable Antiquities
Scheme, and definitely one of Britain's secret treasures. I couldn't have wished to
work with a more passionate champion of Britain's archaeology and antiquities.

My family and friends, who have cheered and chivvied in perfect proportions.

Finally, thank you to the passionate and dedicated members of the public who
find interesting things and share them with the rest of us.